the gardener's weather bible

the gardener's weather bible

How to Predict and Prepare for

Garden Success in Any Kind of Weather

sally roth

RODALE

RODALE

WE **INSPIRE** AND **ENABLE** PEOPLE TO IMPROVE
THEIR LIVES AND THE WORLD AROUND THEM

We're always happy to hear from you. For questions or comments concerning the editorial content of this book, please write to:

Rodale Book Readers' Service
33 East Minor Street
Emmaus, PA 18098

Look for other Rodale books wherever books are sold. Or call us at (800) 848-4735.

For more information about Rodale Organic Living magazines and books, visit us at
www.organicgardening.com

Editor: Deborah L. Martin
Interior Book Designer: Patricia Field
Cover and Interior Illustrator: Michael Gellatly
Layout Designer: Keith Biery
Copy Editor: Sarah Sacks Dunn
Product Specialist: Brenda Miller
Indexer: Lina Burton

Rodale Organic Living Books
Executive Editor: Margot Schupf
Art Director: Patricia Field
Content Assembly Manager: Robert V. Anderson Jr.
Copy Manager: Nancy N. Bailey
Editorial Assistant: Sara Sellar

Cover credits: *Front cover top:* Rodale Images; *front cover bottom:* Rodale Images; *back cover top:* Janet Loughrey; *back cover bottom:* Robert Cardillo/Rodale Images

**Library of Congress
Cataloging-in-Publication Data**

Roth, Sally.
    The gardener's weather bible : how to predict and prepare for garden success in any kind of weather / Sally Roth.
        p.   cm.
    Includes bibliographical references (p.   ).
    ISBN 0–87596–915–1 (hardcover : alk. paper)
    ISBN 0–87596–887–2 (pbk. : alk. paper)
    1. Gardening.   2. Crops and climate.
    I. Title.
    SB453 .R738   2003
    635—dc21   2002151582

Distributed in the book trade by St. Martin's Press

2 4 6 8 10 9 7 5 3 1   hardcover

2 4 6 8 10 9 7 5 3 1   paperback

To Samuel and Benjamin, Jacob and Hannah

Contents

Acknowledgments

My mother had a habit of becoming "lost" a lot during my childhood—but we always knew where to find her. If she didn't answer a call in the house, we knew she must be outside. No matter what the weather, Mom spent at least part of every day puttering in her garden. She was the best kind of teacher you could ask for because the lessons were always hands-on. When the winds roared in, I'd hold the twine and clippers while she did 2 weeks of staking and tying in 10 minutes. On a chilly fall night, she'd take one last look out the door before bed to see if the blanket of clouds was thick enough to keep plants frost-free, or whether the starry sky was telling her to toss a few sheets over the tomatoes or pour a bucket of water over the marigolds. I learned by assisting her and by asking the never-ending "Why?" Sometimes she knew the answer; sometimes she simply said, "Because it works."

For years, I thought my mother had a sixth sense about the weather. Once I had my own yard and plants to take care of, I knew her instinct was born of hours spend outdoors, reading the sky and feeling the air. Like her, I adapt my gardening to fit with the weather: When I guess that rain is coming, I plant seeds and pick a big bouquet of irises and peonies before their petals get battered. When frost seems certain, I cover those plants I want to protect (at least until the Indian summer that usually follows), and I fill the windowsills with big green tomatoes. Not until I sat down to write this book did I realize just how much gardening advice I'd absorbed in the years spent at my mother's knee. Thanks, Mom.

Thanks, too, to the scientifically minded folks who figured out how the weather works and to the practical-minded folks who, like my mom, passed along their knowledge from one generation to the next. Even if the woolly bears I see can't seem to make up their minds, it's still fun to check their predictions. As for the Weather Channel—long may it reign. I'm a confirmed addict, especially when traveling.

Because my concept of the heavenly bodies is as shaky as you'd expect, seeing as how I'm dyslexic about direction, I thoroughly appreciate all those authors who took the time to spell out the workings of the earth, sun, moon, and wind. Writers old and new have added a lot to my understanding of such things as why light changes with the seasons, why cold winds blow from the North, and why it's springtime when Australia celebrates Christmas.

This book began to take shape in the spring, but seven seasons passed before it finally had a heartbeat. Throw in a few rounds of too-close-for-comfort tornadoes, ice storms that knocked out power and heat waves that caused blackouts—not to mention all those days when the weather was great for gardening!—and you get an idea of the logistics that editor Deb Martin had to work with. Going off on a tangent is my habit in both writing and life, and Deb was adept at gently reeling me back in. I'm deeply grateful to her for her endless reserves of good humor in keeping track of all the complicated workings of daily life as well as the content of the pages.

Thank you, too, to copy editor Sarah Dunn, who added a dose of grace and clarity to the sentences on these pages. I'm thankful for her sharp eye—as the first reader of the book, she has been invaluable in strengthening the language and sharpening any fuzzy points.

As a native-born Easterner, I was completely unprepared for living in tornado-prone Indiana. While our neighbors treated the weather with casual disregard, I cowered below the dark banks of looming clouds and waited for the worst. At times like those, I was very grateful to Wayne Hart, the clear-spoken, reassuring, and most important, highly accurate local TV weatherman. There's only so much weather-predicting even an obsessive like me can do herself, and when clouds start to rotate, I want to see the latest radar. Thanks to Wayne, I was always safe and sound in a friend's basement even before the town's sirens wailed their warning.

Speaking of basements, heartfelt thanks to Jim Stinson of New Harmony, Indiana, a friend and neighbor who didn't scoff at my fear of tornadoes but instead extended an open invitation to use the cellar of his bed-and-breakfast home any time we felt the need. Since our house had no basement, we ran the two blocks to his place to take him up on that offer many times. Thankfully, the storms usually veered at the last minute, passing with a gust of wind, while we enjoyed our "tornado party" at the Old Rooming House, playing Old Maid, drinking Cokes in old-fashioned glass bottles, and always keeping an eye on the sky.

"Oh, Boy! It's Raining!"

"Normal" people cozy up on the couch or reach for the remote control on a rainy day, or so I hear.

Not me.

"Oh, boy! It's raining!" I say happily, whenever I look out the window and see anything less than a downpour.

Friends may look puzzled at my cheeriness, but my family has learned what a rainy day means to an addicted gardener. They clear the way as I hurry to pull on my oldest jeans and a pair of battered sneakers. "I'll be in the garden," I call, closing the door behind me 5 minutes later. It's an unnecessary piece of information because when it's raining—in any intensity that's lighter than soaked-to-the-skin-in-5-minutes—that's where I'm bound to be.

I blame—er, thank—my mother for clueing me in to one of the best secrets of gardening. Muddy sneakers on the front steps were such a common sight in my growing-up years that I never gave much thought to them until I was old enough to recognize that others reacted oddly to my mother's rain-or-shine—but especially rain—method of gardening.

When a shower started, she'd greet it as joyfully as I now do and, in those days before baseball caps were ubiquitous, she would grab for her babushka to keep her head dry. Her canvas sneakers were ready and waiting on the front step, crusted with dried mud that there was no sense cleaning off since they'd soon be muddy again.

Totally focused on her garden, she didn't pay any attention to the curious glances of neighbors as she transplanted, weeded, and planted to her heart's content, often "working" right through lunch and supper if rain had been scarce before the current shower.

"Guess I got a little wet," she'd say when she finally came back inside, shaking off her wet clothes like a shaggy dog sheds water. Of course, she'd been wet for hours; she'd just been having too much fun to notice.

Like mother, like daughter. Once I had my own patch of yard to putter around in, I quickly learned that a sky full of rain clouds heralds the best kind of gardening weather. Moist soil, moist air, and no sun to stress the plants—what more could a gardener ask for? (Okay, maybe no raindrops dripping off the end of the nose or gathering on the eyeglasses…)

Moving plants around and putting in new ones is my favorite part of gardening, and a spell of wet weather is the perfect time to do both.

On a rainy day, you can transplant all those perennials that aren't quite in the right spot. You can lift a crowd of bearded irises and untangle those knotted rhizomes (or whack 'em apart with a sharp shovel), knowing they won't miss a beat when they're replanted a half-hour later.

You can move clumps of daylilies or daffodils in full bloom to a more serendipitous spot, with no harm done, during a rainy spell. Even those plants we're warned are nearly impossible to transplant—annual poppies, Oriental poppies near bud stage, established columbines, naked-lady lilies, and other fussbudgets—are worth a try on a rainy day.

A showery day in summer is perfect for adding new plants to the beds. While the drizzle beads on my hair, I transplant seedlings from pots or from my many impromptu nurseries (precious bits of bare space among the plants where I've planted packets of perennial seed or stuck cuttings of cardinal flower, threadleaf coreopsis, butterfly bush, and other fast-rooting stems). Twenty baby coralbells, three dozen 'Moonbeam' coreopsis, more delphiniums than I can count, all charming in their current miniature state but sure to be robust and full blooming by next spring, can go into the soft, moist ground in just a few minutes' time. Poke a hole with a finger, stick in those delicate roots, firm up the soil, and move on to the next. And hadn't I better take a few of these 'Dark Knight' butterfly bushes down the street to that neighbor who's always telling me that she wants to see more butterflies in her yard?

There's so much to pack into a rainy day that it's no wonder I head for the garden as soon as I can when the showers start. It's the perfect time for planting seeds, even though it takes some care to keep the packets of finer seeds from getting wet. They germinate quickly when bathed in gentle rain for hours. Transplants need as many hours of sun-free recovery time as they can get, so I start with the touchiest plants before moving on to the more stalwart bee balm and other easy movers.

Working in the garden on a rainy day means we get to spend all our time playing, and no time at all hauling out the hose or arranging the sprinkler or rigging up the temporary shade. The weather, every gardener's friend and foe, makes it all easy for us.

Weeds yield much more easily in moist soil, requiring only a quick tug instead of a full-bodied yank, and their moist carcasses decompose in a flash when the sun once again streams down upon them.

No need to feel guilty about playing with your plants instead of mowing the lawn, pruning the roses, or deadheading the daisies. Those chores can wait for a sunny day.

Forty-some years of playing in the garden have taught me to keep a weather eye on the sky before I slide the shovel into the ground. If the clouds tell me the rain is going to be a temporary shower, not an all-day soaking, for instance, I keep in mind that any newly situated plants will need watering when the sun comes out to ward off wilting. If the gray clouds hint that they're going to last a long time, I throw caution to the winds.

Gardening and weather go hand in hand. We plant people can't flick a switch or turn a dial to change the weather as those who pursue indoor passions can. Preventive maintenance for us can make the difference between a basket of ripe plums and an empty-handed harvest. Flowers, shrubs, and other ornamental growing things are just as susceptible to the vagaries of weather as food plants are.

Good planning and good plant choices are keyed to our usual patterns of weather and climate: how cold it gets in winter, how much it rains in summer, and other seasonal marks that are as close to "the usual" as it gets with weather. Thanks to decades of weather records, we can figure those benchmarks before we turn the first shovel of soil. But the rest of the gardening spectrum—when to sow, when to reap, when to water, when to weed, and when to do all the other daily caretaking that makes gardening such a never-ending delight— depends on what the daily weather brings to our own corner of the world.

Most of us check the weather forecast on TV or in the newspaper to find out what the next day will bring. That's a fine way to get an accurate handle on the weather, but it's a lot more fun to learn to read the signs yourself.

This book combines the science of weather forecasting with common-sense wisdom. You still won't be able to change the weather—but you will learn why it behaves as it does and how to tell what's likely to be just around the bend weather-wise.

Gardening is a year-round pursuit, no matter how deep your snow gets in wintertime or how hot and steamy the sun gets in summer. On those days when the weather makes it impossible to get out into the garden, we can still find pleasure in planning. In the following pages, you'll discover how to plan for each season according to cyclical weather patterns for your climate. You'll also learn dozens of quick tips and treatments to make the most of whatever the daily weather brings—including plenty of silver linings for those clouds of gardening difficulties that capricious weather can usher in. You'll find out how to drought-proof your garden, how to guard against hail and ice, and how to help plants recover more quickly from weather damage.

I do my best learning in the garden, and the education, it seems, is never finished. On an early fall day a few weeks ago, I noticed that the sunflower seeds planted around the neighborhood by seed-caching jays were sprouting everywhere—despite not having had a drop of rain for at least 8 weeks. That spurred me to take a closer look at the patch where I'd scattered annual poppy seed, figuring at the time that they'd sprout after the fall rainy season began. Was I surprised to discover that not only were my Flanders poppies sprouting fast and furious, but so were the bachelor's buttons, California poppies, oxeye daisies, blue flax, and dozens of other "wildflowers" whose seeds must have been in the soil. Their germination, it seems, isn't as much a matter of moisture as it is of temperature or light—a connection I would have never made had I not noticed the hearty sunflower seedlings.

Just as I was finishing this book, I moved lock, stock, barrel, and senti-mental-favorite seeds from the lower Midwest to the Pacific Northwest. You may have seen photos of luscious gardens in this area, which look as close to an English-garden fantasy as anywhere in North America. That's only half of the story. Like gardeners everywhere, we face plenty of challenges from our old friend, the weather. Instead of southern Indiana's steam-heat summers and spring tornado warnings, we in the Northwest contend with the extremes of a rainy season, when the sun doesn't show its face for months on end, and a dry season, when those lush foxgloves and delphiniums have to withstand what in Indiana would have been serious drought. Somehow they do, even in nonirrigated gardens—a testament to how much we still have to discover about the adaptability of our own plants.

The more time you spend in your garden, the more you'll learn about your plants and their responses to the weather, and the better you'll become at interpreting the feel of the air, the look of the sky, the activity of insects, and all the other hints that alert us to what's in the offing. You may become so adept at interpreting natural clues to weather that you check the daily "official" forecast only to confirm your own. Or, like most of us, you may find yourself combining forecasts from experts with your own observations— deciding that the clouds that just moved into the night sky mean little chance of a killing frost, for instance, even though temperatures had been predicted to fall, and heading for bed instead of out to the garden to cover the tomatoes.

I like to think of this book as an offering of hope to gardeners everywhere. Conjectures about global warming, bolstered by recent cycles of drought and other unusual weather patterns, are scary to think about. Gardening helps bring those great big worries down to day-by-day size. This book will help you keep your garden growing now and guide you in planning for the future. And isn't that what gardening is all about? While we savor the beauty around us every day, we're always thinking, "wait 'til next year."

Sally Roth
Washougal, Washington

CHAPTER 1

"OH, WHAT A BLAMED UNCERTAIN THING
THIS PESKY WEATHER IS;
IT BLEW AND SNEW AND THEN IT THEW,
AND NOW, BY JING, IT'S FRIZ."

—PHILANDER JOHNSON
(WHO ALSO WROTE, "CHEER UP! THE WORST IS YET TO COME!")

Weather, Climate, and Seasons

"DO WE HAVE WEATHER HERE!" MY NEW NEIGHBORS IN SOUTHERN INDIANA hastened to tell me when I moved to that part of the country a decade ago. I couldn't tell if they were bragging or warning, but they were definitely talking about Weather with a capital W.

After a childhood spent in eastern Pennsylvania and a short stretch on the Oregon coast, I was used to weather being a fairly reliable beast. Seasons came and went, with gradual and usually predictable swings in temperature and precipitation. Oh, there were storms now and then—the tail ends of hurricanes in the East, the wind and rain off the ocean in the West.

But none of that prepared me for the weather of the Midwest, where going to extremes is a fact of life. The thermometer can plummet 30 degrees in a few hours. Tornados rule the spring skies. Hailstorms can batter the garden into shreds, rains can run knee-deep in a day, lightning can rend the sky through towering thunderheads climbing impossibly high, and frigid air can come shrieking out of the North like a banshee.

In a speech in 1876, Mark Twain, a midwestern boy himself, noted that he had "counted one hundred and thirty-six different kinds of weather inside of four and twenty hours." His New England audience responded with laughter at what they took for hyperbole. Listeners in the Midwest would have nodded knowingly.

Next time you're inclined to compare your garden to those luscious images of perfection in England, remember it's not just that the British have been tweaking those gardens for centuries longer than we have—here in North America, we also have Weather.

What Is Weather?

Everybody talks about the weather, and for good reason. Weather has a profound effect on our attitude, whether we spend the day in the garden or behind a desk.

The same sunshine that makes our plants grow nourishes more than green things. A sunny day makes us come alive, too. We smile more; we have energy to spare; we look forward to strolling the garden to see what changes have happened overnight.

Too much of a good thing and we wilt just as our plants do in times of unrelenting heat. We also seek out cooling shade and wait hopefully for rain to refresh our gardens and ourselves.

Bring on a storm, and maybe that old broken bone will start to ache, feeling the change in the barometer hours before the thunder rolls or the TV meteorologist announces it. Gusty winds make us hurry to lower the patio umbrella, stake the delphiniums, or, in another season, settle another log on the fire.

To a gardener, weather makes the difference between a good year and a great year—or leads us to console ourselves with "There's always next year."

What's the weather going to be? That's a question so perennially popular that the *Old Farmer's Almanac*, filled with old-fashioned lore and a year's worth of weather predictions, still flies off the shelf more than 200 years after its birth. And maybe it's retro chic, but groundhog forecasters such as

WEATHER: The conditions that exist in the atmosphere over a short span of time; a conglomerate of wind, temperature, humidity, precipitation, and air pressure. Recognizing and predicting weather patterns lets you adapt gardening techniques to take advantage of good weather and to reduce negative effects of bad weather.

SEASONS: Regular periods defined according to the position of the earth in relation to the sun. Because the sun's position determines the length of daylight hours and the intensity of exposure, seasons are marked by noticeable differences in day length and temperature in most areas. The different patterns of heating and cooling air masses due to the shift in the earth's position relative to the sun create seasonal differences in weather, such as snow in winter and rain in summer.

CLIMATE: The conditions produced over a long period of time by daily weather. Knowing your climate is vital to selecting plants that will thrive in your area.

MICROCLIMATE: The conditions produced in small areas by relatively small factors over a long period of time, such as accumulated heat or wind-blocking effects of a masonry wall. Identifying existing microclimates and creating new ones helps you fine-tune plant selection for particular areas and can allow you to coddle delicate plants or extend the growing season.

THE EXTRA WARMTH PROVIDED BY A HEAT-ABSORBING STONE OR MASONRY WALL CAN GIVE TOMATOES THE BOOST THEY NEED TO BEAR FRUIT A FEW WEEKS EARLIER IN THE SUMMER.

Punxsutawney Phil seem to gain a bigger following every year. Meanwhile, the rank upstart in the crowd, television's barely 20-year-old Weather Channel, has quickly become a staple on cable systems across the country.

Whether it's based on the natural signs in front of your nose or the latest computer models, educated guesswork backed by experience can help us make weather predictions for the hours, days, or years ahead.

What Makes Weather?

Our friend the sun would fry us in a heartbeat if it weren't for the layers of air that float above the earth. Only 30 miles of air, the protective blanket we call the atmosphere, is enough to keep us safe from the sun's radiation.

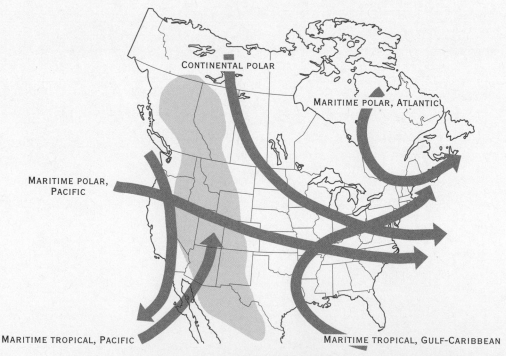

THE MAJOR AIR MASSES THAT MOVE ACROSS NORTH AMERICA ORIGINATE IN MANY DIFFERENT LOCATIONS. AS A RESULT, THESE VAST BODIES OF AIR DELIVER A DIVERSE COLLECTION OF WEATHER CONDITIONS AS CHANGING AIR PRESSURE PROMPTS THEM TO TRAVEL OVER THE CONTINENT.

> ## "Everybody talks about the weather, but nobody does anything about it."
>
> — Charles Dudley Warner (Mark Twain's Connecticut neighbor)

Way up high in our air-filled atmosphere is the stratosphere, home to the ozone layer that protects people and plants from harmful ultraviolet radiation.

Below the stratosphere is the troposphere, the blanket of air that starts at ground level and reaches from 6 to 8 miles over our heads.

"Tropos" comes from the Greek for "turning," and there's the big clue to what makes weather. Inside this layer, air is continually heating and cooling, rising and falling, changing in pressure, and forming big air masses, or cells, that jockey for position overhead. All that energetic activity is what makes weather.

What sets the whole thing in motion to begin with is the unceasing spin of our globe. As the earth rotates dawn to dusk to dawn, over and over, it sweeps the air in the atmosphere right along with it. That contributes to the course of prevailing winds, a major player in the weather picture.

Whether you're sticking your nose out the door, strolling the garden, or watching the weather on TV, what you're actually doing is consulting the current state of four main elements to get a feel for the weather:

1. Temperature
2. Air pressure
3. Moisture
4. Wind

Weather isn't as simple as 1, 2, 3, 4, however. Each of those factors can vary by a little or a lot. Put them together and what you get is an almost infinite number of possible combinations, each of which creates its own brand of weather.

Finding out what the weather is or will be is vital to the garden. When a cold snap threatens, you may want to pile an extra blanket onto plants that might shiver in the chill. When the air is hot and muggy, a snipping pair of pruners

North America has more Weather-with-a-capital-W than England or Russia partly because it stretches so far to the north—well into the Arctic Circle—and so far to the south that it hits the Tropics. When those opposites of cold and warm air collide, they create violent storms and intense winds, and they treat our continent to almost every kind of weather under the sun.

But that's not the whole story. The mountain ranges and oceans in and around Europe and Asia help to moderate cold Arctic air, sheltering those continents from the kinds of wind and weather that Americans take for granted and have grown to expect. Instead of wishing for an English perennial border, we should pat ourselves on the back for being able to grow anything at all!

could be the best tool for maintaining a healthy garden. And when summer slips into sustained drought, a spray of water can be just the pick-me-up your garden needs, as refreshing to your plants as it is to the kids playing in the sprinkler.

As you learn what creates weather—and, just as important, what brings a change in the weather—you can plan a garden that looks great and grows with gusto in whatever weather patterns the skies dish out.

The Sun Starts the Weather

Lift your face to the warming sun in February, and it's easy to appreciate our nearest star's role in making weather. Huge and hot, the sun shoots out heat like a super-duper furnace. Now imagine yourself standing outside in a blast of frigid winter blizzard: The sun is powering that, too.

Warming and cooling air is the secret behind the weather. Because the sun heats different parts of our round planet at different rates, the water, the land, and the air above us are not all the same temperature. All the weather on the globe is simply the result of an effort at achieving balance.

In an attempt to equalize this hot/cold variation, cold air and water flow from the North and South Poles toward the equator, while warm air and water move from the equator toward the poles.

Trade Winds and Horse Latitudes

As the high-pressure air masses near western Europe move toward the low-pressure air near the equator, they create strong and reliable long-distance winds that have carried sailors and their ships for thousands of years without benefit of engine or oars.

Blowing in a constant curve from northeast to southwest, thanks to the rotation of the earth, a ship that caught these "trade winds" near Portugal could sail all the way along to the islands of the Caribbean or to South America, where they could trade for whatever goods their mission required.

Travel too far south, though, and sailors could get stuck in the Horse Latitudes, where air temporarily stalls. The ship was likely to be becalmed long enough to have to pitch the horses on the ship overboard when they ran out of fresh water for them. An even worse fate awaited in the Doldrums, where the wind might not blow for weeks.

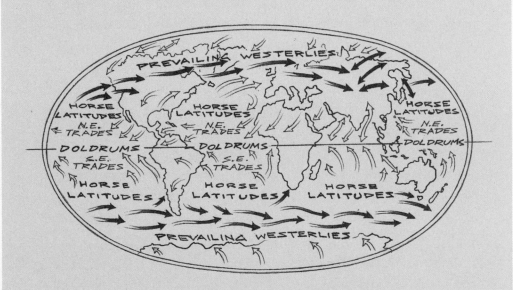

KNOWLEDGE OF THE TYPICAL PATHS OF WINDS AROUND THE GLOBE WAS ESSENTIAL TO EARLY SAILORS, WHO RELIED UPON THESE BENEVOLENT BREEZES TO MOVE THEM AND THEIR CARGO TO DESIRABLE TRADING CENTERS AND BACK HOME AGAIN. EQUALLY CRITICAL FOR SHIPS DEPENDING ON SAIL POWER WAS KNOWING WHERE THE WINDS WEREN'T: IN THE HORSE LATITUDES AND THE DEADLY DOLDRUMS.

Wind Balances the Pressure

Most of us have never stopped to wonder what makes the wind. We know when it's windy and when it's not, and if we give any thought to it, we're likely to picture some fat-cheeked fellow in a storybook, pursing his lips and sending the wind our way.

As far as experts know, there is no icy-browed North Wind fellow, nor any sultry South Wind gal with a flower tucked behind her ear sending us balmy breezes.

Instead we have something even more unbelievable—a home that's spinning around at an astounding 1,000 miles an hour. (So why aren't our skirts always flapping in the breeze? Because we're moving right along at the same rate.)

But although our atmosphere is zipping along through space at 1,000 mph (at the equator; slower toward the poles), the wind that we feel on our cheeks is generated not by the Earth's rotation but by our good friend the sun.

Wind as we know it—the moving air that we feel on our face or watch a hawk soar upon—exists because of a simple fact you learned in third-grade science: Warm air rises. That's why we switch the direction of our ceiling fans in winter, to send the warm air back down to body level. Reverse the fan in summer, and warm air stays near the ceiling, just where you want it.

As the sun heats the land and sea, the air warms, expanding and rising as the temperature increases. Because the air has expanded, its molecules are farther apart, and thus the pressure of the air is lower than that of cooler air.

Why the Wind Blows Sideways

With a troposphere 6 to 8 miles deep, it may seem that wind should blow up and down as well as from one side to another. Thank another primal force, gravity, for the fact that you can turn your back on the breeze. Although winds are generated at various levels in the atmosphere, they always blow in a horizontal direction as gravity yanks them into line.

Trying to balance out the pressure, a mass of cooler air will rush into the lower-pressure area—often with the *whoosh* that we know as wind.

Wind typically blows from high-pressure air masses, or highs, toward low-pressure areas, or lows.

OUR WEATHERMAKING WINDS

An observant man of insatiable curiosity, Benjamin Franklin noticed the weather in his hometown of Philadelphia was often mirrored a short time later by the weather near Boston, where his brother lived. In 1743, he theorized that it was moving air that brought weather from one area to another.

Franklin likely had read of the ideas published by George Hadley, a British weather watcher of the early 1700s, who suggested a pattern of global winds that wasn't far off the mark from what we know today. The power behind the winds, he said, was the difference in temperature between the air at the poles and the air at the equator. Drawing on sailing journals and other firsthand accounts, he came up with a worldwide map that was soundly mocked.

While it's interesting to see how weather travels the globe, what concerns us most is what happens in our own backyards.

Most of us in North America live and garden in a wide area of the Northern Hemisphere that meteorologists and mapmakers call the middle latitudes, or the temperate zone. Regardless of its "temperate" designation, this broad band is filled with weather in the extreme.

Still, despite the violent storms, gasping heat, and bone-chilling cold that sometimes challenge us, this region can be separated from the patterns that rule the air near the North Pole and the equator. As the air masses from the Arctic Circle mix with air that's migrated from the lush jungles way down south, the eternal jockeying for position between cold and warm air creates a strong and constant wind from the west.

Meet the Prevailing Westerlies, the winds that carry the weather across most of North America. The water-laden air that arises over the Pacific Ocean comes onshore on the back of the Westerlies, making Seattle gardeners reach for their rubber boots. But it doesn't stop there. Sweeping up and over the western mountains, the Westerlies keep fronts and weather systems going across Kansas and eventually right on through to the Atlantic.

The Westerlies are prevailing winds, which means that airflow is typically from that direction. That doesn't mean you can always feel them blowing, or that the wind always blows from the west—just most of the time.

Regional or localized air masses can cause a shift in the wind, so that Indiana gardeners accustomed to snugging up their collar against the west wind in winter may feel a warm breath from the south when air masses from the Gulf win the battle for air space.

As you learn to read the clouds in the sky, you'll find that a glance to the west usually tells you what kind of weather is on the way. If you notice the wind is blowing from the north or south, you can bet unusual weather will soon arrive.

IT'S A BIRD, IT'S A PLANE—IT'S THE JET STREAM

High up in the atmosphere, a wind faster than any you'll feel outside of a hurricane is rushing along a narrow path. On weather maps, it looks like a gentle ribbon flowing across the continent, but there's nothing soft-spirited about that narrow band of moving air. The jet stream occurs where gigantic masses of cold and warm air meet. Because of the drastic difference in temperature between the two, especially in winter, extra-strong winds are born; thus, the jet stream. As air masses duke it out, the jet stream is bent and curved like a

> "I saw you toss the kites on high
> And blow the birds about the sky; . . .
> O wind, a-blowing all day long."
>
> —Robert Louis Stevenson, "The Wind"

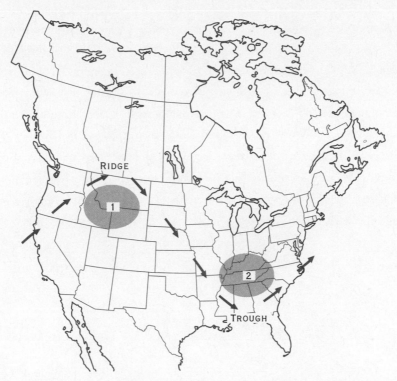

AREAS OF HIGH AND LOW PRESSURE, ALONG WITH MOVING AIR MASSES, ALTER THE PATH OF
THE JET STREAM AS IT FLOWS ACROSS NORTH AMERICA. WHERE A HIGH-PRESSURE AREA
FORMS (1), THE WEATHER IS DRY AND SUNNY; IN THE LOW-PRESSURE AREA (2), RAINY,
MOIST, OR STORMY WEATHER PREVAILS.

ribbon waving over the globe. When it takes a swing to the north, it creates
what meteorologists call a **ridge;** to the south results in a **trough**.

Inside the jet stream, which blows west to east, air may hit a speed of 150
mph or better. That's not as fast as a Boeing 727, but airplane pilots have
learned to put the jet stream to good use. When the pilot of your eastbound
plane announces, "We have caught a tailwind that should bring us into Chicago
10 minutes ahead of schedule," you can thank the jet stream for the extra push.

As with other factors that join to create weather, the jet stream is just another element at work along with warming and cooling air, shifting winds,
moisture, and clashing pressure areas. All these factors are simultaneously in-
teracting to produce the vastly complicated effect we call weather. No wonder
meteorologists sometimes have a bad day!

A High-Pressure Battleground

What goes up, must come down. Therein lies the next element of weather, the eternal battle between high- and low-pressure air.

Cooling air starts to sink because it gets heavy. As pressure builds within the sinking air, a **high** is born. The high-pressure air of a high, which swirls in a clockwise motion (counterclockwise below the equator), brings that crisp, clear, calm-to-slightly-breezy fair weather we all know and love.

When the air is rising as water or land heats up, the air is less heavy and a **low** is created. The air within a low circulates in the opposite direction from a high: It swirls counterclockwise (clockwise below the equator). When a low moves in, it brings windy, cloudy weather, often with rain or snow.

THIS HIGH AND LOW THING CAN GET CONFUSING BECAUSE THE WORDS REFER TO PRESSURE, NOT TO POSITION IN THE ATMOSPHERE. I USE A LITTLE TRICK TO HELP ME REMEMBER: LOWS ARE LIKE A LOW MOOD, GRAY AND DEPRESSING; HIGHS ARE AN EBULLIENT STATE, CHEERFUL AND SUNNY. THANKFULLY FOR BOTH OUR STATE OF MIND AND THE WEATHER, HIGHS USUALLY WIN WHEN THEY CLASH WITH LOWS.

These whirling dervish air masses move across the globe, with highs trying to push into the territory claimed by lows. Weather changes can be fast and furious or slow and easy as one mass of air supplants the other.

Under some conditions, these air masses can remain in one place for days or weeks at a time. But usually the high of cooler, heavier air is moving to shove underneath the low-pressure air. High pressure makes air expand, pushing it outward like Napoleon conquering new territory.

PRESSURE PATTERNS DETERMINE CLIMATE

When air stays in one place long enough, it forms giant masses of like temperature and similar pressure, which then sweep across the globe. In North America, four main areas generate the highs and lows that power our weather:

- Cold air masses build up over Alaska and northwest Canada. They swing southeast, driving the weather in much of North America. Because there are no mountain ranges to stop them, this cold air can swoop deep into the Midwest and even as far as Texas and the Gulf States, bringing the frigid breath of the dreaded "Arctic Express" or "Blue Norther."

- Cool air masses build over the northern Atlantic and Pacific oceans. They affect the weather of the Pacific Northwest and New England. Laden with moisture, the Pacific air masses are responsible for the conditions that created the "temperate rain forest" of the Pacific Northwest.

- Warm air masses form over the balmy Gulf of Mexico and Caribbean, which are well heated due to their proximity to the sun. Pushing northward, they bring weather to the southeast United States. When these air masses are driven by strong winds, they bring steamy humidity to the Midwest because of their high moisture content.

- Other warm air masses form over the well-heated land of Mexico and the Southwest, controlling the climate there. Because they form over land, these air masses are low in humidity, and the areas they affect remain desertlike.

ON THE FRONT LINES

When you see a thick mass of gray clouds low in the sky, covering a big chunk of the western or northern horizon, you're about to experience the weather called a front. A front is exactly what it sounds like: the front of an advancing air mass. In most cases, it's a cold front, marking the leading edge of a mass of high-pressure air that's aiming to displace a low-pressure mass.

When high hits low, all kinds of interesting weather can result. Fronts are where straight-line winds, tornados, and violent thunderstorms often take place. You'll learn more about fronts in Chapter 3. Learn when to expect them and how to identify them, and you'll be better able to keep your garden—and your family—safe during times of turbulent weather.

Wind over Water

Fifty miles inland from where I lived on the Oregon coast, summer brings warm, clear weather, and gardeners and other outdoor types quickly acquire a tan. On the coast, it's another story. The air is heavy with water picked up over the Pacific and released as fog over the land. Chilly winds also blow in summer as the major air masses in the Pacific barrel their way inland. I remember my son playing T-ball games bundled in a winter coat, while we spectators sat wrapped in blankets sipping cocoa—in July!

In southern Indiana, where the Wabash and Ohio rivers converge, the area was once a hotbed of malaria, thanks to the mosquitoes that thrive in the steamy summers. Heat and humidity rule the region, making most folks wait until the cool of evening or early morning to putter in the yard or garden.

Residents of Buffalo, New York, are well acquainted with the effects of wind over water. The big bodies of water called the Great Lakes fuel passing air masses with plenty of water vapor, which translates to plenty of snowfall in winter.

What makes the difference? Weather, of course. Climate patterns depend upon the motion of air masses as well as the tilt of the planet.

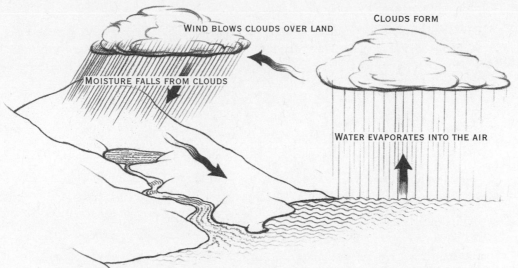

WIND BLOWS CLOUDS OVER LAND CLOUDS FORM

MOISTURE FALLS FROM CLOUDS

WATER EVAPORATES INTO THE AIR

RESIDENTS OF COASTAL LOCATIONS THAT LIE IN THE PATH OF THE PREVAILING WINDS QUICKLY GAIN A CLEAR UNDERSTANDING OF WHAT HAPPENS WHEN AIR MASSES TRAVEL OVER BODIES OF WATER BEFORE REACHING LAND: MOISTURE GATHERED FROM THE WATER IS DEPOSITED OVER THE LAND IN THE FORM OF FOG, RAIN, OR SNOW.

As those air masses of varying pressure battle it out overhead, they also collect moisture. By drawing up—evaporating—moisture from the regions that they form above, they try to achieve a balance in moisture content just as they do in air pressure.

Water is constantly evaporating from the land and seas into our atmosphere, where it is carried as water vapor. Humidity tells us how much water is in the air. As the air approaches its carrying capacity for water vapor, evaporation slows. That's why working in the garden in high humidity in the hot days of summer takes such a toll on our bodies: Without evaporation to cool us off by drying our sweat, our hard-working bodies overheat and we feel like we're about to boil over.

Humidity

As we all know, it's not just the heat—it's the humidity.

Just as high and low pressure are eternally seeking a balance, so are dry and moist air. Dry air sucks up moisture as it passes over oceans, lakes, and rivers, creating the swampy conditions of a southern Indiana summer; the cool, foggy July days of San Francisco and the northern Pacific coast; and the waist-deep snowdrifts in Buffalo, which gets the brunt of the water vapor collected over the Great Lakes.

Moist air eventually reaches a saturation point. Like a sponge, it has sucked up all it can hold. At 100 percent relative humidity, evaporation comes to a screeching halt. The air simply can't suck up one more drop.

The sun is the driving force behind our weather, and it has a major effect on humidity, too. As air heats up during the day and cools off at night, its humidity changes:

- As air warms, its relative humidity decreases, but the warmer air allows more water to evaporate into it before it becomes saturated.

- As air cools, its relative humidity increases. If it becomes cool enough, fog, dew, or frost may form.

Our bodies feel the heat more strongly in humid weather. As the humidity increases, the air temperature feels warmer to us, although the thermometer reading doesn't change. The Heat Stress Index is a scale that uses actual air temperatures and also current humidity levels to come up with the apparent ("real-feel") temperature. On a 90°F (32°C) day with 30 percent relative humidity, we still experience the air as 90°F. But at 80 percent humidity, that same air will feel like 113°F (45°C).

Heat stress caused by humidity and high temperatures may be the biggest weather killer in the country. In one abysmal 2-week period in 1995, the extreme humidity combined with summer heat to kill almost 500 people and 4,000 livestock animals in and around Chicago alone. The apparent temperature during that period soared to 120°F (49°C).

You probably have noticed that your body feels sluggish and tires more quickly when you're outside gardening—or exercising—on a hot, humid day. Listen to your body! If it feels too steamy to garden, take a break, or wait for a change in the weather.

Rain Makers

Look up, and you're bound to see evidence of water vapor in the sky—those streaky, puffy, or lumpy shapes better known as clouds. As moisture accumulates in the atmosphere, the heating and cooling air shapes and reshapes molecules of water vapor into ever-changing formations.

Like other weather factors, clouds tend to fall into recognizable patterns that help us predict what the weather will be. For more on cloud types and the precipitation they can bring, as well as an answer to the fascinating question of what makes it rain, see Chapter 3, "Reading the Sky." The season-by-season chapters later in this book will also give you lots of other information about the various forms water vapor can take when it finally comes back to earth— frost, fog, rain, freezing rain, sleet, hail, snow—and give you tips for successful gardening in the midst of this deluge of weather.

Why Isn't It Raining?

When the meteorologist notes that the humidity is 100 percent, it's natural to expect that rain is falling on your garden. That's not always the case, however. That perfect score simply means that the air has sucked up all the water vapor it can accommodate at its current temperature. It definitely will feel muggy outside, and the air will no longer evaporate water below it, but there may not be any raindrops pelting your plants until other factors signal the air to release its moisture.

Humidity is always expressed as a percentage, but the number is not the amount of water in the air. To arrive at the relative humidity, meteorologists start the equation with the saturation point for a particular air temperature. At 95°F (35°C), for instance, the air can hold a grand total of 4 percent water vapor; that 4 percent figure is the saturation point for 95°F air.

The ratio of the amount of water vapor in the air compared to the saturation amount for that temperature is the percentage of relative humidity. If the instruments show that the same 95°F (35°C) air is holding 2 percent water vapor, the relative humidity is 50 percent. If the air is holding 3 percent water vapor, the steaminess factor rises to 75 percent: The air is at 75 percent of its possible saturation amount.

Sweating is our bodies' way of releasing excess heat. As the moisture on our skin evaporates, our body temperature remains at a safe level.

When that evaporation process gets blocked, our bodies can easily overheat, sometimes to the dangerous level of heatstroke. Before you plan a long bout of energetic gardening, check the relative humidity and take appropriate precautions:

■ When the humidity is below 30 percent, as it often is in desert areas, you're likely to soon be reaching for the lip balm. Air with that low a ratio of water vapor will be evaporating moisture from anything it can find, including your nice, moist lips. If you intend to stay in the garden for long, slather on a moisturizing lotion to prevent dry skin, and be sure to drink lots of water to stay hydrated.

■ Anything less than 40 percent relative humidity will actually make you feel like you have a built-in air conditioner, as air cools your skin by evaporating the sweat. This is a great time to do heavy-duty labor like digging beds, lifting rocks, or planting trees. Replenish your body's moisture with frequent swigs of water and apply moisturizing lotion after your gardening stint, if needed.

■ If the relative humidity is between 40 and 70 percent, you're likely to be in a comfort zone. Weed, transplant, and do other moderate garden work to your heart's content.

■ If the relative humidity clocks in at higher than 70 percent on a warm day, wait until the air cools toward evening (and thus reduces the humidity) to work in the yard.

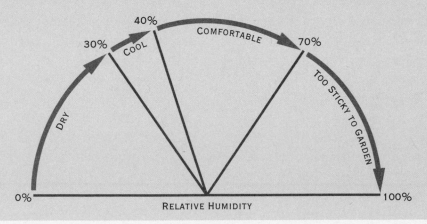

Weather Patterns

Our very lives have depended upon reading the weather since the dawn of human time. If snow was coming, for instance, our ancestors needed to lay in food and fuel and fashion a snug shelter.

Most of us do more hunting and gathering at the local shopping center than in the wilds these days, but we're still at the mercy of Mother Nature when it comes to weather. An unexpected late spring frost can ruin weeks of work in the garden. A record-breaking rain can set off floods that swamp entire towns.

What we call "weather" is a snapshot of the conditions at a given time in our earth's atmosphere. You can step out the door at any time and get an accurate look at current conditions.

But when you want to know what the weather will be in the future, even a few hours from now, the picture suddenly gets more complicated than a quick snap of the instant-camera shutter.

Seasonal Patterns

With so many possible combinations, it's a wonder we can pick out any patterns at all to our weather. For that major miracle, we can thank our lucky star—the sun.

Thanks to our regular 365¼-day route around the furnace at the heart of our solar system, we can start looking at weather with a reassuring knowledge of general patterns.

Death and taxes are supposedly the only sure things in this life, but any gardener can add four more: spring, summer, fall, and winter.

Weather is predictable partly because our beautiful planet keeps to a particular path. In northern areas, farthest from the sun in winter, December and January are cold and the days are short. Farther south, the bulging belly of Earth holds its surface more directly beneath the sun, and so winters are warmer and the days are longer.

Hotter Than Summer, Colder Than Winter

If the start of summer marks the day when the earth gets its most intense dose of sun, how come we swelter more in the dog days of August than in the balmy month of June? As usual, the sun is the culprit behind this weather pattern, too. June 21, the summer solstice, marks the high point of the solar heating season. But in the warm weeks before and after the solstice, heat is building up faster than it can be released. By the time August rolls around, we're seeing the end result of months of accumulated solar energy, a.k.a. heat.

Keep in mind, as you reach for another iced tea to cool your brow, that a handful of short months from June, you can "enjoy" the reverse of the summer heat phenom. December is the start of winter, but January and February are colder because we're losing more energy than we're gaining from the (then relatively weak) sun.

Our route around good old Sol determines the pattern of our seasons. Spring, summer, fall, and winter follow each other year after year, dividing the year into a rhythm that gardeners can count on.

That doesn't mean one spring will be the same as the next, as anybody who's lost their Mother's Day geraniums to an unexpected cold snap can tell you.

Variation is the norm in most seasons. One winter may bring deep snows, the next barely a dusting. But the progression of the seasons is reliable: A slightly later-than-usual snowstorm may blanket your daffodils, but you're not likely to see a blizzard burying your daylilies.

In a few places in North America, such as subtropical Florida and sunny southern California, seasonal changes are much less noticeable, weatherwise. Instead of drastic differences in temperature, the thermometer holds pretty steady. Day length will still vary, though, as the world turns, so the natural year is still played out in the plant and animal world, as flowers bloom and birds nest.

Our Wobbling Earth

If the earth stood up straight instead of leaning on its axis, gardening would change dramatically. That tilt is what determines how much of the sun's rays fall on each region of the earth, and it gives us our seasons.

In June, the top half of the globe is leaning toward the sun like an eager audience, soaking up those rays as if the sun were the best raconteur in the universe. We have longer days and more intense sunlight because our shining star is as close to directly overhead as it's going to get.

Turn the calendar to December, and what we get is just the opposite. Now the tilting earth turns a cold shoulder to the sun, leaning away as if the sun had halitosis. We gardeners pay for our planet's snobbery: Daylight hours are depressingly short, and warm coats and gloves are the haute couture of the season.

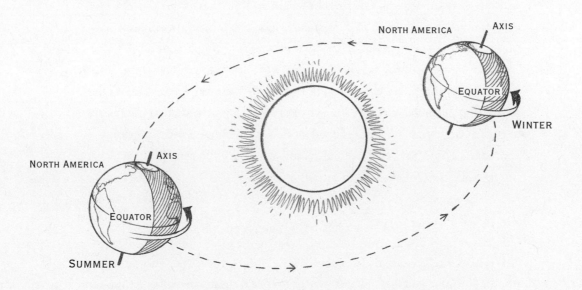

WHEN IT COMES TO THE SEASONS, IT'S ALL ABOUT THE ANGLES. AS THE EARTH MAKES ITS ANNUAL ORBIT AROUND THE SUN, THE TILT OF ITS IMAGINARY AXIS MOVES OUR CONTINENT NEARER AND FARTHER FROM THE SUN. THAT DISTANCE, ALONG WITH THE ANGLE AT WHICH THE SUN STRIKES OUR PART OF THE GLOBE, CREATES THE DISTINCTLY DIFFERENT SEASONS EXPERIENCED OVER MOST OF NORTH AMERICA.

Winter Sun for Indoor Flowers

The sun appears to swing to the south as we enter the seasons of fall and winter. It's also lower in the sky instead of nearly overhead, as in summer.

Take advantage of those low, slanting rays by growing flowering plants indoors in winter. Settled on the floor near a south-facing window, pots filled with summer garden favorites such as geraniums, impatiens, abu-tilons, tibouchinas, fuchsias, nasturtiums, and many others will receive enough light to keep them blooming right through to spring. Experimenting with different plants is half the fun!

If you have a porch on the south side of your house, don't despair: Chances are the sun is low enough in the sky to reach beneath the porch roof to brighten interior spaces.

Because we're on a round ball, not a cube, the actual length of daylight and intensity of sun—or lack thereof—depends on where your pin-dot of a garden lies on the globe. Gulf Coast gardeners can count on much less variation in sunrise/sunset schedules than Minnesotans or Puget Sound folks.

Long winter nights are the bad news for northern gardeners, but long summer days are the reward. When the earth tilts itself toward the sun, it's the northern regions that have the longest days, even though the sun is not nearly as high in the sky as in Miami. It may not be hot enough in Alaska to bring bananas to fruiting stage, but those ultralong days pay off in astounding growth in some plants: 50-pound cabbages, anyone?

Regional Climate

If the earth were completely covered with land of the same elevation, our weather would behave a lot differently. There'd be no tornados whipping across the wide-open plains, no hurricanes swirling up from the Gulf, no humid dog days along the Mississippi Valley.

The elements of weather—temperature, humidity, air pressure, and wind—depend on the movement of air masses across the continent. That's why the lay of the land around us determines the weather in our particular region.

Oceans, lakes, rivers, mountains, woods, and cityscapes all affect what kind of weather we can expect:

■ Air masses pick up moisture over water, so coastal areas are usually rainier than inland. Regions along major rivers tend to be more humid in summer.

■ Air masses heat up quickly over the concrete jungle, so summer temperatures are hotter in city gardens than in suburbs. Individual gardens and the "urban forest" of street trees and backyard trees help to alleviate this rise in temperature.

■ Air masses cool off over the snowy North, so spring is usually chillier in those regions.

■ Air masses rise up and over mountains as they move across the continent, dropping rain on the windward side and creating a rain shadow effect as they descend and leave the leeward side dry.

■ Winds maintain their speed over open, flat land, so plains and prairies are usually windy. But local effects can make for strong winds elsewhere, and it can be windy anywhere there is a strong storm system.

Regional climate usually holds to easily recognizable patterns, which is why it's the first thing to consider when you're choosing plants that will thrive in your garden.

"The season is always a little behind the sun in our climate, just as the tide is always a little behind the moon."

—John Burroughs

USDA Plant Hardiness Zone Map

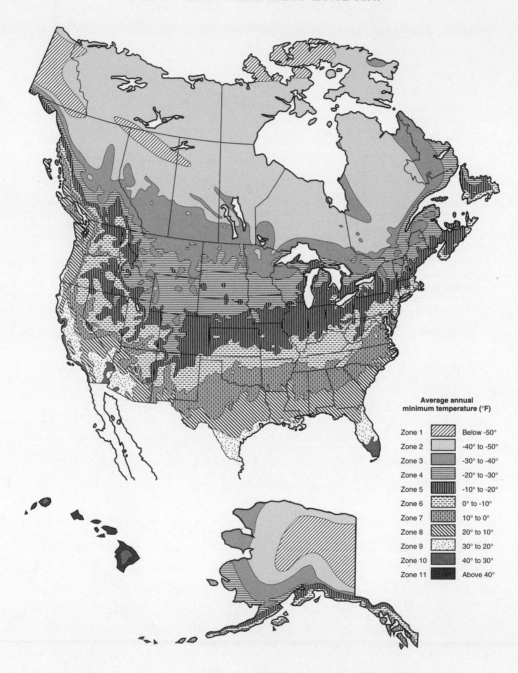

Average annual minimum temperature (°F)

Zone 1		Below -50°
Zone 2		-40° to -50°
Zone 3		-30° to -40°
Zone 4		-20° to -30°
Zone 5		-10° to -20°
Zone 6		0° to -10°
Zone 7		10° to 0°
Zone 8		20° to 10°
Zone 9		30° to 20°
Zone 10		40° to 30°
Zone 11		Above 40°

USDA plant hardiness zones are just the start: These areas are identified solely by lowest minimum winter temperature. If you plant according to USDA hardiness zones, most of your selections will probably thrive. But rainfall patterns and summer humidity are also vital factors to the success of a garden. For example, the Pacific Northwest can count on wet winters and dry summers, so gardeners there plant accordingly: lavender beneath the roses instead of thirsty annuals. Meanwhile, in most years, the Corn Belt in the Midwest can look to summer thunderstorms to keep lawns green and gardens growing. By using winter hardiness as a foundation for your plant choices and then factoring in regional climate conditions such as average rainfall, wind, and summer heat, you can significantly increase your garden's chances for success.

CLIMATE CHANGES

Climate is established over years and years of time. You aren't likely to find a woolly mammoth trampling your prized perennials in Ohio or Kentucky these days, even if the actual bones of such creatures are buried deep beneath your garden. When the mammoth-friendly climate warmed up to something a little less glacial, the shaggy beasts disappeared along with the melting ice.

Climate tends to run in cycles, or so say the experts who study weather records. Winters may be unusually mild for a few years in a row before returning to "normal" levels of snow and cold. Keep in mind that most statistics are averages: A region's average annual rainfall may represent a few very wet years, a number of somewhat dry ones, and not too many "average" years.

Climate can also shift rapidly, especially when the face of the earth is changed in big ways. Slice off the deep forests that create clouds and help circulate moisture, and you can end up with a Sahara—or with the dreaded specter of full global warming.

The worst-case scenario is a scary one: Instead of a 1- or 2-degree rise in temperatures, some experts are now predicting that we may see a galloping leap of 15°F (8°C) within our lifetimes. If 90°F (32°C) makes you sweat now, think how much you'll enjoy a July picnic at 105°F (41°C).

Before you hurry to buy real estate in the Arctic Circle or to order all those Zone 8 plants you lust after for your Zone 6 garden, keep in mind that long-term weather and climate forecasting is still in its scientific infancy. And although significant change has already been wrought during the short course of human history, we may be able to slow the process as we get educated and inspired, so we can keep on tending our gardens for generations to come.

Local Climate

"Think globally, act locally" is a great motto for gardeners to borrow from environmentalists. Choosing a day to set out tender young tomato transplants in your veggie patch means you'll have to consider what's happening hundreds of miles away: Is a cold front barreling down from Canada? A deluge sweeping up from the Gulf? Or will your vulnerable seedlings get their start in a gentle drizzle followed by warm sun to get them growing fast?

Sea Breezes

Land heats faster than water, so in coastal areas in the summer the land is usually warmer than the massive body of water next to it. During the day, the low pressure of the faster-rising air over the land is an open invitation to higher-pressure, cooler air over the water. As the cool air moves toward the warmer air, we feel it as a welcome breeze coming from the sea.

At night, the sea breeze may blow the other way in southerly areas such as Florida. There, the ocean water is warm, and as night falls, the air above the ocean is under less pressure than the cooler air over the land. Highs always move toward lows, so the breeze blows toward the ocean.

Along with its moisture and air, wind from the ocean carries salt, which can affect the plants in a coastal garden. If you live in an area where the breeze usually moves from sea to land, you'll want to make sure to choose salt-tolerant garden plants, such as sea thrift (*Armeria* spp.), as well as plants that stand up to wind.

Choosing an Ideal Garden Site

You can find plants that will thrive any-where other than in concrete—and for those areas, there are always con-tainers!—but if you're beginning a brand-new garden, pick a place where conditions are best for plant growth. Of course, you'll need a location with good drainage and decent (or improvable) soil, but you'll also want to consider how the site is affected by weather.

KEEP ON THE SUNNY SIDE. Most plants do best in sun. If you live in the southern part of the country, afternoon shade is a plus because it gives the plants a reprieve from extreme exposure.

SOUTHERN EXPOSURE FOR A FAST START. Green shoots are the best tonic after a long winter, whether you're nibbling them or just admiring the beginnings of bulbs and perennials. An unimpeded view to the south will give your plants a head start on those rays in spring.

WATCH OUT FOR WIND. If you live in a region with constant wind (the seacoast or the Plains), windbreaks are a must. Wind slows plant growth, dries out the soil, and can topple corn-stalks or snap the stems of heavy-headed flowers like peonies. Learn which direction the winds usually come from during the growing season, and plant a hedge or erect a section of wooden fence or a vine-covered trellis to mitigate the effects.

Being familiar with the smaller scale also leads to gardening success. Living in a valley will give you a different local climate than if your house were perched on a hill. A yard on the outskirts of a housing development adjoining open fields will have a different local weather pattern than a house tucked tightly between neighbors or sheltered by woods. A townhouse on the shady site of the street, oriented toward the north, will need shade-loving impatiens in the window boxes, while its twin across the street, facing south, will do better with sunny portulaca and petunias.

Local climate differences are much less dramatic than regional variations. But they can be just as important when it comes to gardening. Frost tends to settle sooner in a valley, for instance, so your growing season may be weeks shorter than your neighbor's on the hill.

Even closer to home, your own yard includes elements that change the "climate" in small ways. Look for these microclimates in your yard:

▪ Buildings create shade, especially on their north side. Shady areas are slower to thaw in spring; snow lingers longer on the ground. Because shady spots are cooler, they retain moisture longer. They provide shelter from the hot sun for lettuce, young seedlings, and other plants that prefer cooler conditions.

▪ Masonry holds heat. Plant crocuses and daffodils along a sunny wall of your house and they'll bloom at least a week earlier than others in your yard, thanks to the heat collected by the foundation.

BUTTERFLIES FLOCK TO NECTAR FLOWERS THAT ARE PROTECTED FROM THE WIND. TO INCREASE YOUR WINGED VISITORS, PLANT BUTTERFLY BUSH (*BUDDLEIA DAVIDII*) AND OTHER FAVORITES ON THE LEEWARD SIDE OF A FENCE OR OTHER WINDBREAK.

> "I plucked my first dandelion on a meadow slope on the 23d, and in the woods, protected by a high ledge, my first trillium."
>
> —John Burroughs, describing April in *A Year Afield*

- Flagstones and brick paths preserve moisture beneath them. Plants in crevices thrive because of the extra moisture and because the paving protects their shallow roots from the full brunt of the sun.

- Buildings, hedges, and fences break the force of the wind. Put your butterfly garden on the sheltered, or lee, side of windbreaks, and you'll get more winged customers on windy days. Situate hollyhocks, delphiniums, and other plants that topple easily against a wind-breaking barrier.

- Large paved driveways, streets, and city sidewalks boost the heat on summer days. Select heat-tolerant plants for nestling near these areas.

- Sodium-vapor lights used along streets in some areas have a distinctive yellowish glow. Plants growing nearby may be thrown off schedule because of the longer hours of light; deciduous trees, for example, may stay green much longer than usual and thus be more susceptible to injury when cold weather arrives.

CHAPTER 2

"SOME ARE WEATHERWISE, SOME ARE OTHERWISE."

—BENJAMIN FRANKLIN

Developing Weather Sense

THE ONLY THING FOR SURE ABOUT WEATHER IS THAT IT WILL CHANGE. EXCEPT for a very few areas, like sunny southern California, where weather patterns last for months instead of hours, weather is a grab bag.

Making predictions that actually hold true would be a cinch if weather were dependent on just one variable—checking the amount of humidity in the air, for example, to figure out if it's going to rain. But even the most modern forecasting methods are prone to mistakes. Remember the last time you hurried out to stock up on milk, bread, and toilet paper, only to have that blizzard fizzle out to flurries?

We may have a pretty good idea of what goes into making weather, but figuring out just what kind of cake those ingredients will make on a given day is something else again. Put 'em all together, toss 'em up into the air, and the recipe turns out different every time.

Now that you know how weather works, you can begin to develop your own forecasting skills. By watching the changes in heat, pressure, moisture, and wind, you may even be able to outguess the weatherman. Just don't get too proud of your skills. As any player on the wheat futures market knows, weather can turn right around and bite you in the, um, bread basket.

Instruments or Intuition?

Ages before the first weather satellite was sent aloft, folks had to figure out other ways to predict what was coming down the pike. Watching the skies was foremost (and you'll learn more about that in the following chapter). But animals, plants, and insects all offered clues that could be translated into weather forecasting advice.

Just how accurate those methods are is an argument that still generates a lot of heat. Many old-timers and countryfolk swear by their woolly worms and persimmon seeds, while those who put their faith in science prefer to go by predictions based on computer-aided analyses of weather elements. Lots of us follow a path between the time-honored and the modern methods of forecasting. I like being able to tell the difference between a sky that portends rain and one that says sunny days ahead, but I still enjoy my daily fix of the Weather Channel.

Sometimes, I admit, I'm a happier person when I'm ignorant of the long-range forecast. Beautiful day today? Great! But don't ruin it by telling me there's rain moving in for the weekend. And we won't even discuss the sense of impending dread with long-range tornado predictions. At least not until Chapter 5, "Winds, Fronts, and Storms," where we'll talk about "severe weather."

Covering All Points

Thanks to the needs of farmers, pilots, operators of tourist destinations, and tons of regular people who need to know what the weather will bring, the government operates a network of well-equipped stations across the country. At the hundreds of these National Weather Service sites, information about atmospheric conditions is constantly collected, sifted through, and communicated between weather stations.

Data are also gathered from commercial aircraft that relay wind and temperature data back to the National Weather Service from various levels of the atmosphere. Weather balloons are also sent up at more than 100 locations twice per day to measure conditions aloft. All the data go into complex computer programs that predict the future state of the atmosphere up to 10 days in advance.

An Educated Guess

With all this technology at our fingertips, it sounds like we've got it covered, doesn't it? Yet even at weather stations that boast the most sophisticated Doppler radar scans, weather forecasts are still, at best, a well-educated guess. Sneaky old weather can still spring a surprise.

A sudden shift in wind direction or speed, and a squall line can spring into action, flattening trees and sending garden furniture flying. A nudge of any of the weather factors in another direction can mean the difference between a (snow) day off for school kids and just another inch of slush.

Forecasting the weather is still an inexact science, and the weatherman doesn't always get it right. One of the most recent big, bad calls happened in early March of 2001, when meteorologists across the eastern part of the country almost unanimously predicted a major snowfall event (or as we used to call them, a good old-fashioned snowstorm). Schools and workplaces sent their occupants home early, the governor of Connecticut closed schools and banned tractor-trailers from highways, grocery stores were scoured of milk and bread, and pizza shops and video stores did a booming business as everybody battened down the hatches . . . and then the storm fizzled. Why?

Answering that question provided plenty of opportunity for TV meteorologists to tell us how tough their job can be. The giant storm that had been building in the Atlantic stalled farther north than expected, when a high-pressure system over land proved to have more clout than was figured. That kept the low from developing and the snow from spilling. Although some parts of New England did get a couple of feet of snow (winter as usual there), most of the well-warned Northeast saw only a few inches. That darn weather—it just keeps changing.

Forecasting Is Key

Knowing what weather is to come can make a big difference in your garden. If you're unaware of approaching frost, for instance, you won't be able to throw a sheet over your tomatoes or cover up the tender emerging shoots of hybrid lilies. If the forecast signals that a storm is brewing, you can get those stakes in to help hold up delphiniums and other tall perennials, or bring the cushions in from the garden furniture. When it looks like rain is in the picture, you'll want to know so that you can hold off on watering the lawn, get ready to transplant irises and other perennials, or plant more seeds to take advantage of the moist soil to come.

Here's how to tell what your weather instruments—or your knowledge of watching natural signs—means to your garden.

Temperature

A sudden change in temperature announces a front's arrival:

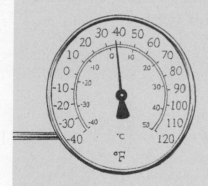

- A climbing thermometer in the early morning hours usually indicates a hot day ahead. Hold off on transplanting, and get ready to haul out the hose if it's been dry. And don't forget to watch the flowers for butterflies, which will be active earlier on a warmer day.

- Temperature is linked to humidity because warmer air holds more moisture than colder. On a humid day, a climbing thermometer may make it too sultry for high-energy gardening activities. You're better off sipping a cold drink in the shade and admiring your garden than redoing that bed today.

- Cooler temperatures are great for transplanting because the plants won't be as stressed after the move as they would be in the heat.

- Checking minimum/maximum readings will clue you in about what your plants are experiencing. If the swings are drastic, such as cold nights and mild days, give your plants an extra blanket of leafy mulch or floating row cover to help them retain heat at night.

Wind

A change in wind direction signals a change in the weather:

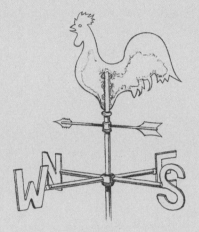

■ When the wind swings to the south, rain is usually on the way. If the season is appropriate, get new plants in the garden so the rain can refresh their roots and leaves.

■ A north wind usually means an extra dose of cold air; protect those marginal plants that may need help to make it through the winter and shelter rhododendrons, boxwood, and other broad-leaved evergreens whose leaves can be desiccated by cold, dry northern winds.

■ Moderate or light north or northwest winds usually mean clear skies; protect against frost as leaves and flowers lose heat more rapidly at night, cooling off to the condensation point.

Pressure

Dropping pressure often means rain is coming, while a rising barometer indicates the approach or arrival of clear weather:

■ Dig in extra compost or other amendments before rain arrives so the water can help work them into the soil.

■ Spread mulch around spinach and other leafy greens, herbs, and ground-hugging flowers like nasturtiums to keep them clean of splashing mud.

■ Freshen or apply mulch before the rain to protect the soil from erosion and help hold moisture.

■ In early spring and fall, clear days (and nights) can mean a cold snap and frost. Protect sensitive plants.

The Home Weather Station

Got a spare million or so in your wallet? Great! You'll need it to set up a weather station that rivals those used by professional meterologists. Oh, you say you're working with a more limited budget? No problem. You can easily plan a working, albeit somewhat more primitive, weather station for the price of a few flats of petunias.

Think about the weather factors you'll need to measure in order to predict what the weather will do next. You can make or buy reasonably reliable instruments to measure wind, temperature, air pressure, precipitation, and humidity—everything you need to know to create your own local forecast.

CHECKING THE WIND

"You don't need a weatherman to know which way the wind blows," sings Bob Dylan—and he's right, of course. All you need to do to discover wind direction is look around: You'll quickly see which way things wave in the breeze. To figure how fast that breeze is blowing, you can depend on a time-tested visual approximation (see "The Beaufort Wind Scale" on page 38), or invest in a sensitive instrument called an anemometer. Or:

- For a cheap and quick wind direction indicator, you can hang a wind sock, like those used by private planes at small air fields. The sock is made of lightweight fabric with one closed end, and it swivels around a pole to indicate direction as its open end catches the wind.

- A lightweight flag, like those sold in home decorating departments and garden shops, will also let you know which way the wind blows. Or tack a few strips of colored plastic or the remains of a mylar birthday balloon to a pole in an open area.

- A metal weathervane perched atop the roof is a traditional way to determine wind direction. But it's usually inaccurate because the holder rusts in its bracket and doesn't let the vane swing freely. It also takes a pretty stiff wind to push a heavy metal flying pig or rooster. Still, a weathervane lends a decorative touch to your weather station setup, even if does nothing more than create a conversation piece and a good-looking focal point for your weather station.

- To measure wind speed, you can invest in an anemometer, which at $40 and up may be the priciest item in your weather measuring lineup. But through rotating cups or other components that catch the wind, this accurate device will let you announce wind speed with authority.

Perfect Placement

Setting up a backyard weather station isn't the same as selecting a site for a bird-feeding station, where the main consideration is how well you can see the birds from inside the house. You're likely to have your various instruments in different places, where they are unimpeded from measuring the various facets of weather. Here are some placement suggestions to increase the accuracy of the measurements you get from each device:

- Position a thermometer where you can read it from indoors. Not only will you know how warmly to dress before you set foot outside, you can also see if you need to hurry out and cover cold-sensitive plants when the temperature takes a sudden plunge.

- Choose a thermometer site in a shady but well-ventilated location to get the most accurate air temperature reading.

- Air pressure within your house changes to match that outside. There's no need to warp the wood of your lovely heirloom mahogany barometer by placing it outdoors; it will do a fine job in the living room. Place barometers near an outside wall, though, so they will pick up changing pressure a bit sooner.

- Mount your wind-direction indicator as high as you can reach so it's not affected by ground-level obstructions like houses or trees, or disturbances like passing traffic.

- Settle your rain gauge in an open area, away from overhanging trees, rooflines, or wires that could affect the drip count.

- Put that yardstick you use to measure snowfall in an area sheltered from wind, which can blow away the snow or drift it higher.

The Beaufort Wind Scale

Lightweight objects are quick to react to passing zephyrs, while heavy things take a strong nudge to get them moving. That's the theory on which the Beaufort Wind Scale is based. Developed in 1805 by an admiral of the British Navy, who included ocean wave changes as well as land indicators for those who hadn't yet set sail, the scale is just as valid today as it was 200 years ago, even though you may have to search hard to find any smoke rising now that leaf and trash burning are things of the past. (If all else fails, light a candle, let it burn for a minute or two to collect some soot on the wick, then blow it out and watch how the smoke trail dissipates.)

Beaufort Number	Description	Miles per hour	Effects
0	Calm	0	Smoke rises vertically
1	Light air	1–3	Smoke drifts; weather vanes remain still
2	Light breeze	4–7	Leaves rustle; some weather vanes move; ornamental grasses sway
3	Gentle breeze	8–12	Leaves and twigs move; weather vanes indicate wind direction; small flags wave
4	Moderate breeze	13–18	Branches move; loose paper and dust blow around

Beaufort Number	Description	Miles per hour	Effects
5	Fresh breeze	19–24	Small trees sway
6	Strong breeze	25–31	Large branches move; whistling noise in window cracks and through wires
7	Moderate gale	32–38	Larger trees sway; walking against wind is hard
8	Fresh gale	39–46	Twigs break off trees; walking into wind is very hard
9	Strong gale	47–54	Shingles loosen; signs blow down; tree branches break
10	Whole gale	55–63	Small trees uprooted; some damage to buildings
11	Violent storm	64–72	Widespread damage to trees and structures
12	Hurricane	73–82	Widespread destruction of trees and structures

MEASURING TEMPERATURE

Thermometers are a bargain. They cost only a few dollars and give years of reliable service. That's why they were popular giveaways for advertisers in days gone by. If your place has a few years of history behind it, you may turn up a Mail Pouch Tobacco or Drink Coca-Cola thermometer in an outbuilding or the attic, or still nailed to a post. In today's collectibles market, some of the rarer oldies-but-goodies can be traded for enough of a stake to cover years' worth of flowering annuals for your garden! If you're shopping for a new thermometer, here are a few things to keep in mind:

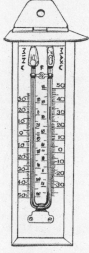

MIN/MAX THERMOMETER

- For less than $5, you can buy a perfectly serviceable thermometer with a simple, unobtrusive design.

- The bigger the numbers, the better: You'll want to be able to read the temperature from inside the house or across the garden.

- Minimum/maximum thermometers are worth the slightly larger price tag, especially if you're away from home for hours at a time. They'll let you know how low the mercury sank during the night, and how hot it got during the afternoon.

MEASURING AIR PRESSURE

Reading the changes in air pressure is like scanning the daily headlines of a developing news story. Increasing and decreasing pressure alert us to what's going on overhead as air masses try to settle their differences.

When a strong low-pressure system wins the battle, the barometer is the instrument that announces the news. When a high-pressure system forms, the barometer will tell you that, too, as its needle swings up the scale. Should that high linger in place, you'll enjoy clear skies, and your trusty forecasting tool will confirm the diagnosis.

Early barometers were 32-inch-long tubes of mercury, set in a dish of more mercury. The level in the tube changed with the air pressure exerted on the open mercury. Barometric pressure is often stated in inches that indicate how far up the tube the mercury would have risen, but the instruments have changed, becoming much easier to work into home decor (without the potential for mercury poisoning). The common dial-type instrument, called an aneroid barometer, hides a vacuum box within its case. As rising pressure squeezes against the vacuum box, a system of mechanical gears moves the needle up or down. In some models, the gears are attached to a pen and cylinder to trace a graph.

The "fixed" arrow of the barometer is made to move—by finger power. Reset it to align with the pressure-sensitive pointer every time you check the gauge so that you can later see at a glance how the air pressure is changing.

Because air pressure changes affect the amount of moisture in the air, hygrometers, which measure humidity, are sometimes used as sort of primitive barometers. One kind uses moisture-sensitive paper to indicate a change: If the shepherdess's skirt is pink, it's a sunny day; if it's blue, you're likely to be feeling raindrops on your head. Another version uses a slim stick that bends up when dry, down when it absorbs moisture from the air. If you decide to add one of these tools to your assortment, mount it on a porch wall, exposed to outside air but out of direct rain. These are simple, fun objects to keep around to entertain friends and family, but fairly useless for long-range forecasting.

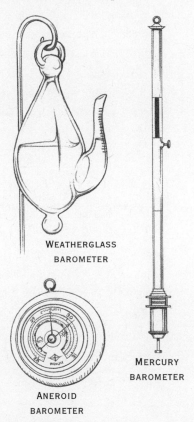

WEATHERGLASS
BAROMETER

ANEROID
BAROMETER

MERCURY
BAROMETER

Baking and breathing are different at high altitudes than at low ones because of the "thinner" or lower-pressure air that is typical of high places. Meteorologists factor this into account when announcing barometric readings so that the numbers don't vary widely depending on where you live.

No matter where the weather station, barometer measurements are translated to what the reading would be at sea level, putting us all on the same level, barometrically speaking, whether our garden is in mile-high Denver or lowland Louisiana. Prices of barometers vary widely, from antiques made of rare wood and brass that sell for thousands of dollars, to bare-bones modern models that you can find for about $15.

MEASURING PRECIPITATION

Accounting for how much rain or snow fell on your garden won't help you forecast the weather, but moisture is one of the biggest answers to the question "Mary, Mary, quite contrary, how does your garden grow?"

Measuring rainfall and snow depth alerts you to soil conditions for future growth, and it also helps you keep track of daily and weekly watering chores. Most experts recommend an inch of water a week for lush lawns and non-desert-garden plants. If your rain gauge tells you that rain has already supplied half of that amount, you can save your water meter a lot of unnecessary spinning by simply making up the difference rather than applying the full amount via your hose.

Rain gauges are the simplest instrument in your weather station. All you need is a vessel that is the same diameter from top to bottom so that you can collect an accurate sample of the amount of water that fell from above. Markings on the tube show how much rain has fallen. Any width will work: A wider mouth container will collect rain from a bigger chunk of sky, a skinny tube from a smaller area of sky. If you're into gadgets, you can also get your rain readings from fancy rain gauges that transmit digital measurements to a base unit inside your house and then empty themselves. Of course, these convenient features cost more than a standard glass or plastic gauge.

HOMEMADE RAIN GAUGE

You can buy a rain gauge for practically pocket change at any discount store or garden center, but making your own is a fast, fun project, especially when you share it with kids. Here's how to do it.

MATERIALS

GLASS JAR

PERMANENT, WATERPROOF FELT-TIP
   PEN, SUCH AS A SHARPIE

TAPE

RULER

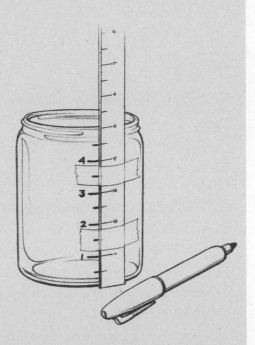

1. Select a cylindrical glass jar whose opening is the same diameter as the rest of the jar. A wide-mouth salsa jar or a tall olive bottle will work just fine.

2. Wash and dry the jar.

3. Tape the ruler to the side of the jar, aligning the ruler so that an inch marking falls exactly where the inside bottom of the jar begins.

4. Use the felt-tip pen to make a line on the outside of the jar at each inch and half-inch mark on the ruler. You can also mark quarter-inch increments, but use shorter lines so they're easy to tell apart from the more major measurements.

5. Remove the tape and ruler. Number the markings at each inch with the corresponding number, beginning at the bottom of the jar and going up (that is, 1 is the marking that is 1 inch from the inside bottom of the jar, 2 is the next inch marking, and so on).

6. Set your rain gauge on a brick or other flat surface, away from overhanging branches or wires. Wait for rain, or set up the sprinkler to give it a test run.

Developing a Weather Eye

Anybody who spends a lot of time outside eventually becomes a weather forecaster of sorts. When someone says, "Looks like rain," you can bet that every head that nods in agreement belongs to a gardener, farmer, golfer, long-distance cyclist, sailor, or anyone else who by vocation or avocation spends time under the open sky.

That kind of knowledge may seem to come by osmosis, but it actually is an accumulation of months and years of paying attention to small signals that many of us overlook.

A weather eye is actually a weather brain—much of the input becomes semi- or even unconscious after a while, making the output effortless: "Looks like rain;" "Feels like snow;" "Fixin' to blow."

I think of it as being like learning a foreign language. Eventually, you don't have to painstakingly translate your observations word by word into English; you begin to think in weather terms.

Getting Educated

Simply looking upward is the best thing you can do to develop your own weather eye. Whether it's sunny and clear or gusty winds are blowing up a storm, a frequent glance at the sky will familiarize your brain with the cloud formations that spell out oncoming weather to the experienced observer.

Weather education is best learned at Mother Nature's knee. Learning the names of clouds and what a barometer reading means is a great start, but experience, just like your parents tried to tell you, is still the best teacher.

> "It is not so much what we see
> as what the thing seen suggests."
>
> —John Burroughs

Oh, Those Aching Bones

Air is invisible, but that doesn't mean it goes unnoticed. A formerly broken bone or arthritic joints can signal the advent of falling pressure. "Feeling it in your bones" is a recognized phenomenon, probably due to the bones reacting to changes in the pressure. My own left leg, snapped in three places when I was 7 years old, warns me with a slight but persistent ache at least a day ahead of a big storm. An ankle, badly sprained a decade ago, often chimes in with a second opinion, especially for snow.

Sudden weather-related pressure shifts, as in hurricanes or tornados, can make you feel it in your ears, too. The sensation is similar to that uncomfortable stopped-up feeling and the consequent "pop!" when you drive up or down a mountain or fly in a plane. Such signs occur when the eustachian tubes in your ears close because of unequal pressure on either side of the eardrum, causing that thin sliver of tissue to bow outward (lower pressure outside) or bend inward (higher pressure outside) and our vocal chords to go "ouch!" Chewing gum or yawning helps open the tubes again, letting your poor eardrums return to normal position.

A modern twist on aching joints is the idea that changes in air pressure may also affect our brains. In times of low pressure, folks tend to feel moody and irritable and have a lower level of energy. When the barometer heads back up, depression clears like the skies, and we're sunny and active again.

Once may be enough to put you on alert for a certain kind of weather ever after. Seventy years after a particularly vicious tornado flattened a path from Texas to Indiana, old-timers I know, who were children at the time of the disaster, still get apprehensive when the sky is tinged with any hint of yellow or green. A sickly yellowish hue settled over the area just before the monster roared in and destroyed their hometown of Griffin, Indiana.

On a sunnier note, your first delightful surprise of a big, wide rainbow is likely also to be a lesson in weather lore, causing you to look to the sky every time the sun breaks through rain clouds.

Chapter 3, "Reading the Sky," will help you learn to recognize cloud formations and what they mean. Couple that with lots of looking up, and you're on your way to holding your own with any old-time farmer.

Weather Signals

The battles of air pressure over our heads are constant, but the only news you'll find about who's winning is written in the sky. Clouds tell us just about everything we need to know about what's happening over our heads—and what's going to happen in days to come.

The shape of clouds, their size, their speed, and their changes reveal the current state of the weather and provide a host of clues as to what's to come in the next day or so. The following chapter includes lots of details and examples of clouds to help you learn the language of the skies.

Other big hints to approaching weather systems are held in the glories of sunsets and sunrises. The clouds—or lack of them—in the sky at these times, plus their colors, are the calling cards of weather. You'll learn more about those, too, in the next chapter, but in the meantime, you can start planning to

THE THICK, LOW CLOUD LAYER OF AN APPROACHING FRONT SIGNALS TO THIS GARDENER THAT RAIN WILL SOON BE SWEEPING IN. TIME TO PUT AWAY THE LAWN MOWER AND MAKE SURE THE RAIN GAUGE IS EMPTY SO ITS NEW MEASUREMENT WILL BE ACCURATE.

Flowers on the January Air

When all the world is cold and bleak and winter seems like it will never lose its grip, a whiff of fragrant flowers can lift you out of the doldrums in a single breath. It can also make you doubt the accurancy of your senses!

But the phenomenon is no mirage— when a strong system sends wind northward from the eternal spring of the Deep South, the scent of frangipani, jasmine, and other sublime flowers may ride along for incredible distances. Next time the wind swirls from the south or southeast in wintertime, draw in a deep breath— through your nose—and you might smell springtime on the wind.

make a regular occasion of sunset watching. If you're an early riser, you'll find that sunrises also hold many helpful clues to what the day's weather will bring.

Current weather can help you figure out future weather once you start playing detective and putting the clues together.

Weather rides in on the wind, so you'll want to pay attention to its speed and shifts. When a north wind swings around to the east, for example, warmer temps are likely to result. Speed and direction alert you to how fast and how dramatic the changes will be.

With all its interwoven factors, the weather picture is as complicated as a Persian mosaic. You can easily pick out all the blue tiles, all the red ones, all the yellow. But to get a true sense of the image those interwoven tiles are creating, you need to step back and consider them all together.

Combining scientific instruments and intuition bred of experience will help you see what picture the elements of weather are really displaying.

Science and Common Sense

I use my weather instruments for both an early-warning system and a confirmation of what I see happening around me. When my creaky weathervane swings around to a new direction, for example, chances are I've already felt the shifting breeze on my own skin or read a change in the clouds above my head.

Combine your readings at your weather station with your observations of the sky, and you're likely to get a more accurate forecast than with either one alone. Perhaps your falling barometer alerts you to an approaching low-pressure system, likely to bring snow at this time of year. By checking the cloud formations, you can get an idea of how fast the storm will blow through or how big the drifts will be.

A third way of predicting weather is based on natural lore—the signs of plants, animals, and insects, which you'll find discussed in Chapters 11 and 12.

Perfume Enhancers

A rose is a rose—except on a hot, humid day, when it will smell better than ever. Heat encourages the release of molecules of fragrant oils from flowers and foliage, and on a humid day, water vapor in the air connects with those scent molecules, making it easier for our nose to detect them.

Herbs and shrubs with aromatic leaves, including Carolina allspice, citrus, and spicebush, are also more fragrant in humid weather. Try the sniff test often in your garden and see if you can notice the weather-related difference by nose alone.

When I visited the Southwest desert for the first time, I was struck by how different the air smells. In temperate regions, much of the fragrance picture is the sweet smell of decomposition: The earthy note of humus forms an almost constant background to other fragrances. In desert areas, fragrances are much more discernible, like dabs of perfume applied here and there instead of swimming in a humus stew.

Although desert air is dry, the scents were so distinct that I could easily follow my nose to find the source of a new fragrance. If I'd had a tail, I would've been wagging it like a golden retriever on the trail of its favorite soggy tennis ball.

Some of these are more reliable than others, but they all take some measure of how living creatures respond to changes in atmospheric conditions. For example, bees are more active in warm weather because heat produces more nectar in the flowers. And bird feeders will be crowded with customers before a snowstorm, just like the checkout lanes at the grocery store.

Other nature-based weather lore— that intended for long-term prediction— has a long history but few scientific studies to back it up or disprove it. In areas where persimmon trees grow wild, countryfolk split the seed to see if a "spoon" or "fork" is inside. If the shape in the seed looks like a spoon, hard winter coming; a fork means it'll be a milder

BIRDS SEEM TO KNOW WHEN HEAVY WEATHER IS COMING—A CROWD AT THE FEEDER, COUPLED WITH A FALLING BAROMETER AND LOW-HANGING CLOUDS, IS A PRETTY GOOD INDICATION THAT SNOW WILL SOON BE FALLING.

season. You'll find many of these old-time bits of weather lore in the chapters that follow, but take them with a grain of salt. When it comes to predicting the weather, nobody—feathered, furred, or armed with the most modern equipment—can say for certain what's to come.

> "Close up these barren leaves,
> Come forth, and bring with you a heart
> That watches and receives."
>
> —William Wordsworth

A Weather Diary

Jotting down a few notes about the daily weather gives you a basis for comparison from season to season and year to year. Matching up one month to another is an eye-opener, especially if you include planting dates in your journal as well as daily weather data such as rain, temperature, frosts, and other high points.

The Human Thermometer

My favorite parlor game is one I play outside with gardener friends. We call it "What's the temperature?" and that's about as simple as it gets. I've been playing this game by myself all my life, so I have the advantage of experience, but it's fun to see how quickly brand-new players catch on.

Guessing the current temperature may not seem to have modern application, but it boosts your awareness of your surroundings, and it's valuable to gardening. You can change your clothes according to the temperature, but plants can't: They'll appreciate a helping hand from you in the form of a cooling drink of water on a hot day or a blanket of leaves on a chilly night.

I credit my seemingly intuitive sense of temperature to my trusty thermometer, which I glance at a dozen times a day while strolling the garden. After years of such a seemingly trivial pursuit, my brain has learned to "take the temperature" almost automatically. Sometimes I'm right on the nose, but usually I'm within 3 degrees on either side of the actual reading. Try it yourself:

1. Stand still near the thermometer, at a time when you haven't been exerting yourself physically, but don't peek yet. Close your eyes and become aware of the temperature around you.

2. Look at the thermometer and see what the temp actually is.

3. Close your eyes and again become fully aware of the temperature of the air.

4. Repeat, at least once a day, at various times—early morning, high noon, twilight, and night.

5. After a few weeks, try to guess the temperature before looking at the thermometer. Soon you will be able to guess within about a 20-degree range—"must be near 70," for instance, is a good guess for anywhere from 60° to 80°F (16° to 27°C).

6. Congratulate yourself, and keep practicing.

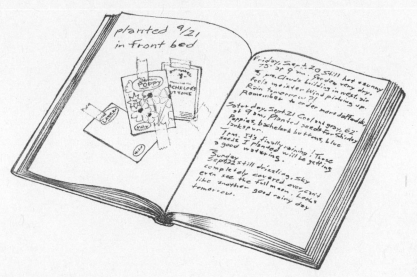

The handwritten journal notes in the image read:

planted 9/21
in Front bed

POPPY

BACHELOR'S
BUTTONS

Friday, Sept 20 Still hot & sunny
75° at 9 am. Garden very dry.
5 pm. Clouds building in west, air
feels moister. Wind picking up.
Rain tomorrow?!
Remember to order more daffodils.

Saturday, Sept 21 Cool and gray, 62°
at 9 am. Planted seeds for Shirley
Poppies, bachelor's buttons, blue
larkspur.
1 pm. It's finally raining! These
seeds I planted will be getting
a good watering.

Sunday
Sept 22 Still drizzling. Sky
completely covered over, can't
even see the full moon. Looks
like another good rainy day
tomorrow.

YOUR WEATHER DIARY WILL BE MORE HELP THAN YOU KNOW WHEN YOU SEE GREEN SHOOTS POKING UP THROUGH THE SNOW—A PEEK THROUGH THE PAGES WILL TELL YOU WHAT CAME UP THERE THIS TIME LAST YEAR.

Over the years, I've noted the date of my first planting of peas and Shirley poppies—my earliest spring crops because I try to sow as many plantings as possible while the weather is cool—as early as February 4 one warm spring, and as late as March 28 a cold year.

That's a 7-week stretch in the very same garden, caused entirely by vagaries of the weather. In the exceptionally early year, the weather was so mild all winter that the soil never froze any deeper than a thin crust on top after a chilly night. In the unusually late year, the garden was treated to deep snow that didn't melt until the sun got strong as spring progressed.

After four decades of good intentions and not so good follow-through, I've learned that no matter how pretty my garden journal may be, my daily jottings soon peter out to nothing once the gardening season clicks into gear. Now I content myself with using my annual wall calendar as a weather and garden diary. A felt-tip pen hanging nearby makes it easy to scribble a few notes beside the date. Since you can see a whole month at one glance, the calendars are easy to compare side by side to get a snapshot of weather and its trends and tendencies in your garden.

CHAPTER 3

"SOME READERS MIGHT ARGUE WITH THE AUTHOR IN SAYING THAT
PEOPLE WERE BETTER EDUCATED OVER A CENTURY AGO THAN THEY
MAY BE NOW IN THIS AGE OF SPACE FLIGHT. YET IT IS TRUE THAT
ALMOST EVERY FARMER KNEW THE STARS AND THE COMPLETE
ROUTES AND TIMETABLES OF THE SUN AND THE MOON."

—ERIC SLOANE, IN *DIARY OF AN EARLY AMERICAN BOY*,
A BOOK BASED ON THE 1805 JOURNAL OF 15-YEAR-OLD NOAH BLAKE

Reading the Sky

PUT YOURSELF IN A BIG IMAGINARY BUBBLE MADE ENTIRELY OF OPAQUE MATERIAL except for the top, which is clear. You're completely insulated from the outside world and its winds and warmth, but you can still see overhead. Believe it or not, with a little practice and experience, you would soon be able to describe what kind of weather is happening at the moment—and what is likely to happen tomorrow.

With amazing accuracy, the sky overhead tells us what kinds of forces are at play. National and even regional forecasts can miss the mark when weather patterns make a slight shift. But if you keep an eye on the sky, you're likely to come up with a fine forecast for your very own garden.

Besides, even the late local news is over by the time frost falls—or doesn't. Your TV meteorologists may miss that all-important weather bulletin, while you can simply step outside to check the sky and see if it makes sense to protect vulnerable plants.

Clear Skies

We're so used to seeing clouds decorating the blue bowl overhead that their absence is something remarkable. (Even more striking to folks who are accustomed to keeping an eye on the sky was the lack of jet contrails that occurred for a few days following the incidents of September 11, 2001.) A completely cloudless sky is a rarity that usually lasts for only a few hours, as pressure changes and wind usher in new conditions that lead to cloud formation.

A clear sky means clear weather. Sun will shine. (At least for today.) As for tomorrow, you'll have to wait and see what the sunset signals, or what clouds move in to make the future more clear.

Fair-Weather Gardening

Our gardens love sun—to a point, that is. The energy-giving rays of Old Sol encourage plant growth, coax blossoms into opening, and bring our sweet corn and apples to full, bursting ripeness. Too much of a good thing, though, and fair weather can seem most foul. When the air reaches a temperature above 100°F (38°C), it's not only the gardener who feels like she's melting. Plant growth slows, pollinators seek shelter, and leaves and flowers wilt because moisture is being lost faster than the roots can replace it.

When extended sun is coupled with a lack of rain, any garden not stocked with unthirsty desert or deep-rooted plants will soon show signs of distress. Here's how to make the most of sunny days—and head off any ill effects that too much sun can cause. You'll also find seasonal specifics for fair-weather gardening in the "Spring Weather," "Summer Weather," "Fall Weather," and "Winter Weather" chapters later in this book.

The Sun and Its Strength

Picture a basketball. Now picture a pea next to it. That pea is our planet; that basketball, our sun. Good thing that bright ball is so far away and we are protected by Earth's personal air conditioner, our blanket of air.

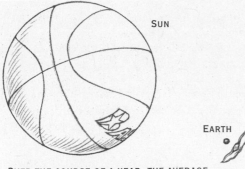

SUN

EARTH

OVER THE COURSE OF A YEAR, THE AVERAGE
DISTANCE BETWEEN THE EARTH AND THE SUN IS
150 MILLION KILOMETERS. AT THE SHORTEST POINT
IN EARTH'S ORBIT AROUND THE SUN, OLD SOL IS
STILL 147 MILLION KILOMETERS AWAY.

With a surface that at 11,000°F (6,000°C) is way too hot to handle even with oven mitts, the sun is powerful enough to fry an egg on concrete—or wither any garden in which the plants are not well adapted or are struggling to survive a drought.

Watering is a pleasurable activity, but you don't want to drag a hose out day after day to keep plants alive against the will of the sun. That's why it's vital to select plants that will grow well in your own climate.

Here's where local climate and microclimates become big players in the weather picture. Our changes to the natural landscape also cause changes to the local climate.

HOT ENOUGH TO FRY AN EGG

That old trick actually works. In summer, the sun sends us so much energy that we can turn sidewalks into cookstoves. This is definitely a trick you can try at home. But don't attempt to wow your kids or neighbors by preparing eggs Benedict on the lawn—grass doesn't heat up nearly as well as concrete.

Because of this heat-holding ability, our masterpieces of human construction—the cities—make human life more trying in hot weather. All that masonry absorbs heat, boosting the temperature by roughly 10 degrees over that of greener areas. Cities may have earned the nickname "concrete jungle," but they're really more of a concrete desert.

In recent years, many municipalities are realizing the problem—bolstered perhaps by complaints about high energy bills for air conditioners—and hiring "urban foresters" to implement a program that can be summed up as: Plant, plant, plant. The more trees, flowerbeds, and grass, the cooler the air and the

10 To-Dos for Clear Weather

1. *Keep* old bedsheets handy for frost protection at night.

2. *Apply* sunscreen, or wear light clothing and a hat to reduce sun exposure.

3. *Play* with the hose to make mini-rainbows.

4. *Mulch* your garden beds and plants.

5. *Water* in early morning so plants soak up moisture before it evaporates.

6. *Enjoy* watching the butterflies at your flowers.

7. *Water* your container gardens and window boxes more frequently.

8. *Prepare* new beds or deeply cultivate existing ones.

9. *Patrol* your plantings for wilting plants to move to shadier sites.

10. *Mow* the lawn and let grass clippings lie. They'll dry quickly, making a light-weight, fine-textured mulch that's perfect for seedlings.

EVEN AT MID-MORNING, THE SUN'S LATE SPRING RAYS ARE STRONG. WATERING GENEROUSLY AROUND THE ROOTS KEEPS THE SOIL MOIST SO YOUNG PLANTS DON'T WILT AND DRY OUT FROM THE EVAPORATING EFFECTS OF THE SUN.

Why the Sky Is Blue

Our sky is blue only during the day. At night, it's black, just as it is far out in the immensity of space. But air isn't really blue or black at all—catch a boxful, day or night, and it's colorless.

The magic happens when the light from the sun encounters the air molecules of our atmosphere. Sunlight is full-spectrum light—it includes all those classic rainbow colors you see when a prism catches the rays. If air molecules were faceted prisms, they'd make a sky full of rainbows. But the tiny particles happen to be exactly the right size and shape to scatter only the blue and violet colors of the sun's possible spectrum. Mix them together and you end up with "sky blue." Those waves of blue light spread in all directions through the atmosphere, making the sky appear blue from the heavens to the horizon.

You've no doubt noticed that the exact hue of "sky blue" varies from day to day. Water vapor in the air causes a hazy gray or pale blue effect because the molecules are bigger than air molecules, so they cause more of the sun's light to scatter, like putting a whitewash over blue paint. Toss a city's worth of smokestacks, car exhausts, and wood stove chimneys into the air and you get a brownish sky because those bigger particles scatter other colors from the sun's spectrum.

Water droplets and ice crystals in the sky can be big enough to send the sun's entire spectrum scattering. The result is white light—which we see as clouds.

less strongly we have to squinch up our eyes against the glare. You can test this yourself in your own yard: Step barefoot on a paved area and your feet will quickly curl in protest at the heat. Move onto the grass, and your soles will say "aah." Repeat the exercise a few hours after the sun goes down, and you'll see the pavement is still holding heat.

The cooling effect of greenery is caused by both the amount of sunlight absorbed instead of reflected and the natural process of transpiration, in which leaves give up moisture from the plant to the air. Other surfaces absorb and reflect sun at differing intensities, so in a very real way, your local geography puts its own spin on the climate.

Soaking Up the Sun

Sunlight translates into heat, which is why dark forests are warmer than bright, snowy fields in winter. (Wind, of course, also has an effect on temperature, but even on a perfectly calm day, the North Pole will bring a "brrr.")

Light-colored surfaces reflect more sunlight than they soak up. The amount of light absorbed also varies according to the angle of the sun in the sky. The heat trap effect of cities is caused by solar energy: Transferred from the sun to solid heat-absorbing objects, it accumulates faster than it can be released. So, even after the sun goes down, cities are still sweltering.

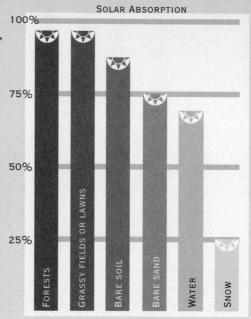

SOLAR ABSORPTION

100%

75%

50%

25%

FORESTS / GRASSY FIELDS OR LAWNS / BARE SOIL / BARE SAND / WATER / SNOW

In the Shadows

Beginning artists often turn out pictures that look flat and unnatural because they forget to put the shadows in. We pay hardly any attention to shadows, but take them away and we're quick to notice something's missing.

That little companion that dances along attached to your heels is born when your body blocks the sun. Houses, big trees, and other large objects don't move about much, so their shadows stay in one place. That's what we call shade.

Unless your yard lies deep in a narrow valley, overshadowed by a big hulking mountain range or a solid block of skyscrapers, the sun will eventually sneak around obstacles as it tracks across the sky. As we move through the seasons, the sun slides sideways, migrating from a southerly route to a northerly one. As we cycle through the day, the sun moves up and down. So even though fixed obstacles stay in place, their shadows (and therefore, the shade) shifts position along with the sun.

In deciduous woodlands, the spring wild-flower show is a brief extravaganza, crammed into a few short weeks between the time the soil warms and the time the trees overhead leaf out. By the time shade blocks the sun, the plants have ma-tured and receded for another three sea-sons of sleep until the next spring brings them back to life.

These briefly blooming wildflowers are called ephemerals, and they're per-fect for planting under deciduous trees on your property—but not for a year-round shady site, such as the north foundation wall of your house. Although the woods where spring ephemerals are found are densely shaded in summer, the plants do not thrive in year-round shade. They need that spring burst of sun to make food for the next year's growth. Order them from specialty catalogs or nurseries in your area, and enjoy a show that starts with bloodroot (*Sanguinaria canadensis*) and hepaticas (*Hepatica* spp.), spreads into spring beauty (*Claytonia virginica*) and tril-liums, and finishes with a burst of Virginia bluebells (*Mertensia virginica*).

FLOWERING TREES AND SPRING-BLOOMING WILDFLOWERS AND BULBS MAKE A STUNNING—AND WELCOME—DISPLAY OF COLOR BEFORE LEAVES ARRIVE LATER IN THE SPRING.

That full-shade strip behind your house, for instance, may stay in the dark until June, when the sun has moved high enough overhead to shine some light on that situation.

Keep alert for changing shade patterns as the seasons progress. You may need to serve extra water to plants that sit in late summer sun, or move shade lovers to keep them in the cool, dim light they thrive upon.

The hours of sunlight in a part-shade spot are likely to increase and decrease with the sun's seasonal movements. Nearly all plants can compensate for the change. Watch out, though, for part-shade plants exposed to the still-intense rays of afternoon sun in the lower half of the country. They may wilt during the heat of the day, ruining the effect of the bed, or flowers or foliage may discolor from sunscorch. Transplant to a more shaded site if you can.

For more about gardening in shade or creating a patch of temporary or more permanent shade, see "Creating Shade" on page 205.

Cloudy Skies

Chances are you already know some of the secret code of clouds. One look at puffy white masses against a rich blue background, and you know it's a great fair-weather day to spend in the garden. When those innocent white puffs start to show bottoms of ominous gray and pile ever upward into huge masses, you can guess that it's time to speed up the staking of your flopsy hollyhocks because strong winds will soon be ushering in a thunderstorm. When you see a sky thickly layered in shades of gray, you know it's time to put the tools and lawn mower in the shed because a long rain is likely in the offing.

Mackerel sky and mares' tails

Make lofty ships carry low sails.

—Folk saying

Congratulations, weather detectives! You already know the basics of forecasting by cloud code.

Clouds herald the weather because they form in response to changes in wind direction, moisture, and even temperature. As you gain experience at matching up cloud types with the weather they portend, you'll soon be able to glance at the sky and know what garden activities to plan for the day.

"Cool enough for summer, warm enough for winter," claimed an advertising campaign for thermal bed blankets, which are woven in loose layers of interlocking stitches. That's not entirely true—you'll still want a quilt on cold nights—but the blankets were pretty effective at evening out the extremes of the room's temperature. Clouds work in a similar fashion. When cloud cover is thick and continuous overhead, the sun's rays are deflected so it stays cooler at ground level. And on chilly nights, cloud cover blocks heat from rising away from the surface, thus staving off frosts.

Most important for our gardens, clouds are the rainmakers.

What Is a Cloud?

It may be streaky, wispy, speckled, layered, or a classic cotton puff, but every cloud is made of the same thing: water. The number and size of those water molecules—along with their frozen or liquid state—accounts for what the cloud looks like.

Water vapor is present throughout the air, as we learned in the section about humidity in Chapter 2. So why aren't clouds spread across the sky?

It's a trick question that depends on a nitpicky answer: Water vapor is not the same thing as water. Water vapor has a paradoxical name, but it's the vapor that wins out over the water—this is a gas, not a liquid. The liquid water has evaporated (see that word "vapor" hiding in there?) into a gaseous state.

Water vapor is always present in our air; the humidity is never 0 percent. On days of low humidity, when the percentage of moisture is very slim, you can't see it or feel it. When the humidity builds, the water vapor forms a haze against the blue, making the sky look paler.

Water vapor molecules move so fast and furious, they aren't inclined to cluster together. But give them something they can stick to—a tiny particle of pollen in the air, a speck of sea salt, a smidgen of soot, or any other *condensation nucleus* they can find—and the molecules of gas will glom on to it and to

The Ultimate Recycle

Here's a factoid to boggle your mind: All the water on earth is never added to or subtracted from. It just changes forms.

That cloud sailing across the blue may have once been part of the Pacific Ocean. Or the Arctic ice cap. Or the Nile River. Or the icicles on your eaves. Or even, not quite as pleasant to think about, the sweat on your brow.

Vast oceans evaporate just like the morning dew, transferring water (or, to be precise, water vapor) to the air. Air holds the water vapor like a giant reservoir suspended over our heads. When conditions cause the water vapor to condense back to a liquid, it turns into clouds or touches the earth as dew, frost, rain, or snow.

Over and over the cycle repeats: evaporation, condensation, evaporation, condensation, and so on, with rounds of freezing thrown in here and there to add the third state of ice.

Wouldn't it be fun to know where the soft April raindrops falling on your pea patch have been?

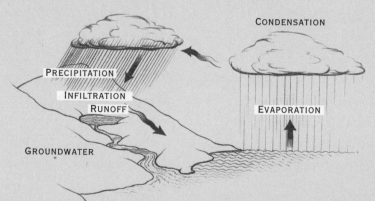

WATER IS CONTINUALLY RECYCLED AROUND THE WORLD, THANKS TO ITS ROLE IN THE WEATHER. WATER EVAPORATES INTO THE AIR OVER OCEANS, LAKES, SNOW, AND MOIST LAND AND THEN RETURNS TO EARTH AS RAIN OR SNOW. ON LAND, THE WATER RUNS OFF INTO CREEKS AND SOAKS INTO THE SOIL, REACHING THE GROUNDWATER. EVENTUALLY, THE WATER RETURNS TO THE OCEAN.

each other, the first step toward reaching condensation point, when water vapor transforms from a gas back into a liquid.

Those molecules are the building blocks of all the forms of moisture we experience—drizzles and downpours, flurries and blizzards, slanting sleet and marble-size hail—but also the gentle mists of fine droplets we call dew, fog, and frost.

No, it's not raining yet! Those tiny droplets may eventually become big enough and heavy enough to fall, but much more often, they simply condense and stay in the air. When the air cools to its dew point, you can bet on seeing grass wet with dew or iced with frost when you step out in the morning.

Higher up, where temperatures are cooler, air reaches dew point over and over. That's where the magic trick of turning gas into liquid takes place in a way we can see from below. Liquid water molecules are way bigger than gaseous water vapor molecules; put a bunch of 'em together and our own two eyes see the result every day. When water vapor turns back to water, a cloud is born.

DEW POINT

Think of dew point as a drum roll: It's signaling that the time has come for the climax of the air's big act. That dew point temperature is the exact moment when gas turns to liquid:

- If the air is doing a high-wire routine at the time, we see clouds overhead.

- If the trick takes place at a lower level, we may see fog, walk through grass wet with dew, or find our late-fall asters iced with frost.

> Frost or dew in the morning light
>
> Shows no rain before the night.
>
> —Folk saying

Fog—A Cloud You Can Touch

To plants and people, fog feels moist. It's a welcome breath of moisture to plants, on whose leaves it will settle and move toward the roots. Fog feels moist because it is saturated with water, just as clouds are.

In fact, fog *is* a cloud! The air has reached that magical dew point number—when invisible water vapor turns to water droplets—close to ground level instead of overhead.

The effects of fog aren't long lasting, but that gentle mist can make a difference to a drought-stressed garden. One brutal summer, when newspapers were full of photos of the cracked, parched earth and my garden had reached the stage of survival of the fittest, I was thankful for the fogs that formed over the nearby Ohio and Wabash rivers. Their moist, cool breath was enough to keep some struggling plants going until the fall rains settled in.

Fog usually doesn't last long. As the sun warms the air, the water in it moves back to vapor state, and the fog "burns off." By midmorning, there's usually no trace left of the gauzy blanket that settled on us overnight. Here are a few more fascinating facts about fog:

- Fog is more likely on a clear night. Without a blanket of clouds, the ground—and the air near it—cools more quickly.

- Fog is more common near the coast, especially the Pacific. Moisture-laden air cools as wind sweeps it across the cooler ocean, forming fog over the water. When the breeze blows it inland, you get the famous San Francisco fog.

- Fog is more common in dirty air. Extra particles of soot, wood smoke, and other pollutants give vapor molecules more to hang on to, making the air more saturated. London is known for its fog, but the cloud was choking rather than charming a couple hundred years ago, when coal particulates poured out of smokestacks.

- Fog is likely to form at night when the late-afternoon temperature is close to the dew point number. When the sun goes down, the air close to ground level will cool off to sound that drum roll for the condensation trick.

Portland, Oregon, is so notorious for its rainy winters that its residents take a perverse pride in keeping track of the number of consecutive days with precipitation. In 2002, it looked like the city was on its way to a record-breaker—33 days of rain had been recorded, only 1 day fewer than the 34-day record. Even the Weather Channel was keeping count.

Then a gray day came when the clouds looked promising but no rain fell, not even a drizzle. Oh no! Was this the end of the string? Nope, declared meteorologists at the weather station. True, no rain had actually fallen—but there had been a fog that was heavy enough to register on the precipitation gauges. Even with help from the precipitated fog, the 2002 rainy run ended at 34 days, tying the record years of 1948, 1950, and 1953, but still one day short of record-breaking status.

FROST OR DEW?

Objects that are any cooler than dew point will receive a beading of dew, like a spider web in autumn, or a glass of iced tea at a Fourth of July picnic. If that magic dew point number is 32°F (0°C) or lower, say goodbye to tender plants because the coating will be ice instead of water.

Local meteorologists often adopt tones of significance—or even roll their eyes—when announcing a dew point, but most of their audience probably has no idea why we should be concerned about it. Here's why those numbers are important:

Frost alert. Overnight temperatures usually cool to about the dew point number, as long as there are no significant winds to blow away the moist air. So any number at or below the 32°F (0°C) freezing point can mean frost.

Fan alert. In summer, dew point affects our well-being more than that of our gardens. Warmer air, with its greater capacity to hold water vapor, has a higher dew point than cooler air. If the dew point is high, humidity and temperature are also high. The air feels muggy and uncomfortably warm. When the dew point is 68°F (20°C) or higher, you're apt to be complaining about the heat and humidity. A dew point in the mid-70s will make you moan even louder. And when the dew point hits 80°F (27°C), you're in conditions that rival an equatorial rain forest. No wonder the weatherman is making fanning motions when he announces the bad news!

Light Frost, Killing Frost

Snow flurries on your arm are like a light frost is to plants: Although their own stored-up heat may not be enough to melt away those delicate ice crystals of frost, the plant's heat keeps its "body" safe from freezing. The leaves of particularly sensitive plants like impatiens may droop, but they'll probably perk up again after a few hours of sun.

When the air is colder, there's a slimmer margin of safety. Now the plant is likely to suffer frostbite at the edges of its leaves, leaving them darkened or

Tough or Tender?

Plants run the gamut in their level of susceptibility to cold, and there's no way to tell the delicate from the tough just by looking. Bedding geraniums, for instance, look like stout types that would shrug off cold, but they collapse just as easily as watery-stemmed impatiens. Exotic fuchsia and even roses look like they should have a hot-blooded nature, but they're usually darn tough when it comes to standing up to cold weather.

Hardiness zones will tell you whose roots will live through winter, but the question of who suffers first from frost is something few plant labels address.

Plants that originally hailed from cold-winter native homes—and that bloom in early spring or in fall—are tops on the list of frost survivors. Snowdrops, crocuses, and other spring bulbs are well adapted to laugh at spring frost (and even snow); perennial asters and goldenrod keep on blooming right through fall frosts. Meanwhile, the tender stems of impatiens and portulaca—both plants from warm-winter regions—keel over at the first strong nip of cold weather.

SAUCER MAGNOLIA

drooping when the sun shines the next morning. Gardeners who plant saucer magnolia (*Magnolia soulangiana*), an early-blooming species with white or rosy pink flowers like water lilies, are often dismayed when a late-spring frost sneaks in to turn those full-blown petals to brown mush.

Late-spring frosts can be heartbreakers, and they're well worth guarding against with a quick flip of a bed sheet over the blooming bush or the vegetable garden bed.

But by the time fall rolls around, we know that cold is coming. Protecting against frost now is merely a question of delaying the inevitable. It's still a shock, though, to see the proud leaves of the pumpkin patch looking like crumpled crepe paper.

The "killing frost" of fall is really a killing freeze. When the air sinks to below freezing temperatures and stays that way for hours, plants suffer an extreme case of "frostbite" as their water-filled tissues turn to ice. The result is dramatic: The plants collapse into a bedraggled heap, their leaves and flowers turn brown, and all growth comes to a screeching halt.

If you're a late sleeper or don't stroll your garden until after you get home from work, you may not even be aware when light frost has fallen. But there's no way to miss the calling card of a killing frost.

CONDENSATION IN MIDAIR

Lying on your back watching clouds form in the sky is a calming way to spend time, but the picture isn't nearly as peaceful as it seems. Water molecules are mind-bogglingly small. It takes a congregation of billions of them to form just one droplet of water in a cloud, which gives you an idea of the frenetic activity going on invisibly overhead.

As air rises, it expands and cools off, eventually reaching its dew point, the temperature at which condensation occurs. At dew point, the air is completely saturated and relative humidity is 100 percent. Welcome to the birth of a cloud.

For an entertaining demonstration of how this works, find a cloud forming in a clear blue sky. If you had X-ray vision and an eagle's-eye view, you'd see that below that brand-new cloud is a particularly warm area, like a blacktopped parking lot. That air warms faster than the air above the surrounding cooler surfaces, which makes it collect more moisture and rise faster—and also reach condensation point faster. When the warm air rises until it is surrounded by cooler, lower-pressure air, it spreads out or expands, and itself begins to cool.

The formation of a cloud is an announcement that the air has reached dew point, and its gaseous water vapor molecules have collected around condensation nuclei and turned back to water. A lone cloud doesn't last long. While you watch, you'll see it shred and shrink as winds shift the air and the cloud's edges evaporate into drier surrounding air. The condensation point has been changed, at least temporarily. As warm air continues to rise from that parking lot, the cycle repeats.

Mountain Weather

Planning a day of hiking in the mountains? Don't forget your sweater. Air cools as it rises, at the rate of about 5.5°F (3°C) for every 1,000 feet. It may be a mild 70 degrees at the bottom of that valley in Virginia's Blue Ridge, but by the time you've climbed to 3,000 feet, you're bound to be shivering. While you've been rising, so has the air, which lessens its pressure and cools its temperature. Gain the summit and the temperature will be a shivery 54 degrees.

Gardeners in mountain states know that spring comes later the higher up you go. Planting dates are delayed, frost protection is needed longer, and early-season perennials may come into bloom weeks after those in the lowlands. Mountain gardens get a double whammy: Because of that cooling air, winter comes sooner.

Watching clouds takes just a small nibble out of the day, but it's a pastime you and your kids will remember forever. Even with competition from TV, old-fashioned imagination remains a delight.

Lying on your back is the best position for cloud-gazing, so get comfortable right on the grass, or settle onto a chaise lounge if you're a little creaky in the knees. Cloud shapes can shift quickly, so keep scanning the sky to see what you can see. Linger as long as you're having fun.

The best cloud picture I ever saw was so remarkable, I pointed it out to strangers on the street. I had just left a diner after breakfast when I glanced up at the sky (as is my habit) and spotted the shape of North America. There was the Florida peninsula, there was a tail petering out into Mexico, there was the Baja peninsula, why, there was even Maine and a hook that could've been Cape Cod.

"Look! Look!" I hollered, pointing. "It's America! In the clouds!" By the time folks figured out what I was talking about, the continent was breaking up faster than tectonic plates can shift, but enough was left to still give a rough idea.

RAIN (OR SNOW) FALLS AS AIR COOLS

CLOUDS FORM ON WINDWARD SIDE OF MOUNTAIN

AIR WARMS AS IT TRAVELS DOWNWARD; MOISTURE CONTENT HAS ALREADY BEEN REDUCED

MOIST AIR; PREVAILING WIND DIRECTION

VALLEYS ARE AT THE SAME ELEVATION, BUT THE LEEWARD VALLEY IS WARMER AND DRIER

WHEN AIR COOLS AS IT RISES OVER A MOUNTAIN, CLOUDS FORM AS THE WATER VAPOR CONDENSES, CAUSING THE SIDE OF THE MOUNTAIN FACING THE PREVAILING WINDS TO RECEIVE MORE THAN ITS SHARE OF RAIN. BY THE TIME THE AIR CRESTS THE MOUNTAIN, VERY LITTLE MOISTURE IS LEFT IN IT. THE LEEWARD SIDE OF THE MOUNTAIN IS IN THE "RAIN SHADOW"— IT'S MUCH DRIER AND WARMER.

For an eye-opening excursion, take a drive up a steep mountain when spring is going full throttle in the valley below. As you climb, you can see spring retreat before your eyes: Tree leaves become smaller and then are just budding; flowers and insects are on a whole different schedule. But the downhill stretch will reverse the process, and you can have the fun of driving through 2 or 3 weeks of spring in an hour's time.

Mountains have another trick up their sleeve: They make their own clouds. As air flows upward along the windward slope of a mountain, it cools and condenses, forming clouds. Enough water in those clouds, and they'll drop rain or snow on the slope. The other side of the mountain gets short shrift. The air on that side is much drier, falling in the "rain shadow" of the mountain.

In western Oregon and Washington, the windward side of the steep Cascade Range is so soaked with rain that it qualifies as a temperate rain forest. Thick, long moss cloaks every available surface, and trees grow to incredible height. Pass over the mountains and you enter the desert, where rainfall is sparse and sagebrush and junipers eke out a living in the dry soil.

Clouds Are Clues

Entire books have been written about forecasting weather by interpreting clouds, but a few basics—which you already have—and your own experience will give you a good foundation for making an educated guess at the weather. Remember that air masses are constantly jockeying for position overhead, changing pressure and temperature and generating winds.

The story of these changes is written right above your head, and usually it follows the same plot line:

1. High cirrus clouds, made mainly of ice, start the cycle in a clear sky.
2. Low, water-bearing clouds form next, their form and intensity determined by wind and temperature.
3. Rain or snow occurs.
4. The sky clears, and the cycle repeats.

The instability of the air that holds the clouds is what causes storms and winds. You'll find out more about the ways this shapes clouds and affects weather in Chapter 5, "Winds, Fronts, and Storms."

LEARNING CLOUDSPEAK

Learning the lingo of clouds is like learning the names of your neighbors: You can call hello without knowing each other's names, but once you become Jim and Mary, you feel more like friends.

If you enjoy learning the names of the plants you pass along your garden paths, you'll also have fun getting to know clouds by name. Just like plants,

> Mountains in the morning,
>
> Fountains in the evening.
>
> —Folk saying

animals, and every other natural thing under the sun, clouds are classified by Latin scientific names.

Years ago, every schoolkid learned that clouds come in four distinct types: cumulus, cirrus, stratus, and nimbus. Simple, right? Not so fast. These names apply only to cloud shape, not to placement in the sky. They also fail to cover a few zillion (okay, maybe a dozen) variations on the basic models.

(continued on page 76)

CLOUD IDENTIFICATION

Use this quick reference to tell you at a glance what the weather's doing outside.

	PREDOMINANT CLOUD TYPE	CURRENT WEATHER
	CUMULUS	Fair
	CIRRUS	Clear and windy
	STRATUS	Rain or snow

Many folks gave names of their own devising to clouds, usually likening them to everyday objects, just as they named the flowers and plants they saw frequently. My grandfather used to call cumulus "cauliflower clouds," but I think that was a moniker all his own.

Learning the clouds by their old-fashioned nicknames is often easier than remembering the Latin because they're so lively with description. On the other hand, I've never even seen a mackerel, which apparently has speckled skin.

CIRRUS: Hen feathers, mares' tails, spiderwebs

CIRROCUMULUS: Mackerel sky

CUMULUS: Woolly cloud, wool pack

CUMULONIMBUS: Thunderhead

MAMMATOCUMULUS: Bunch of grapes

DISTINCTIVE-LOOKING MAMMATUS CLOUDS (*CUMULUS MAMMATUS*) MAY RESEMBLE FLUFFY POPCORN OR HEAVY BUNCHES OF GRAPES, BUT DON'T LET SUCH INNOCENT ASSOCIATIONS FOOL YOU—THESE CLOUDS TEND TO APPEAR IN THE COMPANY OF THUNDERSTORMS AND OTHER SEVERE WEATHER.

FORECASTING BY THE CLOUDS

Clouds change throughout the day as atmospheric conditions shift. A look skyward at any time will tell you the current state of the weather; checking the clouds late in the day will alert you to changes in store for tomorrow.

CLOUD SHAPE	CLOUD NAME	CLOUD'S FORECAST
	CUMULUS	Generally sunny, but brief shower possible
	CIRRUS	Clear if winds from north to west; rain possible in a day or so if winds from east to south
	CIRROCUMULUS	Rain possible, especially if cloud is seen in early morning

CLOUD SHAPE	CLOUD NAME	CLOUD'S FORECAST
	ALTOCUMULUS	When seen in morning, possible thunderstorms in afternoon
	ALTOSTRATUS	Warm front approaching; possible rain
	NIMBOSTRATUS	Rain or snow likely, usually of extended duration
	CUMULONIMBUS	Heavy rain, strong wind, thunderstorms, hail, or snowstorm possible

With so much variety in cloud shapes, it's quite a feat to separate them into general groups. Certain similarities, no matter what the particular details look like, put clouds into three main categories:

Cumulus clouds are like chickadees—everybody can name them. They're the classic cotton-puff clouds, often building to enormous size. You can clearly see where a cumulus cloud begins—the edges are sharply distinct against the blue.

Cirrus is another widely recognized type of cloud. *Cirrus* comes from the Latin for "curly," and these clouds are often swirled like giant Cs, to match their name. They are wispy and thin, with edges that trail off to nothing instead of being clearly defined, and they usually change rapidly.

10 To-Dos for Cloudy Weather

1. *Divide* perennials.
2. *Transplant* divisions or entire plants, which will lose less water through their leaves in overcast weather.
3. *Harvest* herbs, whose volatile oils are at their highest levels on gray days.
4. *Take* pictures of the garden; the lack of stark shadows and sunlight will give better results.
5. *Add* new plants to the water garden; the diminished amount of reflection from the water will reduce stress.
6. *Notice* the lower number of honeybees, butterflies, and other pollinators; nectar is less abundant on cloudy days.
7. *Rake* leaves in fall before rain makes them heavy and wet.
8. *Watch* for sun dogs—small patches of rainbow—and other rainbow-colored phenomena in cirrus clouds.
9. *Set out* slug traps if slugs are a problem in your area; snails and slugs are more active in cloudy weather.
10. *Keep* birdfeeders brim-full in fall and have sand and snow shovel ready.

Stratus means "layer" (it's the singular form of *strata*, or layers), and these clouds reflect the accuracy of that name. They're long and flat. Stratus clouds can also occur in multiple layers stacked together.

Nimbus is an "extra": It used to be used alone to describe a dark cloud, but today it's more commonly added as an adjective indicating "dark." Nimbostratus clouds are deep gray; cumulonimbus clouds are the dark-tinged thunderheads that build to towering heights.

Cloud shapes are often a mixed bag, showing characteristics of more than one type. Then they are pegged with compound names: A flock of wispy but puffy lumps is called a cirrocumulus cloud, for example; a cirrostratus cloud looks like a big spiderweb stretched long and flat.

Higher clouds get the adjective "alto" attached to their type: Altostratus clouds, for example, stack their layers high in the sky. Dedicated cloud experts who want to converse about their specialty (no matter what their native tongue) use an additional set of Latin words as adjectives, such as *fibrous* (thready, wispy), *tranlucidus* (translucent), *perlucidus* (light breaking through in places, pearlescent), *uncinus* (hook-shaped), *undulatus* (wavy parallel lines), and others to pinpoint cloud types. *Altocumulus undulatus*, to be exact, is a high cloud formation of parallel bands of slightly puffy clouds separated by bands of sky.

CLOUDS PLUS WIND

A sky full of gray clouds suggests that rain or snow is on its way. Before you wax the runners of your Flexible Flyer or get ready for reading under the covers while rain patters on the roof, consult with the wind to see what the odds might be:

- If cooler, drier wind arrives from the north to west, the clouds will not be so inclined to drop that moisture in the form of rain or snow.

- If a warmer, moisture-laden wind swings in from the south to east, pull out the umbrella and ready the rain gauge.

CHAPTER 4

RING AROUND THE MOON,
RAIN IS COMING SOON;
LARGER THE RING,
NEARER THE RAIN.

Reading the Night Sky

THANKS TO THE POWER OF THE SUN, THE DAYTIME SKY IS A PLACE OF OFTEN RAPID and extreme changes. Clouds boil into towering masses or tear apart and dissipate as moisture evaporates. Nighttime weather is usually less shifty because the sun isn't heating things up.

The night sky also holds important information about coming weather. Unfortunately, much of our modern view of that vastness overhead is obscured by light pollution from streetlights, buildings, cell phone towers, and the neighbor's dusk-to-dawn security light. Still, no matter how poor your viewing, you'll be able to spot the moon and at least a few bright stars or planets—enough to allow you to deduce what's happening in the heavens.

The night sky can give you big hints about what your garden will look like tomorrow. You can start gathering clues as soon as the sun begins to sink.

Sunsets and Sunrises

We all know the sky is blue—except at sunrise and sunset, when every other color of the rainbow may be visible. At those times, that's exactly what you're seeing: the leftovers of a rainbow.

It may seem like the sun is nearest to us at the beginning and end of daylight because it's as low to our horizon as it can get. But at neither time is that actually the case. At sunset, the earth is spinning away from the sun as fast as it can go. And at sunrise, the sun is just entering our perspective as we rotate toward it.

When the sun is higher in the sky, its rays don't have to travel as far to illuminate our sky. But when it's low to the horizon, the light has a long way to go to reach our eyes. During that trip, the blue and violet colors get bounced around first, due to the air molecules they're shooting through, which are perfectly sized to scatter them. As the blue and violet get "used up," so to speak (see page 57), the rest of the rainbow shines on through.

Red, orange, and yellow, in any and every combination, are the show-stoppers. Overlay their colors on blue, and you get every hue of pink and purple, plus an occasional clear aquamarine or turquoise.

A GLORIOUS SUNSET, FULL OF PINK, ORANGE, RED, AND PURPLE CLOUDS, FORETELLS GOOD WEATHER THE NEXT DAY. ENJOY THE SHOW AND PLAN YOUR GARDEN ACTIVITIES ACCORDINGLY.

In the Garden at Sunset

There's plenty to do while the sun says goodnight. Here are some ways to take advantage of one of the most beautiful times of day. Don't forget to look up and admire that sunset!

- Plant. The air is cooler and the sun will soon be gone, so the watered soil will stay moist longer.

- Transplant. This late in the day, the sun won't dry out the leaves and wilt the plant, so divide daylilies, iris, hostas, and others; set out seedlings from pots into garden beds; or move evergreen shrubs.

- Plant containers. Fill your window boxes and plant new containers for the patio in the dusky hours, when the plants will stay fresh and the soil will hold moisture longer.

- Observe night-opening blossoms. Watch the moonflowers (*Ipomoea alba*), evening primroses (*Oenothera* spp.), angel's trumpet (*Datura metel*), and birdhouse-gourd blossoms twirl open as evening draws nigh. If you're lucky, you may spot a sphinx moth making the rounds of newly opened offerings.

- Notice how flower colors change as the light dims. Certain pinks and yellows seem to almost glow across the garden, while darker blues recede into invisibility.

MOONFLOWERS AND OTHER NIGHT-BLOOMING PLANTS MAY BRING NECTAR-SEEKING SPHINX MOTHS TO YOUR GARDEN. WITH ITS STRIKING MARKINGS AND A WINGSPAN OF MORE THAN 3 INCHES, A VISITING SPHINX MOTH MAY REMIND YOU OF A NIGHT-FLYING HUMMINGBIRD AS IT DARTS FROM FLOWER TO FLOWER.

Flaming Colors

Sometimes the display at sunrise or sunset is subtle, a simple wash of color in an uncluttered sky. Other days, the whole sky seems to be on fire.

What makes the difference? Water—and dirt.

The water suspended in clouds gives us those fire-in-the-sky sunsets and sunrises. When the rays of red, orange, and yellow light hit the water molecules, they scatter, making us ooh and aah.

GLORIES AT NIGHT, GARDENER'S DELIGHT

The colors of the sunrise usually report what has passed, rather than what's to come. Weather in the eastern sky is usually on its way out since winds blow generally west to east. Any clouds lingering to greet the rising sun will soon be history—unless the wind is from the east to south, in which case you'd better take heed!

It may be old news in the eastern sky, but in the western sky you can see signs and portents in the colors that light the sky. The clouds that glow with color at sunset are carrying the weather toward us. Their colors are a hint of the state of water within them—which may be falling on our heads before long.

Figure on the sunset forecast being good for the following day. If strong winds sweep in, though—from any direction—all bets are off.

"We are climbing Jacob's ladder..." goes the hymn, but the ray of light we sometimes see, especially near sunset, won't get you up to Heaven. The "Jacob's ladder" effect is caused by dust particles scattering the sunlight as it streams through a break in the clouds.

Dirt particles in the air scatter light, too, and encourage the water vapor in the air to form cloud-level water droplets. When I lived on the coast of Oregon, I was disappointed by the lack of flaming towers of clouds. Most of the sunsets were of the clear-wash-of-color variety—I suspect because the ocean-swept air was relatively clean. Volcanoes are famed for creating fantastic sunsets—once the major ash cloud has settled. Huge amounts of sulfuric acid molecules create a haze that sets the sky on fire with red, orange, and yellow.

SUNSET COLORS	PROBABLE FORECAST
The fiery classic: brilliant red, pink, orange, purple, with patches of clear, pale lavender-blue sky peeking through high clouds	Fair
Gray, with faint wash of color	Fair
Red and yellow on very low clouds	Unsettled; may bring rain
Rosy pink on high clouds	Fair
Golden yellow	Wind
Pale yellow	Rain within the next day or two
Gray clouds against a bright white background	Rain
Ball of sun is fiery red, no clouds	Fair

The Moon as Gardening Aid

Some full-moon nights, the glow from our celestial night-light may be bright enough to weed by, but don't worry: We're not going to put you to work in the garden 24 hours a day!

Instead of laboring by the light of the moon, spend the next full moon night sitting on that garden bench that stands vacant during the day (because you're always pulling just one more weed). Old-time gardeners relied upon the moon. They used it to guide their planting times, their harvests, and the cycle of their lives. Some folks still garden by the moon, putting their faith in the wisdom of the generations of gardeners who handed down the lunar lore.

Planting by Moon Phases

All of the water on the earth moves with the moon, or so goes the theory. We know that the rising and falling of ocean tides keeps time to the moon's cycle. Perhaps the sprouting of seeds and the fattening of potatoes follow the moon, too.

Time-honored gardening lore guarantees success if you sow and reap according to the phases of the moon. It's fun to try your own experiments with planting "in the growing of the moon" (waxing) or pulling weeds "on the old of the moon" (waning). But getting more familiar with the moon is worth it by virtue of beauty alone. And, the more you learn about the moon's movements, the more you'll grasp about its workings in relationship to the earth and the sun. Here are some moon facts to get you started:

- The moon has no light of its own: Moonlight is simply sunlight reflected off the moon's surface.

- Half of the moon is always lighted. It's the moon's place in orbit around the earth that determines how much of it we see illuminated. A skinny crescent moon is placed just right to show us only a curved sliver of its lighted side.

- A full moon rises just as the sun sets. At that point in its orbit, the moon is on the far side of the earth from the sun.

We still know a full moon when we see it, but that's the extent of most of modern society's knowledge about the moon. You can remedy that just by looking up more often. The 29-day cycle of the moon's waxing and waning is easy to keep track of.

WAXING OR WANING?

The phases of the moon begin at new, when the moon is between Earth and the sun. They gradually fill from earliest crescent to first quarter to gibbous to full, then diminish in similar stages until the moon "disappears" to new again. The full orbit takes 29 days, 12 hours, and 44 minutes, to be exact.

You can tell whether the moon is increasing toward full (waxing) or decreasing toward new (waning) by watching its outer curve:

▪ If the outer curve is toward the right, the moon is waxing. This period is also called "the growing of the moon" or "on the new moon."

▪ If the outer curve faces left, the moon is waning. This phase is also known as "the old of the moon" or "the darkening of the moon."

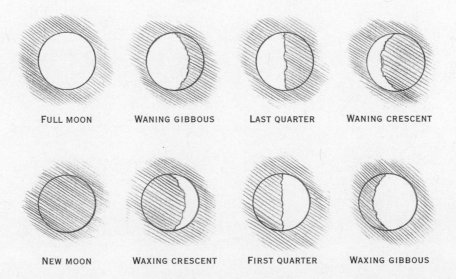

FULL MOON   WANING GIBBOUS   LAST QUARTER   WANING CRESCENT

NEW MOON   WAXING CRESCENT   FIRST QUARTER   WAXING GIBBOUS

Root-vegetable planters and night-garden admirers aren't the only souls you may meet by the light of the moon. Rabbits are unusually active on full-moon nights, especially during courtship season. You may spot them playing an Olympics-worthy game of leapfrog—or should we say leapbunny?

Part of the dating game among cotton-tail rabbits involves running at full speed toward each other, then leaping high into the air. Watch for this ballet in your own backyard on moonlit nights in late winter to spring. Then watch for more bunnies nibbling your lettuce later in the summer.

MOON PLANTING CALENDAR

Now that you know as much about the moon as your great-granddaddy did, you're ready to start gardening by the phases. Be forewarned, though: If you didn't absorb this info as a youngster, it may take years until you get it all down. Here are some moon-planting tips to start with:

Planting. Plant all things whose edible parts are above the earth while the moon is increasing (waxing). Plant all things whose edible parts are below the earth while the moon is darkening (waning). Plant flowers while the moon is in the first quarter. Never plant anything on the first day of the new moon.

IF YOU WANT YOUR PATCH OF SWEET CORN TO THRIVE, PLANT THE SEED WHEN THE MOON IS INCREASING, OR WAXING. GARDEN LORE RECOMMENDS THIS TIMING FOR ALL CROPS THAT BEAR THEIR FRUITS ABOVE THE GROUND, WHILE ROOT CROPS SUCH AS POTATOES AND CARROTS SHOULD GO IN WHILE THE MOON IS WANING. IT'S FUN TO TRY PLANTING YOUR GARDEN BY THE PHASES OF THE MOON—AND YOU MAY BE SURPRISED BY THE RESULTS!

Grafting. Graft when the moon is increasing.

Weeding. Pull weeds or turn sod on the fourth quarter of the moon.

Harvesting. Pick apples, pears, and other tree fruits in the old of the moon; they will rot if picked while the moon is increasing. Dig turnips, carrots, and potatoes on the old of the moon; they will keep better.

Preserving. Make preserves and jelly in the last quarter of the moon. Can vegetables when the moon is waning.

I STILL HAVE TO RESORT TO THAT GRADE-SCHOOL DEMONSTRATION AND USE AN ORANGE, AN APPLE, AND A FLASHLIGHT TO FIGURE OUT WHY THE MOON WAXES AND WANES, BUT I HAVE NO TROUBLE RECITING THE NAMES OF THE MOON'S PHYSICAL FEATURES. THE WORDS ARE PURE POETRY: SEA OF TRANQUILITY, SEA OF SERENITY, SEA OF FERTILITY, SEA OF NECTAR, OCEAN OF STORMS, SEA OF TEARS, LAKE OF DREAMS, BAY OF RAINBOWS. WHY, IT'S A GARDENER'S YEAR!

Full Moon Names

Native American tribes marked time by the full moon, and many gave their own names to each month (or "moon") according to the weather-related events that took place in that period.

MONTH	NAME	EXPLANATION
JANUARY	Wolf Moon	Wild animals are hungry and howling in the cold woods.
FEBRUARY	Snow Moon	The deepest snowfalls can be expected this month.
	Hunger Moon	Food stores are getting scarce, and bellies are rumbling.
MARCH	Sap Moon	Time to tap the sweet stuff rising up through maple trees.
	Worm Moon	Small piles of earthworm castings on the soil's surface show that life is stirring, a reason to hope for easier days to come.
	Crow Moon	In the far North, crows are the traditional harbinger of spring.
	Windy Moon	March comes and goes like a lion, roaring gusty winds.
APRIL	Grass Moon	New growth of slender grass blades means a time for rejoicing because milder weather is on the way.
	Flower Moon	The reappearance of early wildflowers is a sign for celebration.
	Fish or Shad Moon	Shad, which live in the ocean as adults but spawn in fresh water, move upstream now to lay their eggs.
MAY	Corn Planting Moon	Time to get the main crop in the now-warm soil.
	Flower Moon	Peak wildflower season in many places.
JUNE	Strawberry Moon	Just as beloved in the old days, sweet strawberries, ripe for the picking, were important enough to name the month.
	Green Corn Moon	Time to feast on tender, milky-kerneled corn.

MONTH	NAME	EXPLANATION
JULY	Buck Moon	Male deer are rubbing the velvety coating off their new antlers.
	Thunder Moon	Warmer summer air sets the stage for collisions with cold fronts, sparking thunderstorms.
AUGUST	Red Moon	Haze on the horizon often colors this month's moon blood red or deep orange as it rises.
	Corn Moon	Fully ripe corn is delicious blackened in its husk over a fire.
SEPTEMBER	Harvest Moon	A busy month for picking squash, pumpkins, shell beans, ear corn, and other staples in the moon's extra light.
	Nut Moon	The season to gather walnuts, hickories, beechnuts, pecans, hazelnuts, and any other nut you can find.
OCTOBER	Hunter's Moon	Deer, turkeys, squirrels, and other game animals are plump, and winter isn't far away. Time to stock the larder.
	Harvest Moon	Still a good time for bringing in the sheaves.
NOVEMBER	Beaver Moon	With cold weather, these animals grow thick, soft fur. This is a timely month to trap them to make warm blankets.
	Frost Moon	An icy layer on grass and plants often greets the eyes on a November morn.
DECEMBER	Cold Moon	Full winter, and long hours of dark and cold.
	Long Nights Moon	Plenty of hours to gaze upon the face of this month's moon.

Moon Phenomena

With so many of us away at work during the daylight hours, nighttime strolls in the garden are no longer reserved only for the romantically inclined. After dark may be the only hours available for yanking a few weeds, watering, or just enjoying the pleasures of your garden.

The moon will be your companion on most nights of the month and, like all things in the sky, this lunar body holds some good clues to deciphering the weather that's to come. Notice any clouds that it illuminates: They will have the same attributes as daytime clouds, except that they're more difficult to see clearly!

> "Though the hut is hidden fairly deep among the trees, they have now planted five banana trees to make the view of the moon more arresting."
>
> —Matsuo Basho, 17th-century Chinese poet

The moon glows only with reflected light, so the view of your garden won't be nearly as clear as when the sun illuminates matters at hand. Even the brightest full moon can muster only about 0.02 foot-candles of light. A "foot-candle" is the amount of light that falls upon a 1-square-foot surface that's placed 1 foot away from an ordinary taper. The full moon produces one-fiftieth of that illumination! Think about how many candles you need as a centerpiece for a dinner by candlelight, and you'll quickly see how feeble moonlight is. But our marvelous eyesight can adjust even to such dim light, so while you may not be able to appreciate the true colors of your garden at night, you'll be able to see well enough to tell an iris from a peony.

As you get into the habit of keeping an eye on the moon, you're likely to spot one of the phenomena it occasionally treats us to. As with any sky show, these out-of-the-ordinary sightings are a hint that weather-makers are going on overhead.

RING AROUND THE MOON

The most common moon trick is the prosaically named "ring around the moon," which looks exactly like its name. The ring may be narrow and near the moon, wide and far away, or any combination in between. It can be so dim you have to look twice to see if it's there, or a hazy but bright halo. It may be creamy or golden or it may even be tinged with faint rainbow colors.

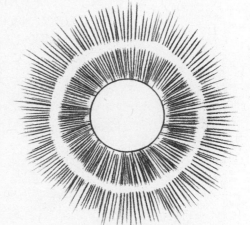

WHILE WEATHER LORE TELLS US THAT A RING AROUND THE MOON FORETELLS RAIN, THIS DISTINCTIVE NIGHTTIME DISPLAY DOESN'T ALWAYS RESULT IN PRECIPITATION. PAY ATTENTION TO YOUR BAROMETER TO SEE IF THE MOISTURE THAT GIVES THE MOON ITS HALO WILL WIND UP ON YOUR GARDEN.

Spotting a ring around the full or almost-full moon is easy because the circle of light is definitely different from what we're used to seeing. Spend a little time appreciating the niceties of a ring around the moon whenever you see one, and you'll discover that their nuances are as beautiful as those of rainbows.

Like a rainbow, the ring is caused by light reflecting off the moon, then hitting water or ice droplets in the air. As the already-weak moonlight refracts through the water, it creates a round-the-moon rainbow—not nearly as bright as the spectrum made by sunlight, but still noticeable and lovely in a subdued way. If you're lucky, you may sometimes even spy a double ring around the moon.

On a full moon night with a cloudy sky, the patterns of color the moonlight makes can be glorious. One night I watched the moonlight play off a bank of speckled, striped "mackerel" clouds, illuminating them with a wide, ever-changing band of color that shifted from apricot to deep, dusky purple. It looked like the shaded stripes of a tiger, so striking that I roused some nearby friends out of their house to watch with me.

Weather watchers over the years have developed various interpretations of the meaning of a ring around the moon. Here are a couple such observations that prove true more often than not:

- A ring around the moon means rain, or so the saying goes. This maxim bears out much of the time because the ring is a sign that quite a bit of moisture is in the sky. Whether you'll wake up to a drizzle depends on how the wind shifts during the night, or how air pressure changes. When you see the ring, check your barometer: If it's falling, you can bet on rain within a day or two.

- A ring around the moon means not much chance of frost during those iffy late-spring and fall weeks when we're trying to wiggle a few extra days out of the beginning or end of the garden season. As we saw in Chapter 3, a cloudy sky holds heat closer to the earth, so a frost is less likely when there are enough clouds to bend moonshine into a ring.

MOONBOW

Most rainbow aficionados reserve the word "moonbow" to describe a faintly colored arc created by refracted moonlight, not the full circle called a "ring around the moon."

Moonbows are much more rare than the ring effect. Even though moonlight is much weaker than sunlight, you can sometimes see a moonbow created by moonlight shining through a spray of water that's way down here on earth. On a clear night within a day or two of a full moon, moonbow pilgrims make the trek to waterfalls in hopes of catching the phenomenon. The moonbow at Victoria Falls in Zimbabwe, Africa, is internationally famous, but if a trip to Africa isn't in the plans, you can also catch a moonbow at these three public sites:

- Cumberland Falls State Resort Park, eastern Kentucky

- Yosemite Falls, California

- Middle Falls on the Genesee River, New York State

I keep meaning to experiment with creating my own moonbow closer to earth—by angling the spray from a hose with a mister head on a full moon night in hopes of getting that elusive angle just right. One of these months, I'll remember to try it.

Starry, Starry Night

When people who spend a lot of time studying the skies talk about nighttime pollution, they're not discussing the kind that turns the sky brown or makes you wrinkle your nose. It's light, too much of it, that "pollutes" our skies during the darkest hours.

The light produced by streetlights, city lights, and the dusk-to-dawn light on your neighbor's garage all chip in to create a constant glow over heavily populated areas. Take a cross-country trip at night through the wide-open spaces of Montana or Arizona, and you'll be able to see a glow from approaching civilization while you're still 50 miles away. That can be comforting when you need a motel or a gas station, but when you're trying to read the night skies, light is a definite hindrance.

Still, no matter where you live, you can still make out at least a few of the brightest natural night-lights. The moon is visible even over Times Square, and in most places you can also pick out nearby planets like Jupiter and Venus, and a few of the brightest stars. Those few points of light in the night sky are all you need to determine the clues for coming weather.

"But my friends ask what I will do when I get there. Will it not be employment enough to watch the progress of the seasons?" —Henry David Thoreau, *Walden*

Starlight Weather Indicators

By checking whether the moon or usually visible stars are shining bright or obscured, you'll also be able to determine if the sky is cloudy:

- In winter, clouds at night keep temperatures near ground level warmer. Frosts are more likely on clear nights.

- In summer, nighttime clouds make the air feel more humid. Heavy dew and fog are possibilities when the night sky is cloudy.

Planting by the Signs

As little as a generation ago, clear skies were the norm, not the exception. Every gardener—and that was mostly everybody, because if you didn't grow it, you probably didn't eat it—knew winter was approaching as soon as they spotted the great hunter Orion stalking the sky. Time to dig the potatoes, cure the pumpkins, and get ready for a season of cold.

Today it's unusual to find anyone who knows the stars by name. Most of us never set foot outside our houses at night unless we have dogs to walk or plants to hurriedly cover against a frost. In Appalachia and other pockets where knowledge is handed down from one generation to another, planting "by the signs," a system that relies on the constellations that make up the zodiac, is still in service.

The art of planting by constellations was most likely developed in response to a verse from Genesis:

Let there be lights in the firmament of the heavens to divide the day from the night; and let them be for signs, and for seasons, and for years (Genesis 1:14).

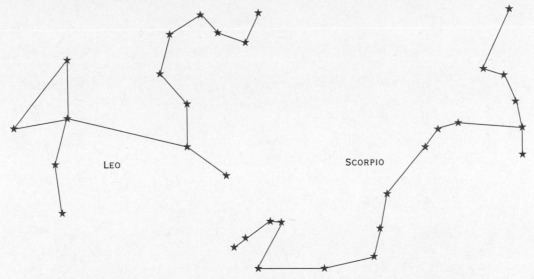

LEO

SCORPIO

NOTING THE REGULAR PATH OF THE 12 ZODIAC SIGNS ACROSS THE NIGHT SKY IS ANOTHER WAY OF MARKING THE MONTHS. OLD-TIMERS ASSIGNED THEM ATTRIBUTES THAT MADE SENSE IN THE GARDEN CALENDAR. WHEN FIERY LEO THE LION (*LEFT*) ROARS OVERHEAD IN LATE APRIL, IT'S TIME TO FOCUS ON WEEDING. SCORPIO (*RIGHT*), PROMINENT IN JULY, IS A FRUITFUL OMEN FOR PLANTING FLOWERS, FRUIT TREES, AND VEGETABLES.

The Zodiac Zoo

The 12 zodiac constellations—the same ones you may check daily to see what your horoscope foretells—follow each other on a slowly revolving path through the sky, with each one appearing overhead for 2 or 3 days of the month it "rules." (You won't see that particular sign on those days, though, because the sun will be in it; 6 months later is when it will reign visibly in the night sky.)

Each zodiac sign (except for Libra) is named for an animal. After that it gets murky: Each is also assigned a part of the human body and a planet and element that is associated with it. Capricorn the goat, for instance, is associated with the knees, the planet Saturn, and the element earth. Each sign is also classified as barren, fruitful, very fruitful, masculine, feminine, airy, fiery, moist, or a host of other attributes.

We'll let astrologers worry about why. Zodiac-conscious gardeners will be too busy attending to the literally hundreds of rules that govern living by the signs.

(continued on page 98)

An Easy Constellation

I've never been much of a map reader, and the first time I tried matching up a guidebook to the night sky with that jumble of stars overhead, I was totally lost. Then I learned the easy way to get to know the stars: Start with one constellation.

The 12 star pictures that make up the zodiac—what's your sign?—wheel through the heavens continually as the earth turns, following the path of the sun. Some get lost in the sunlight when they're positioned overhead during daylight hours; others rise at inconvenient times. But every season at least 3 of the 12 will be visible during prime viewing time.

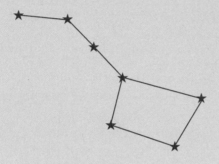

THE BIG DIPPER: Simple and bright—a great star-pic to start with. Find the handle, and then you'll be able to quickly pick out the scoop.

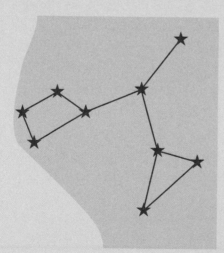

SAGITTARIUS AND THE MILKY WAY: "I'm a little teapot, short and stout . . ." That's what Sagittarius looks like, even though the heroic legend tells us he's an archer. In summer, look low in the southern sky to spot Sagittarius—and the "steam" rising from his spout, which is actually the billions upon billions of faraway stars of the Milky Way. On a clear night, away from city lights, you can follow that cloud of stars all the way across the heavens.

for Every Season

And since the zodiac constellations are spaced fairly equidistantly, once you know where one is, you can make a good guess where others will be. If the sign for Taurus, for instance, is overhead, that of Scorpio—6 months away on the zodiac calendar—is on the opposite side of the earth.

Along with the 12 zodiac signs, a slew of star pictures from grand to puny decorate the night sky. Those illustrated here are among the easiest to discern; once you can recognize them, you're on your way to becoming a connoisseur of constellations.

TAURUS: I love constellations that actually look like what they're supposed to be. It's easy to see the red-eyed bull with his eye-catching V of bright horns. A cluster of stars marks the bull's hip; that's the Pleiades, or Seven Sisters, once seen on the hoods of Subaru cars. Since Taureans are born when the sun is in this zodiac sign in April, you'll spot it overhead 6 months later in October.

ORION: No matter how new you are to stargazing, you'll be able to pick out the three close, bright stars of hunter Orion's belt. Look closer and you'll see his short hanging dagger. On a winter night, when your breath steams in the cold, clear night air, Orion strides across the sky in full glory.

Here's a sampling of those rules that apply to gardening:

- Always set plants out in a water or earth sign.

- Plant in the fruitful signs: Scorpio, Pisces, Taurus, or Cancer.

- Root flower cuttings when the signs are in the knees or feet.

- Plant beans when the signs are in the arms.

- Don't plant potatoes when the signs are in the feet, or they will grow little toelike nubbins all over the main tuber.

COMMONSENSE CALENDAR

This system is not as fanciful or as complicated as it seems at first. A lot of it is common sense. Remember that most folks in long-ago days did not use a printed calendar, just the one in the heavens. They knew, just by checking the position of the stars in the zodiac, how far along the year's cycle was. The moon told them what week or day it was.

"Plant beans when the signs are in the arms" is just another way of saying "Plant beans in May"—about the same time we who get our learning from seed-packet instructions poke our limas into the soil.

Plan a Night Garden Party

Admiring the night sky is a great excuse to show off your garden. Plan the event for a night that coincides with the peak of an annual meteor shower, and you may end the evening with a finale of Mother Nature's fireworks. The Perseids appear reliably every August, sending shooting stars across the heavens. That happens to be the time when many summer flowers—especially night bloomers—are at their peak. What a fitting way to bid adieu to summer!

Begin the evening before sundown so that you can share the thrill of watching flowers open before your eyes. Evening primroses (*Oenothera biennis*) are a fun flower for the garden. Their pale yellow blossoms unfurl with an audible snap!

NIGHT BLOOMERS, NIGHT FRAGRANCE

Try these flowers to delight guests at a night garden party.

FLOWER	FEATURES
Angel's trumpet (*Datura metel*)	Huge white trumpet blossoms open in the evening; annual
Moonflower vine (*Ipomoea alba*)	Blossoms open in the evening, attracting hummingbird (sphinx) moths; annual
Japanese iris (*Iris kaempferi*)	White cultivars look like huge white butterflies in a dark garden; perennial
Sweet alyssum (*Lobularia maritima*)	Increased fragrance at night; white cultivars show up well in the dark; annual
Evening primrose (*Oenothera biennis*)	Fragrant; flowers open in evening; biennial
Petunias (*Petunia* spp. and hybrids)	Increased fragrance at night; pale colors show up well in the dark; annual
Roses (*Rosa* spp. and cvs.)	White cultivars show up well in the dark; be sure to plant those with distinct fragrance, which carries well at night; perennial shrub
Night phlox (*Zaluzianskya capensis*)	Supreme night fragrance, white flowers show up well in the dark; annual

CHAPTER 5

"THE STORMY MARCH HAS COME AT LAST
WITH WINDS AND CLOUDS AND CHANGING SKIES."
—WILLIAM CULLEN BRYANT

Winds, Fronts, and Storms

WHEN YOU HEAR THE WIND RUSTLING THE *MISCANTHUS* GRASS, IN MOST PARTS OF the country you can bet that a change in the weather is on the way. Wind drives the weather: It sweeps storm clouds in and out, brings moisture picked up over the ocean to sprinkle onto our tomato plants, and breathes icy polar gusts over our sleeping perennials and down our collars.

Wind also has a big hand in determining the climate in which you tend your tomatoes and grow your perennials. Regular, seasonal wind patterns are the culprit behind hot or humid summers, mild or cold winters. The mild, rainy winters of the West, the knee-deep snows of New England, the February daffodils of the South: All are thanks to the wind's effect on climate.

Whether they're humongous or middling in size, moving air masses can cause gardeners major headaches when they collide. Along those front lines of battle, damaging storms and sudden shifts in temperature make us rush to protect our arborvitae, add another blanket to our borderline-hardy perennials, and practice positive thinking to send that hailstorm in another direction.

The Cycle of Wind

Long-term or local, wind is nothing more than moving air. Remember the beautiful big blue marble revealed by the first pictures from space, with the spun silk of clouds swirling over its surface? Even at a distance, we can see weather happening around the world. Masses of clouds move over the surface, stretching and thinning, spinning, growing, and otherwise showing the patterns of wind at work.

Just as we can interpret low-level winds from watching the smoke from a chimney or the grasses in our garden, the motions of the clouds show wind at work at higher levels.

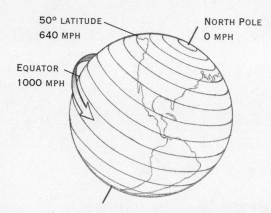

50° LATITUDE
640 MPH

NORTH POLE
0 MPH

EQUATOR
1000 MPH

OUR MAJOR WEATHER MAKERS

Two gigantic air masses, which are constantly forming and moving, are the primary forces behind the weather of most of temperate North America.

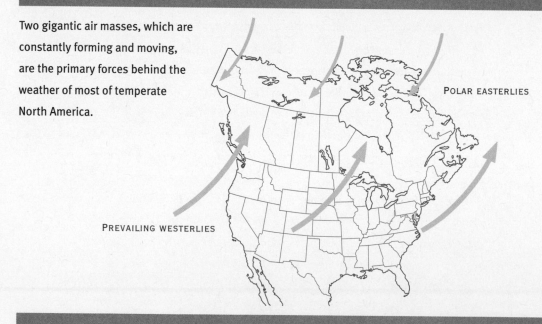

POLAR EASTERLIES

PREVAILING WESTERLIES

All this activity starts from a very simple source: warm air rising, cool air falling. Over and over the cycle repeats, with masses of warm air replaced by cooler air, and vice versa. The more drastic the temperature difference, the stronger the wind.

The Biggies Build Climate

A few giant masses of air—following regular routes—are what determine the regular weather patterns that give us our climate. A garden of cacti and succulents in Arizona, a bed of columbines and alpines in the Rockies, and in March, the deep-drifted yards of Minneapolis and the fantastic display of azaleas in Charleston, South Carolina, are all thanks to air movements we can count on year after year.

AIR MASS AND SOURCE	WEATHER RESULT	COMMENTS
Hot, moist air from the tropics sails into the mid-latitudes, but it's warmer aloft (at 5,000–15,000 feet)	Sunny and hot; possible high humidity.	Warm air rises—but the warmest air is already on top. This is a stable situation because there's no huge difference in temperature or, therefore, in pressure.
Hot, moist air from the tropics sails north, with cooler air above.	Thunderstorms	Warm, moist air at the surface with cold air above is unstable and yields thunderstorms when fronts or other triggers are present to get them started.
Warm, moist air from the south glides up over cold, polar air, but it's stable.	Widespread "steady" rain or snow	This is usually warm-front-type precipitation.

The Earth's surface heats at uneven rates, thanks to its varied surface. As the water and land are warmed by the sun, the air above it is likewise affected.

"Warmed" is a relative word, however! Near the Equator, tropical seas soak up the sun's rays at close range and remain warm year-round as does the balmy air above them. Far up north in the land of the white bear, the eternal snow reflects most of the sun's warming rays, so its attending air is pretty darn chilly.

Meanwhile, in the mid-latitudes—our home—more moderate warming is taking place, setting the stage for action.

Other air masses also migrate around the earth, affecting the weather over large areas. The Pacific Coast air mass of summer brings cool days and fog from California to Alaska. On the other side of the continent, the Atlantic Coast maritime air mass swings air cooled by frigid North Atlantic waters over New England, creating a welcome respite from the heat and humidity of summer elsewhere.

Local or Long-Term

Regional geography determines whether the wind whistles down your yard for sustained periods often enough to earn your climate the title "windy." Gardens in the windswept Plains region are exposed to the nearly constant presence of moderate wind, a given in that region. Move eastward, and the climate is much calmer.

In the Southwest, wind can seem almost constant. My family and I were caught in what felt—to us—like a once-in-a-lifetime windstorm in Deming, New Mexico, one year. We hung on for dear life, trying to make ourselves as heavy as possible, while our SUV rocked like a wicker chair in the gusts. Finally we limped into town, driving carefully to avoid dust devils rising over the desert and trash barreling across the road. Pulling open the door of a diner with all our strength, we piled inside, gasping a collective "Whew!"

"Quite a windstorm!" we remarked to the regulars, who were eyeing us with curiosity.

"Windstorm?" they laughed. "It's always like this." Seems the wind was a near-daily occurrence, kicking in almost every afternoon and dying out with nightfall. Warm air rising can definitely create some strong currents.

Your local geography also can make your yard a windy one. Mountainsides are treated to more wind than sheltered valleys. Big-city gardeners enjoy the challenge of wind racing down "canyons" of tall buildings. A sheltering woods or even a belt of trees can create an oasis of calm in a normally windy region.

Local weather is the instigator behind those sudden winds that herald a storm. You'll learn more about winds that roar—once in a while—in the later section on storms.

Dealing with occasional locally strong wind calls for crisis planning so that your defenses are ready when the wind roars in. In the following pages, and in later chapters on seasonal gardening, you'll learn nifty tips for keeping your garden safe during powerful storms.

A garden besieged by long-term winds calls for strategic planning to make the most of it. Thanks to the regularity of the wind, you can successfully take steps to counteract its effects by choosing plants that are suited to windy conditions—and also by erecting barriers to diffuse the gusts, and adapting your watering routine to mitigate the side effects of the wind's hairdryer-like power.

Prevailing Winds

Dry summers or snowy winters are the first things that come to mind when we decide what plants to pick for our gardens. But climate also includes wind, which is another factor that can mean the difference between a good garden and a great one.

Which Way Does the Wind Blow?

Air is invisible—only when it's in motion can we "see" it. No matter how wildly the blades of your clump of *Miscanthus* grass are swaying, we're seeing not the wind, only its effects.

To figure out the direction of the prevailing winds in your garden, take another look at the *Miscanthus*—in fall or winter, after its blades have dried. Like a hairdo stiffened in one direction by a blow dryer, your long grass will show you which way the wind usually blows.

TALL, FLEXIBLE ORNAMENTAL GRASSES LEAN AWAY FROM THE PREVAILING WIND. WHEN THEIR STEMS DRY IN FALL, THEY STIFFEN INTO THAT WIND-BENT POSTURE. IF YOU PREFER AN UPRIGHT LOOK, SHIELD THE CLUMP WITH A WINDBREAK IN SUMMER.

We've all seen the ravages of a gusty windstorm, when broken branches litter the ground and whole trees lie like giants felled by a slingshot. Even less extreme winds can wreak havoc, toppling your proud row of sunflowers or snapping the stems of your prize dinner plate–size dahlias.

It's hard to guard against rare outbursts of strong winds. But you can protect your garden from the usual winds that blow through it.

The prevailing paths of major air masses create the prevailing winds that blow in our home gardens. For most of us, that means wind from the west. Gulf Coast gardens may experience more wind from the South; coastal gardens get their breezes from the direction of the ocean.

The Windy Garden

Plants grow more slowly when they have to fight the force of frequent wind:

- Water evaporates more quickly from the soil and from leaves.

- Wind rocks plants, dislodging their roots—either entirely or just slightly, which is still enough to cause a setback.

■ Flowers don't last as long because the petals are blown off by the breeze instead of lingering until they naturally fall. Tulips, poppies, and other flowers with large, single petals are most at risk.

Windy conditions affect the wildlife in your garden, too. Butterflies aren't apt to test the abilities of their delicate wings against anything but a light breeze, and hummingbirds also prefer calmer conditions. Most of us think of these winged visitors as merely ornaments in our gardens, but they're really doing important work—pollinating the blossoms they visit. Other pollinators may also lay low on windy days.

Gardeners have it tougher in windy areas, too. You'll be depending more on stakes and other plant supports than those who tend their

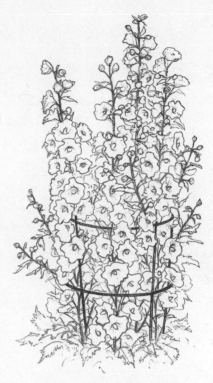

STURDY PLANT SUPPORTS ARE A MUST FOR TALL FLOWERS IN WINDY SITES.

Protecting Pollinators

For many fruits and vegetables, pollinating insects are the magic ingredient for a successful crop. Without bees and wasps buzzing around the blossoms on your berry bushes, few fruits would form. Likewise with squash, pumpkins, apples, cherries, and lots of other favorites.

Windy conditions present challenges for flying insects. If your pumpkin patch or apple tree is exposed to the full force of prevailing winds, the pollinators you need may be seeking shelter instead of doing their duty when the flowers bloom. Give 'em a break by growing insect-pollinated crops in sheltered nooks of your garden. Plant fruit trees on the leeward side of buildings, and place the vegetable garden behind a sheltering hedge or wall.

plants in calm conditions. You'll also need to keep a close eye on soil moisture levels. Plants that wilt will usually recover, but you'll lose days of active growth, and flower buds are likely to suffer injury.

10 To-Dos for Windy Gardens

1. *Apply* and renew mulch to slow the evaporation of moisture from the soil.

2. *Position* plant supports before plants reach full height. (Commercially made ones are excellent for keeping plants upright.)

3. *Buy* a bundle of thin bamboo canes, and keep them handy for quick support if needed.

4. *Enrich* potting mixes with compost to improve their water-holding capabilities; further reduce watering chores with capillary matting or drip irrigation for your container plants.

5. *Prune* roses back to half their height in late fall to prevent the roots from rocking when winter winds catch the topgrowth.

6. *Ensure* roses, clematis, and other trellised climbers are well supported. If you can cause the structure to lean by pushing against it with your hand, better hammer in another supporting post.

7. *Use* antidesiccant sprays to prevent boxwood and other broad-leaved evergreens from drying out in winter.

8. *Plant* dill, yarrow, and other plants with clusters of many small flowers to encourage the presence of pollinators.

9. *Grow* tulips, poppies, peonies, and flowering cherries, whose petals are easily blown off days before they would naturally fall, in the shelter of a building, wall, or hedge, or on the leeward side of a strong arbor or trellis.

10. *Anchor* garden netting, spun row covers, and plastic plant protectors like milk jugs so that they don't end up halfway down the block.

If winds are a regular occurrence in your yard, as they are in many areas of the Midwest and on the coasts, a windbreak is a permanent solution to creating conditions more conducive to plant growth.

SMART SELECTIONS

Natives, naturally, are a great starting point in any garden with difficult conditions. Look around at what grows wild in a similar location, or ask a local native-plant nursery for suggestions.

Common sense is the best aid for choosing plants for a windy garden. Not only do you want to find plants that flourish in a windy space, you'll also want to select things that won't suffer cosmetic damage in the wind.

Look for these attributes when choosing plants for a usually windy site:

Low growth. The best adaptation to protect plants from windy conditions is when they grow too low to blow.

Bare, tough, or wiry flowering stems with blossoms at top. Less foliage means less wind resistance; stems are apt to bend but not break in a stiff wind.

Silvery, felted leaves. A clue that the plant is adapted to the dry conditions usually prevalent in windy areas.

Succulent leaves. Thick, fleshy, juicy leaves store moisture that helps a plant survive in times of drought.

Waxy leaves. Another adaptation to cut water loss, especially important in winter.

Twiggy growth habit. Shrubs with many branching stems will break the force of the wind.

Deep roots. A taproot is much tougher to dislodge than more shallow, branching roots.

Small or needlelike leaves. Will not shred or snap off in stiff wind.

Clusters or spikes of small or many-petaled flowers. Will shelter each other from wind and hold petals longer.

Strappy or grassy foliage. Will yield to wind without snapping or splitting.

Here's what to avoid and why:

Ferns. Adapted to the moist, calm conditions among sheltering trees, they will struggle in an open, windy garden.

Big-leaved foliage plants. Plants like Rodgersias, large-leaved hostas, cannas, bananas, and ligularias have supersize leaves, which are likely to become tattered in a windy site.

Tall, heavily flowered spikes. Delphiniums, sunflowers, and hollyhocks are striking vertical accents, but they won't stand up straight under the force of constant wind.

Tall, leafy flower stems. Large-flowered dahlias, with their lush, leafy flowering stems and heavy blossoms, are also great wind-catchers, much to their detriment. Unless you're prepared to solidly stake them, choose more flexible types.

Big petals. Like a flag that's been left too long on the pole, flower petals soon show signs of wear under the wind. Bearded irises, tulips, poppies, and others with large, simple flowers are best planted behind a windbreak.

GROW LOW, STAY SAFE

Ever wonder why those coveted "alpine" perennials and shrubs are so delightfully downsized? Not to charm us gardeners, I'm sorry to tell you—these plants are diminutive for survival, pure and simple.

Climb to the top of a mountain, and you'll notice an interesting thing: The higher you go, the smaller the plants get. Mountaintops are inhospitable

Look to the Prairie

Early descriptions of the unspoiled prairie weren't much for originality, but most used a common theme: the sea of grass. They were talking about its unbroken sameness, but also about its waterlike ripples in the wind—a constant force in the great grasslands down the middle of the continent.

Those glorious stretches are long gone, replaced by just-as-uniform sweeps of wheat and soybeans, but we can still take a lesson from prairie plants. Many of the "forbs," or flowering plants, are just as striking in gardens as they were in the sea of grass. And more important, they're naturally adapted to stand tall against the wind. Ironweed (*Vernonia noveboracensis*), perennial sunflowers (*Helianthus* spp.), compass plant (*Silphium laciniatum*), gayfeathers (*Liatris* spp.), and dozens of others have exactly the attributes you're seeking: tough, flexible stems, usually nearly bare of foliage, and small to medium flowers that won't tear to shreds in the wind.

Visit a nursery or browse a catalog specializing in prairie natives, and you'll find plenty of wind-worthy warriors for your garden.

GROUND-HUGGING PLANTS ARE PERFECT FOR A WINDBLOWN GARDEN BECAUSE THEY NEED NO STAKING OR OTHER PROTECTION. THEIR DENSE MATS OF FOLIAGE AND THE ROCKS AROUND THEM HELP KEEP THE SOIL MOIST IN THE FACE OF DRYING WINDS.

to plants. The soil is thin, the air is colder than in the valleys below, and the wind whistles cruelly. Poke your head out a car window and you'll quickly get a feel for what mountain plants have to put up with. A tall, lush-leaved plant would soon have all its lushness sucked right out of it. But a plant with smaller leaves that hugs the ground provides much less wind resistance.

Alpines can be a lifelong addiction. Open a catalog from a specialty nursery, and you'll find enough small treasures to experiment with for decades.

Other low-growing plants are often well suited for windy gardens. To counteract the drying effect of constant wind, seek out plants with felted foliage or succulent, water-storing leaves. A windy site is a great excuse to explore the pleasures of hens-and-chicks (*Sempervivum* spp.), basket-of-gold (*Aurinia saxatilis*), lamb's ears (*Stachys byzantina*), artemisias, wallflowers (*Erysimum* spp.), creeping phlox (*Phlox stolonifera*), sedums in all shapes and sizes, and small-flowered species tulips (*Tulipa tarda* and many others).

SUPPORT YOUR PLANTS

Supports stiffen the backbone of wind-susceptible plants. Install them when plants are about half their ultimate height; any earlier and your garden will look like a plot of sticks and wire. Fasten your plants to the supports loosely, allowing the plant some room to wiggle so that your garden isn't standing at enforced attention. Any of these will help your plantings stand tall:

- Twiggy sticks are perfectly functional—and free. Stockpile the prunings from your privet hedge or other shrubs. Poke them into the soil with care; stems are brittle once they dry out.

- Wire supports come in all shapes and sizes. Most gardeners develop their own preferences after trying out several types.

- Homemade stakes can be fun to make if you have the right tools. An evening with a wire cutter, needle-nose pliers, and an ample supply of wire coat hangers can keep all your dahlias from drooping!

THINK OF A PLANT SUPPORT AS A LITTLE EXTRA STIFFENING FOR THE BACKBONE, NOT AS A RIGID BRACE. ALLOW YOUR PLANTS A LITTLE WIGGLE ROOM WHEN YOU ATTACH THEM TO SUPPORTS, AND THEY'LL LOOK MORE NATURAL. TWIGGY PRUNINGS ARE GREAT FOR HOLDING UP PEA VINES, WHILE WIRE SUPPORTS AND GREEN BAMBOO STAKES ARE VIRTUALLY INVISIBLE IN THE FLOWER GARDEN.

- Bamboo canes are slim and ultrasturdy. Use them for delphiniums, hollyhocks, and other plants of height and erect posture.

- Wire loops and squiggle supports don't require fasteners to hold the plant in place. Vertical canes and stakes will need your aid to hold the plant to the pole.

- Figure-8 fasteners. A quick twist of the wrist and your plants are in place with these inexpensive and well-designed devices.

- Twist ties. A favorite for decades—save them from bread and veggie bags, or buy a roll to cut to the desired length. Because they're reinforced with wire, you'll need to remove them at the end of the season to prevent accidental jabs should they get mixed into compost.

Windbreaks

Solid windbreaks, such as a wall, don't work quite as you'd expect them to. Wind slams into the solid wall, and turbulence is the result when the currents get confused.

On the leeward side of a wall, the force of the wind is much less. But don't get complacent—the effect lasts only for a short distance, close to the wall. As you move away from the wall, turbulent overflow causes areas of windy confusion as the wind sweeps up and over the wall, then swirls around on the far side.

If you want to protect a relatively narrow bed along the wall, the solid mass is fine. For bigger gardens, a hedge is a better choice because it shelters a bigger area. It softens the wind, breaking its force with its twiggy branches and foliage, and redirects the flow.

Height makes a difference in windbreak effect: The taller the hedge or structure, the bigger the reduction in wind. A hedge will protect a garden bed; a windbreak of shrubs and trees or a pergola of vines is needed to shelter the seating in a patio area.

How to Plant a Windbreak

For a casual windbreak for occasional or breezy winds, a single row or grouping of large shrubs should do the trick. Choose plants that form a large mounded or irregular shape, with branches close to the ground so that wind is filtered throughout their height.

Interestingly, some of the best plants for windbreaks are those you can buy really cheap! They're the old-fashioned shrubs that graced frugal Grandma's garden—forsythia, weigela, privet, rose-of-Sharon, and others—that were popular because they grew quickly and looked good. Look for bundles of young, bareroot common shrubs in spring, usually packaged with their roots in plastic packed with peat—or buy in quantity from no-frills catalogs—and you may get the makings of a windbreak for less than $20.

To protect a garden or create a wind-free sitting space in an area with frequent winds, plan on a permanent serious-business planting:

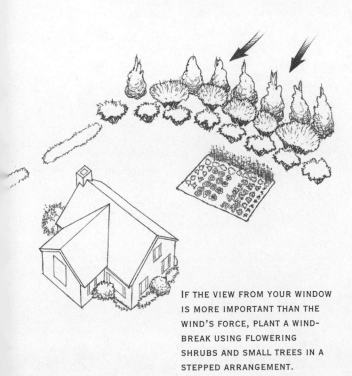

IF THE VIEW FROM YOUR WINDOW IS MORE IMPORTANT THAN THE WIND'S FORCE, PLANT A WINDBREAK USING FLOWERING SHRUBS AND SMALL TREES IN A STEPPED ARRANGEMENT.

1. Plan a triple row, staggering the plants.

2. In the outside, windward row, plant shrubs that have a shorter ultimate height than the trees in the middle row. Large, dense, fast-growing, branching shrubs—weigela, forsythia, deutzia—are ideal for this outer row.

3. In the middle row, plant wind-resistant small trees or taller shrubs, including holly, privet, mountain ash, rose-of-Sharon, or hawthorn.

4. In the third, leeward row, again use large, branching shrubs.

Upright Plants for Windy Gardens

Gardening in a windy site doesn't have to mean going without tall plants to provide vertical accents in your beds and borders. Choose from this list of upright perennials that will manage to stand tall even when a stiff breeze is blowing. In addition to these stalwart perennials, don't forget to include some ornamental grasses in your plan. Born to wave in the wind, little bluestem, big bluestem, switchgrass, maidengrass, and others will acquire a leeward lean over the season, in no way reducing their charm.

Name	Height	Flower Color	Comments
'Coronation Gold' yarrow (*Achillea* 'Coronation Gold')	2 to 4 feet	Golden yellow	Flexible stems keep these tall plants from collapsing in wind.
Japanese anemone (*Anemone* × *hybrida*)	2 to 3 feet	White, pink	"Anemone" means windflower, and this sturdy perennial offers height, too, holding its flowers on bare stems above the dark foliage.
Asters (*Aster* spp.)	1 to 5 feet	Blue, pink, purple, red, white	Wiry or tough branching stems diffuse the wind's force and bow without snapping, standing straight again once the wind has passed.
Crocosmias (*Crocosmia* spp. and hybrids)	2 to 3 feet	Red, orange, yellow, bicolors	Wiry flower stems and flags of foliage don't snap or flatten.
Perennial sunflowers (*Helianthus* × *multiflorus* and others)	4 to 6 feet	Yellow	Supertall and prone to running rampant in a garden setting, but good candidates for adding a splash of gold in areas away from prized beds.

Name	Height	Flower Color	Comments
False sunflower (*Heliopsis helianthoides*)	2 to 6 feet	Yellow	Multibranched stems of sturdy constitution keep the clump upright.
Gayfeathers (*Liatris* spp.)	2 to 5 feet	Lavender, pink, purple, white	Upright spikes packed solid with small feathery flowers are tougher than they look and stay rigidly erect.
Faassen's catmint (*Nepeta* × *faassenii*)	1 to 2 feet	Lavender to blue	Fine flowers and foliage diffuse the wind.
Violet sage (*Salvia nemerosa*)	2 to 4 feet	Blue, pink, purple	Erect, skinny spikes of tiny flowers won't topple in the stiffest wind.
Compass plants (*Silphium* spp.)	3 to 5 feet	Golden yellow	These thick, square, supertough stems barely quiver in strong winds. Some species spread aggressively; corral them in an out-of-the-way corner.
Olympic mullein, other mulleins (*Verbascum olympicum* and other spp.)	To 6 feet	Yellow, white, pink, purple	Stout, single stems stay straight.

STRAW-BALE WINDBREAK

You can make a windbreak in a weekend by stacking bales of straw against the windy side of an unprotected garden. Disguise it with fast-growing annual vines and trailers cascading over the top, and it will give your plants a full season of shelter. Whole houses are being constructed with baled straw for walls, so why not a windbreak? It's cheap, fast, and within a few weeks it will be so prettified no one will ever know its humble origins!

1. Lay a double row of straw bales along the windward side of a new or established garden bed.

2. Place a second row of bales over the first, placing the first bale so that the joints are staggered and the ends look like steps.

Hide the straw bales with fast-growing annual sunflowers, decorative red-leaved corn, and other tall plants at the back of the bed. Sow seeds of scarlet runner beans, hyacinth bean, or plain old pole beans along the bales, and train the vines upward to cover them. For a more elaborate finishing touch, use a large knife to saw out holes 10 to 12 inches deep and wide in the tops of the bales. Fill the holes with garden soil and compost, and use as planters for bright annuals. Include trailing nasturtiums, licorice plant, verbena, and other sprawlers to clamber across the tops of the bales.

BALES OF STRAW—NOT WEED-CARRYING HAY—ARE CHEAP, FAIRLY LIGHTWEIGHT, AND STACK QUICKLY TO MAKE A HARD-WORKING WINDBREAK. DISGUISE THEM WITH RUNNER BEANS OR OTHER FAST-GROWING FOLIAGE.

Mitigating Wind Effects

Step out of the shower, switch on the blow dryer, and notice what happens to your hair: Voilà! It dries, even if you keep the setting on "cool." That's the evaporative action of wind at work, and it has just as dramatic an effect on your garden plants and soil as your trusty hair dryer has on your flowing tresses.

A two-pronged approach is the best strategy for dealing with a windy garden's tendency to dry out quickly: (1) Select plants adapted to dry conditions; and (2) preserve precious moisture with all the tricks you can muster.

WELL-SUITED PLANTS

Turn first to plants that hail from regions where water is scarce and the natives have learned to make the most of it. Desert plants with succulent leaves keep their own reservoir for times of need; those with silvery, furry foliage deflect the sun's drying rays and also physically slow down evaporation. Prairie plants have amazingly deep roots: They often go as far into the earth as the plant rises above it! A mature clump of big bluestem grass, for instance, may have roots that stretch 4 feet deep—where moisture is apt to linger even when the surface is bone-dry.

A good rule of thumb in choosing garden candidates is to plan for the worst: Pick plants that will not need much help from you to survive the extremes of your climate. Sure, your Nebraska winters are snowy and

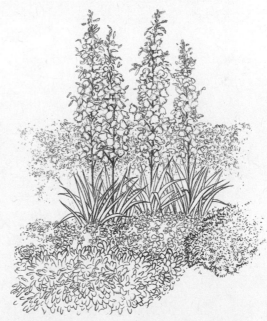

PLANTS THAT TRACE THEIR ORIGINS BACK TO WINDY HOMELANDS, AS THESE YUCCAS DO, HAVE EVOLVED TO STAND TALL EVEN AFTER SUSTAINED GUSTS. THEY WON'T NEED STAKING OR OTHER EXTRA SUPPORT.

your springs rainy, but if you fill your garden with lush, thirsty perennials, your water meter will be spinning like a merry-go-round when the dry summer arrives. Refer to "Smart Selections" on page 109 to find more tips for choosing easy-care plants.

Conserving Water

Of course, we all like to try plants that aren't a perfect fit for our gardens—otherwise, we'd all let our yards go wild. That's when it pays to have a few tricks up your sleeve to make those foreigners (as well as better-adapted plants) flourish in difficult conditions. In a windy garden, conserving water is the key.

Wind evaporates water anywhere it finds it, which is why your moist lips chap quickly on a windy day. As the wind evaporates moisture from plant tissues above the ground, the roots try to prevent the plant from drying out by drawing more moisture from the soil to send to the upper growth. A good plan—as long as the soil is moist. In dry soil, you'll quickly see the sad results of the wind's actions: Plants droop and wilt, leaves yellow and drop, petals fall, and buds shrivel.

Try these conservation techniques in your windy garden, and you can prevent your plants from suffering:

"A Gardener's life

Is full of sweets and sours;

He gets the sunshine

When he needs the showers."

—Reginald Arkell, *Green Fingers*, 1934

Water deeply in early evening or at night. We're often cautioned not to water at night, for fear of encouraging fungal diseases. In a nonwindy garden that's good advice, but when winds blow regularly, the extra moisture will be gone long before mildew or other fungus gets a start.

In between deep waterings, spray foliage in early morning. Plants absorb water through their leaves, too, which is one reason your garden looks so refreshed after a rain. Use a mister head on your hose to create a gentle shower.

Mulch, mulch, mulch. It's your best defense against dry soil.

Aim at the roots. For deep watering, use drip hoses, soda-bottle root soakers, or other devices that direct water straight to roots.

Add soil amendments. Dig in compost and other organic matter—or grow tillable cover crops—to increase the water-holding capacity of your soil.

Use a timer. Be sure your plants get enough to drink by using a timer to control watering. It screws into your hose line and shuts off the water flow after the specified length of time.

Invest in self-watering containers. They save work and water by supplying a reservoir of water that's available to plants as they need it. They also prevent potted plants from suffering dry-soil setback—for these focal-point gardens, you'll want the best display you can get.

Apply antidesiccants. Antidessicants are primarily wax-based products that you spray onto the foliage of your plants to reduce moisture loss through the leaves. Antidesiccants are best used in winter, when foliage dries out at an accelerated rate because plants can't pull water from the frozen ground. It takes time and money to apply antidesiccants, so save them for your most vulnerable broad-leaved evergreens, and adopt other strategies for a more naturally adapted garden.

Seed Dispersal

Wind is one of nature's favorite mass transportation devices—for seeds. If you're a seed collector, you'll need to keep a close eye on maturing seedheads so that you can beat the wind at its own game. Stems of annual poppies, for instance, are easily bent by the breeze, scattering those pepper-shaker seeds in all directions. Tufts of butterflyweed (*Asclepias tuberosa*) seedpods loosen quickly under the wind's encouragement, sending parachutes of what you'd hoped would be future generations of flowers to who knows where.

PLANTS TAKE ADVANTAGE OF WIND BY PRODUCING SEEDS ATTACHED TO A BIT OF FLUFF, WHICH SERVES AS A PARACHUTE FOR THE PROGENY. THESE MILKWEED SEEDS WILL SPROUT WHEREVER THE FOUR WINDS BLOW THEM.

The wind will also bring you gifts from afield: Unfortunately, mostly weeds. Dandelions are notorious for cultivating new territory through windblown seed, but daisy fleabanes (*Erigeron* spp.), wild asters (*Aster* spp.), hawkweed, and others may also blow into your beds or lawn. There's nothing you can do to stop them, so you may as well just admire these ingenious dispersal mechanisms at work.

> "Trust much to gentle showers, to make crops. But . . . the clouds pour down heavy rains, and the soil melts and runs rapidly away."
>
> —N. T. Sorsby, *Horizontal Plowing and Hill-Side Ditching*, 1860

WIND EROSION DOES ITS WORST IN THE WIDE-OPEN SPACES OF NORTH AMERICA'S PRAIRIES. WITHOUT A PROTECTIVE COVERING OF PLANTS AND THEIR SOIL-HOLDING ROOTS, BARE SOIL IS AT THE MERCY OF THE STRONG WINDS THAT BLAST ACROSS THE MIDDLE OF THE CONTINENT. GARDENERS ARE FORTUNATE TO WORK ON A SOMEWHAT SMALLER SCALE, WHERE WINDBREAKS AND MULCHES CAN MODERATE ALL BUT THE MOST DEVASTATING EFFECTS OF THE WIND.

Soil Erosion

Close your eyes quick—the dust is blowing! When wind sweeps across bare soil, especially dry bare soil, it easily airlifts particles onto the breeze. Unfortunately, the soil at surface level is the best of the bunch: It's topsoil, renowned for fertility and tilth.

The infamous Dust Bowl was the result of uninformed farming techniques. Those who tilled the land forgot to take the power of the wind into account. Although wind erosion can't be totally eliminated in vast open stretches, it can be mitigated by smart farming practices like contour plowing and hedgerows.

It's much easier to prevent a dust bowl in the home garden. The quickest cure is mulch. Keep soil surfaces covered, and you won't have to worry about your precious topsoil sailing away.

Fronts: Where Titans Clash

If you think you have a hard time figuring out a congenial seating chart for the Thanksgiving dinner table, be glad your relatives aren't literal windbags! Politeness is a foreign concept when one of the air masses overhead runs into another. Instead of agreeing to seek a mutual level of temperature and moisture, they argue with roaring winds and crashing lightning bolts. Here's what happens:

■ The colder air slides under the warmer, like a wrestler going head-down to overthrow his opponent.

■ The warm air fights back by rising in a tower of turbulent air, swirling with wind and electricity inside.

The line of battle, or front, where air masses collide is often a place of unsettled weather. Winners are usually determined quickly, which is great news for us on the ground, who have to bear the fallout of the battle in terms of hail, thunderstorms, or straight-line winds that can topple a 100-year-old oak.

How Far Off, I Sat and Wondered

Apologies to singer Bob Seger ("Night Moves"), but rock stars pondering life in the dark hours of the soul aren't the only ones who wonder how far away a thunderstorm may be. Gardeners have a vested interest too: You'll need time to put in any last-minute stakes, carry in the trays of seedlings, or fasten down the row covers before the brunt of the action hits.

Here's how to tell just how much calm you have before the storm:

1. When you see a flash of lightning, start counting off seconds. "One-groundhog, two-groundhogs, three-groundhogs..." spoken at a normal rate without pauses will give you a good approximation.

2. Sound travels about a mile in 5 seconds. If your count is at five groundhogs when the thunder rolls, the storm is a mile away. Ten groundhogs, it has 2 miles to travel. Half a groundhog, better scurry!

Some areas are famed for seasonal winds that blow steadily for days. Residents of those areas may feel like a blast furnace has moved in; complaints about the wind affecting sanity, or at least peace of mind, are frequent. In the words of author Raymond Chandler, "It was one of those hot, dry Santa Anas that come down through the mountain passes and curl your hair and make your nerves jump and your skin itch . . . "

NORTH AMERICA

Chinook: Hot, dry wind sweeps down the eastern slope of the Rockies eastward into the Plains; the word means "snow eater," and the warmth, although unusual, is welcome to many winter-weary folks.

Santa Ana: Hot, dry winds arise in high-pressure areas east of California's mountains and sweep westward into southern California. These are responsible for exacerbating many rapidly spreading wildfires.

OTHER CONTINENTS

Haboob: Wind picks up dust over the Sudan and creates gigantic dust storms northward.

Monsoon: Summer monsoon winds develop over the southern Indian and Pacific oceans, carrying deluging rains and devastating floods to Southeast Asia and China. Winter monsoons start in China and Siberia and sweep dry air southward, bringing a dry spell to Southeast Asia.

Sirocco: Hot, dry wind blows across the Sahara to the Mediterranean.

When the cold air prevails, the march continues as a cold front, creating a line of gray squall clouds at its leading edge and colder weather after it sweeps through. Should warm air win out, the warm front meanders in, usually with milder winds than a cold front, and with mellow temperatures in its wake. When the battle is a draw, we call it a stationary front—which usually doesn't last for long.

Severe weather, the kind that brings tornados, hail, and damaging winds, occurs when the differences between colliding air masses are large. Let a blast of icy Arctic air collide with a sultry tropical air mass, and whammo! It's time to batten the hatches.

Thunderstorms

Storms may be front-page news to gardeners, but in the big weather picture, they're local events. They thrive on instability, the condition created by competing air masses of different temperatures and moisture levels.

Instability is warm, moist air at low levels, combined with sufficiently cold air above it, so that if the surface air begins to rise, it will accelerate upward much like a helium balloon unleashed. The thunderstorm's heart is a plume, or constant stream of warm, moist bubbles that rise up through the colder air aloft. That rising air condenses out precipitation into rain and hail.

Some of that rain begins to fall to the ground and evaporates beneath the cloud base or along the edge of the cloud and cools the air. That cooled air then accelerates downward as a downdraft, hits the ground, and blasts outward as a cool, gusty, sometimes-damaging outflow. The mature thunderstorm contains both a strong updraft and a downdraft simultaneously,

Stable or Unstable?

Air masses, which are several miles thick and up to about 1,000 miles wide, each have their own conditions of temperature, pressure, and moisture. Variances in those conditions between air masses are what create the push and pull that give birth to wind and storms. Unstable air creates unsettled weather as nature tries to realign air masses to get back to the preferred state of stability.

- Stable condition: Cooler air is below warmer air.

- Unstable condition: Warmer air is below cooler air.

Interestingly, old-time weather forecasters sometimes tried to predict weather by the phases of the moon. If the new moon was stormy, the first quarter would be clear, for instance. They weren't altogether out in left field: Weather systems typically take 3 or 4 days to move across the country, creating weekly weather patterns that seem to keep time with the moon's cycle. For example, a mass of cold, dry air moving from the Rockies may move through the High Plains in the following day or two, then be in Illinois a day later. Meanwhile, another system is brewing for the next week's weather.

Jefferson's Lightning Rods

Tall trees are notorious targets for lightning, which is why you're too smart to seek shelter under that big maple in the backyard during a storm. But how to keep that maple from losing its top when lightning is crashing all around it? An antique idea is the answer.

Founding father Thomas Jefferson was a guiding force of American gardening as well. He swapped seeds and ideas with kindred spirits—and like any gardener, fretted over the workings of weather in his patch. One of his garden ideas is well worth putting into practice

if you have large shade trees: the time-honored lightning rod, which you can still see in place on venerable trees at Monticello, Jefferson's home.

Strapped to the topmost branch of a tree, a metal lightning rod attracts the electrical charge during a storm, sending it down a wire cable into the soil. If the tree were zapped instead of the rod, a split and charred hulk would result. Consult an arborist for installation of lightning rods; climbing tall trees can be hazardous to your health even in fair weather!

separated by a few miles. Falling, melting hail can also cool the air and trigger the downdraft.

If the storm creates hail, the hail usually falls before the rain settles in, while lightning and thunder are at their peak. Hail forms in intense, very high clouds, where the temperature is cold enough to change water droplets to ice. As the pellet of ice falls and then rises on the strong updraft, it gets bigger and bigger with each ride through the cloud. When the cooler downdrafts eventually win out over the warmer rising air, the electrical charges dwindle and the storm simmers down. After the storm passes, the air is drier and cooler.

June damp and warm

Does the farmer no harm.

—Folk saying

Donner and Blitzen

This pair of well-known reindeer names comes from the German words for thunder (*Donner*) and lightning (*Blitzen*). (Continuing the foreign-language lesson, *Donnerschlag* is a thunderclap; *Donnerblitz*, a thunderbolt.)

Thunder and lightning leap into activity when the air is unstable, with cold air and warm air quarreling over territorial rights. In the clouds, electrical charges build up—and even today, nobody knows exactly how.

10 To-Dos for an Oncoming Storm

1. *Be safe:* Storms can move fast, and you need to be safely indoors when lightning is nearby.

2. *Avoid* handling any metal objects when the storm gets near. Metal conducts electricity easily, and that golf club in your hand makes a great path for that jolt to travel from ground to cloud.

3. *Steer clear* of faucets or sprinklers. Water pipes also conduct electricity.

4. *Put* potted seedlings in a safe place where they won't get battered or swamped by rain.

5. *Empty* the rain gauge so it's ready to record.

6. *Stake* any prized plants you would hate to see topple: delphiniums, hollyhocks, tall bearded iris, Asiatic or Aurelian lilies.

7. *Store* lightweight lawn furniture to prevent it from blowing into beds.

8. *Set* heavyweight lawn furniture over plants you want to protect from possible hail: hostas, dwarf bananas, peonies in bloom.

9. *Move* portable containers under a tree, picnic table, or other shelter to prevent washouts.

10. *Cover* herb, flower, or vegetable seedlings with floating row covers to break the force of the rain and to prevent soil from washing away from their roots.

What they do know is that the ground below the cloud acquires a positive charge. Put a strong enough negative force near a strong enough positive force, and stand back! You've just created lightning. Those zigzag bolts that Zeus supposedly aimed at mortals whenever he was displeased are made of electrical energy, and they can be deadly.

Thunder is the sound that lightning creates as some of that bolt's immense electrical energy is transformed into sound waves. It is—excuse the expression—a lightning-fast process:

1. The lightning sears the air to more than 40,000°F (22,000°C), which makes it expand—in a big hurry!
2. When the air expands, it quickly cools, causing it to contract like a balloon with the air gone out.
3. All that in-and-out expansion/contraction galvanizes the air molecules into a superfast back-and-forth motion. Like a whip singing through the air, that rapid motion creates sound waves. Kaboom!
4. Sound travels more slowly than light (so unless the storm cloud is right over your head, you'll see the lightning before you hear the thunder).

CHAPTER 6

RAIN BEFORE SEVEN
CLEAR BY ELEVEN.

Rain, Ice, and Snow

WHAT GOES UP MUST COME DOWN. ALL THAT WATER VAPOR IN THE AIR EVENTUALLY condenses and comes back to earth, and that's a subject of vital interest to those who wait below. Will rain come at all?

Will it be a gentle shower to nurture seedlings? An all-day soaking that makes us smile as we watch the plants practically growing before our eyes? A glaze of ice that may crack branches or freeze the forsythia? The "onion snow" of early spring that tells us it's time to get cold-hardy crops in the ground? Or that first real snow of the winter season, a signal that we can put away the hoe for the year and start to dream over seed catalogs?

Forewarning of what the clouds will drop gives us time to plan garden activities to take advantage of, or guard against, the upcoming wet weather. In this chapter, you'll learn how to bolster the expert advice of TV meteorologists with the visual aids of clouds, the instruments in your backyard weather station, and your own weather sense. You'll also learn how to practice "preventive gardening" so you can prepare your plants and soil for precipitation.

Rain, Rain, Come Again

That's the usual garden mantra, and for good reason. Water is essential to plant growth. April showers bring May flowers, May showers bring June strawberries, June showers bring Fourth of July corn on the cob, and so on through the garden year.

A few centuries ago, North American explorers were fooled by the incredible height of the trees in the West: At last, they believed, they had found the richest soil in America, fit to nurture 300-foot giants. They were wrong, but understandably so. The incentive for such astounding growth wasn't fertility, but rain. With a steady 6-month diet of drizzle, trees grew to enormous proportions. (The most fertile soil actually lay beneath the great grasslands of the Midwest, the home today to waving fields of grain.)

In the damp Pacific Northwest, it's not only trees that grow to outsize proportions. In my Oregon backyard, a butterfly bush (*Buddleia davidii*) that I expected to reach about 10 feet at maturity topped 20 feet in just 3 years!

When rain is scarce, growth slows down. Fewer new leaves are produced

Essential Autumn Rains

Every gardener delights in a delicate April drizzle, but to our plants, especially evergreens and containerized specimens, a cold November downpour is even more vital. A plant with its roots in dry soil going into winter can suffer drought stress, even if you can't see the signs of wilting leaves.

Plants go into slow motion in colder regions in the winter, so their roots don't need to draw nearly as much water as when the plant is in active growth. But they still need to sustain enough moisture throughout the plant's tissues to keep it alive.

Evergreens are particularly susceptible to the effects of a dry autumn. Their leaves continue losing moisture to the air, which is often drier in winter than in summer. You probably won't see any alarm signs until spring, when you may spot dead, tan foliage here and there—or, on deciduous plants, dry, dead twigs. To prevent such setbacks, water containers and permanent plants deeply in fall if natural rainfall is scarce.

and stems stop expanding. But after a good rain, you can almost see plants leap with new growth. Their growth rate goes into overdrive as roots take up the moisture, almost as if they'd been doused with a quick-release fertilizer. Essentially, that is exactly what happens.

Regular doses of rain keep the garden flourishing because:

- Rain is absorbed by roots and moves into plant cells, plumping up and stiffening leaves and stems.

- Rain liquefies nutrients in the ground so that plant roots can absorb them.

- Rain increases soil moisture, benefiting the micro- and macroorganisms that are doing the work of decomposition that feeds plant roots.

- Rain washes leaves and blossoms, making them look fresh.

- Rain removes dust and other particles from plant leaves, allowing them to "breathe" freely.

- Rain moistens the soil, making it easier for plant roots to physically penetrate.

How Much Is Enough?

The answer depends on what's growing in your garden. Many experts recommend an inch of water—either from rain or supplemental water—a week. That's a generous helping of H_2O, and that amount will certainly keep your bluegrass lawn looking lush. An inch a week will also keep your veggie garden flourishing.

But gardening habits and soil types can make a big difference in water needs:

- Soil that is unprotected by a layer of mulch will dry out much faster than a thickly mulched garden.

- Similarly, a mature garden or cottage-style planting, with plants cramming every inch, leaves little soil surface vulnerable to the drying effects of the sun and wind.

- A more formal planting, with open space around each plant, means more water loss.

Fee-Fi-Fo-Fum! Smell the Rain about to Come!

It's not those approaching droplets that make the air "smell like rain," but the intensified scents of soil, flowers, decomposition, and myriad other backyard smells that usually stay at a low-level hum. Fragrance molecules bind to the bigger water molecules in the air as conditions reach rain stage, making them easier for our noses to notice. Usually, it's the aroma of humus that makes you first take a deeper sniff to check your senses: It's an earthy smell, like that released when you turn the compost pile or hold a handful of fresh-turned soil to your nose. The perfume is that of decomposition, the chemicals released as organic matter in the soil gets recycled by big and little organisms, from worms to bacteria. That humusy aroma is extrastrong after rain hits the soil, and it's carried along on the wind that brings in the rain clouds. To most gardeners, it's as good as ambrosia.

As with all at-home weather prediction, becoming aware of the signs around you will make you a sharper forecaster. Get in the habit of frequently sniffing the air, and you'll soon educate your nose to discern a host of other aromas beyond the can't-miss scent of, say, new-mown lawn. When your sniffer picks up the pleasant, rich scent of decay, you can bet that rain is on the way.

One summer, I was strolling the heart of Philadelphia on a day that felt like rain, thanks to high humidity and brooding clouds, when I suddenly noticed a change in the city smell. The air took on a tangy, almost sour scent, with an undertone of stirred-up dust. Minutes later, the wind swept in and brought the rain. In a big city or beside a major highway, the slightly sour smell of wet concrete or a brew of dust and oil are likely to alter the perfume that reaches your nose before a rain and lingers afterward.

■ Soils, too, vary in their ability to retain or drain water: In slow-draining, heavy clay soil, you may find an inch of water per week creates your own version of a bog garden.

If your climate is a drier one, or you're not inclined or not allowed to help out Mother Nature with the hose, you can find plenty of plants that are able to get by on much less moisture.

If you're having trouble getting your hair to behave, you may be getting an early warning of wet weather on the way. The high humidity that often precedes rain is what causes the frizz or makes your flip go flop. Hair absorbs water from the air, and the added moisture forces apart the protein and other molecules in the strand. When that happens, curly hair turns into flyaway fuzzies, and straight hair loses its bounce and hangs limp. A bad hair day is likely to be a good day for your garden!

Rainfall Patterns

Annual rainfall figures are deceiving. The 45 inches of average annual rainfall in Massachusetts is not equal to the 45-inch annual figure of northern California. Here's why:

- First of all, that annual rainfall might not be all rain. It could also include snow, ice, and even particularly heavy fog, all of which are converted to equivalent inches of rain.

- Even more important from a gardener's standpoint, the number of inches of rainfall says nothing about when it falls. In most of the eastern two-thirds of the continent, precipitation is pretty regular year-round: perhaps an average of 5 inches in December, 4 inches in June, 3 inches in July, and so on. Seasonal differences are usually moderate and account for whether the precipitation is clear liquid or white stuff. In the West, it's a much different story. There, climate changes are marked not only by temperature (which is often much less dramatic in seasonal shifts than in the East) but also by extended rainy "seasons" that alternate with lengthy dry "seasons."

- In some regions of the West, such as east of the Cascades, east of the Rockies, and throughout the Southwest, that wet/dry pattern is partnered with low annual rainfall. Successful gardening in these areas demands plants that thrive in arid conditions.

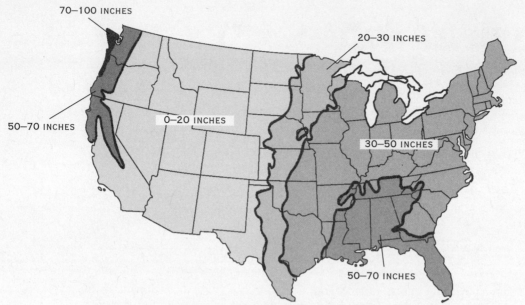

70–100 INCHES

20–30 INCHES

50–70 INCHES

0–20 INCHES

30–50 INCHES

50–70 INCHES

AVERAGE ANNUAL PRECIPITATION: AVERAGE PRECIPITATION FIGURES GIVE YOU A GOOD IDEA OF WHETHER YOUR CLIMATE IS DESERT-DRY OR RAINFOREST-WET. BUT ACTUAL YEARLY TOTALS MAY VARY WIDELY FROM THAT AVERAGE FIGURE.

"Average" rainfall may not be anywhere near what you actually get in a given year. A region's precipitation can vary widely from one year to the next, and rainfall patterns may change for a few months or for years. Historic droughts have ruined entire civilizations, and are still occurring in various places today. The El Niño ocean current of the 1990s resulted in sweeping shifts in weather patterns, including rain and snowfalls. The ongoing research into global warming suggests that even more dramatic changes to climates worldwide may be on the horizon.

WET SEASON, DRY SEASON

When I moved to Oregon from Pennsylvania, I knew I was leaving behind the brilliant colors of fall for a mostly evergreen palette. But average annual rainfall was pretty similar in the two locations, so I thought I'd be gardening with many of the same plants. Big surprise! From November till April in Oregon, rain fell nearly every day. From May through October, nary a drop. If the plants I put in couldn't cope with 6 months of drought, they were goners. Not willing to depend on the hose to keep my garden alive, I learned in a hurry to choose plants that were well adapted to this seasonal shift. Luckily, many of my old favorites, such as azaleas and heathers, were tolerant—once their roots were well established and protected by a deep layer of mulch. Others, such as fireweed (*Epilobium angustifolium*) and western bleeding heart (*Dicentra formosa*), were new pleasures to play with. My garden was still full of bloom, only from February through November (instead of April to September)—and the cast of characters was different.

Low Annual Rainfall

Desert dwellers, you know who you are. No matter whether you garden in the saguaro country of Arizona or the high sage of Colorado, it's easy to tell

What, Where, When

Rainfall patterns and amounts determine what to plant, when, and where. Look at your neighbors' yards—those who don't have an irrigation system installed!—to see what grows well in your climate. Ask for recommendations at a local garden center or nursery, and read labels and catalog descriptions carefully. You'll also find plant suggestions for seasonal rainfall patterns later in this chapter.

Looking at rainfall patterns also helps you decide where to plant. Slopes drain water more quickly than the lower places at their feet. Plants with heavier water needs must be sheltered from winds that cause them to dry out even faster. If you plan to do supplemental watering (a hot issue in many areas, and deservedly against the law when an official drought is declared), group plants of like needs together so you don't waste water on drought-tolerant types planted side by side with thirstier plants.

In a climate with year-round precipitation, you can plant any time the soil and temperature allow it. But in an alternating, either/or wet/dry climate, you'll want to get seeds and transplants into the ground soon after the beginning of the rainy season to avoid being held hostage by the hose.

at a glance that yours is a region where rain is scarce. Natural vegetation is mostly gray-green or silvery, with a few dabs of very dark green plant life. Lush, leafy greens are just about nonexistent, except after spring rains and in irrigated yards. Tall trees? Only along natural watercourses or in well-irrigated landscapes.

Luckily for you, plenty of fabulous plants are adapted to making do on a very skimpy drink of water. Plants that wilt to mush in wet areas are at their bright, beautiful best in your garden—golden desert marigold, for instance, and hummingbird-heaven desert willow. No, you'll never have an English garden—but a bed of delphiniums in Tucson would look as out of place as an adobe in London.

Lots of low-water plants display zingy color, and you'll discover an abundance of red and purple flowers, custom-made to advertise their attraction to hummingbirds and butterflies. *Xeriscaping* is the word for dry-land gardening. Consider it a benefit instead of a challenge, and enjoy getting to know the unique and wonderful plants that thrive in your area.

You can also enjoy the knowledge that visitors from water-abundant regions are envious of your terrific plantings—and even your exotic weeds! On my first

Well-Seasoned Advice

Gardeners love to share. A clump of iris handed over the fence, an envelope of seeds from a special plant, a recipe for mint tea—and especially advice, asked-for or not! In recent years, regional gardening books have sprung up like dandelions, and they're a treasure trove for benefiting from seasoned advice. Some are professionally printed, while others are home-grown jobs; all are valuable aids, no matter how slick (or not) the cover is.

Ask at local bookstores, libraries, or garden clubs and search the Internet to find a book of shared experience for gardening in your particular region. While you shouldn't depend on the Internet alone—some regional guides are distributed only via old-fashioned ways—your search may also turn up like-minded folks and message boards at regionally related Web sites, yet another place to turn for reassuring advice.

Drought-Insurance Plants

These annuals, perennials, and grasses do well in dry conditions with very little water, but they also will flourish in gardens that receive reliable rainfall. Although most hail from desert regions, they will quickly adapt to life in a garden with more abundant water. That's good news during dry spells or when cyclical drought settles in your area—unlike thirsty plants, these hardy sorts will quickly adjust to the lower moisture levels. Note that "ample water" doesn't mean standing water: Be sure to give these plants a site and soil that drains well.

ANNUALS/TENDER PERENNIALS

CAPE MALLOW
   (*ANISODONTEA CAPENSIS*)
CALIFORNIA POPPY
   (*ESCHSCHOLZIA CALIFORNICA*)
CALIFORNIA BLUEBELL
   (*PHACELIA CAMPANULARIA*)
MOSS ROSES (*PORTULACA GRANDI-
   FLORA* AND HYBRIDS)

PERENNIALS

'WARLEY ROSE' STONE CRESS
   (*AETHIONEMA* 'WARLEY ROSE')
AGAVES (*AGAVE* SPP.)
ALOES (*ALOE* SPP.)
BLUE HIBISCUS (*ALYOGYNE HUEGELII*)
MOUNT ATLAS DAISY (*ANACYCLUS
   PYRETHRUM* VAR. *DEPRESSUS*)
PIMPERNELS (*ANAGALLIS* SPP.)
PUSSY-TOES (*ANTENNARIA DIOICA*)
SEA THRIFT (*ARMERIA MARITIMA*)
WINECUPS, PRAIRIE POPPY MALLOW
   (*CALLIRHOE INVOLUCRATA*)
RED VALERIAN (*CENTRANTHUS RUBER*)
ROCK ROSES (*CISTUS* SPP.)

CROCOSMIAS (*CROCOSMIA* SPP.
   AND HYBRIDS)
FOXTAIL LILIES (*EREMURUS* SPP.
   AND HYBRIDS)
GAURA (*GAURA LINDHEIMERI*)
BEARDED IRIS (*IRIS* HYBRIDS)
SILVERLEAF
   (*LEUCOPHYLLUM FRUTESCENS*)
PRICKLY PEAR CACTI (*OPUNTIA* SPP.)
OREGANOS, MARJORAMS
   (*ORIGANUM* SPP.)
CAPE LEADWORT
   (*PLUMBAGO AURICULATA*)
MATILIJA POPPY (*ROMNEYA COULTERI*)
SEDUMS (*SEDUM* SPP. AND HYBRIDS)
HENS-AND-CHICKS
   (*SEMPERVIVUM* SPP.)
IRONWEED
   (*VERNONIA NOVEBORACENSIS*)
CALIFORNIA FUCHSIA
   (*ZAUSCHNERIA CALIFORNICA*)

GRASSES

BIG QUAKING GRASS (*BRIZA MAXIMA*)
SWITCH GRASS (*PANICUM VIRGATUM*)

trip across this great country, one of my many moments of truth—or should we say comeuppance—occurred while I stretched my legs in the vacant lot next to a gas station in west Texas. I was pretty proud of my knowledge of plants and wildflowers, but I'd never been to the desert before. Humming a few bars of Marty Robbins' old hit "El Paso," I scanned the lot and was humbled to discover that I recognized only 1 of the maybe 50 species growing there—the common sunflower. Naturally I wanted to ask for a sample of each, but I restrained myself from getting down on hands and knees then and there. Having killed many a potted cactus by overwatering, I figured these desert dwellers wouldn't last long in the very different climate of the Pennsylvania garden I was returning to.

You can't always judge a plant's adaptability at first sight, though. Twenty years after that western trip, I was surprised to find pots of bright cerise poppy mallow (*Callirhoe involucrata*), which I'd first encountered out near the West Texas town, offered for sale as prized newcomers at my local Midwest nursery. I'm happy to report that despite the lack of cowboy boots, these desert dwellers flourished in southern Indiana. From ½ inch of annual rainfall to 45 inches—this plant, and many others, are amazingly able to adapt.

Don't Kill with Kindness

Generous watering may seem like a kindly thing to do for your garden, but you could be setting your plants up for a fall. A lush plant is a thirsty plant: Plants treated to ample water respond by growing shallower roots, plus they put out lots of topgrowth that may not be supported should watering dry up. Frequent spraying with the hose or a sprinkler isn't helpful, either, because only the very top inch or so of the soil gets wet, so that's where most of the roots stay.

When the water supply is cut off—such as when you leave for vacation—these plants will suffer because they haven't grown the roots necessary to seek out deeper reserves. Infrequent but regular, thorough watering—either through natural rainfall or supplemental irrigation—encourages strong survivors. If water is scarce in your area, experiment to determine the minimum needed for good performance, instead of overdosing your plants with kind-hearted hosing.

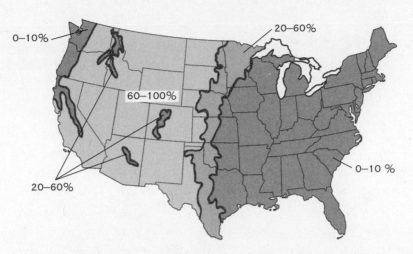

PERCENT OF YEARS IN WHICH DROUGHT OCCURS: THE MINIMUM YEARLY PRECIPITATION GARDENS AND FARM CROPS NEED: 20 INCHES. SOME AREAS OF THE COUNTRY ARE MORE PRONE TO OCCASIONAL DROUGHT YEARS THAN OTHERS. IN THOSE REGIONS OF HIGH DROUGHT RISK, IT MAKES SENSE TO BUILD A GARDEN WHOSE BACKBONE IS MADE OF PLANTS THAT TOLERATE DRY SOIL.

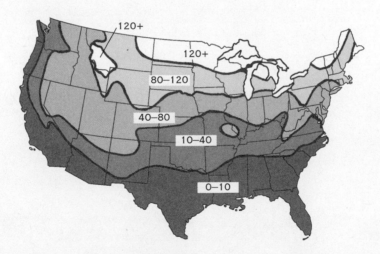

AVERAGE ANNUAL DAYS OF SNOW COVER: "PRECIPITATION" IS ANY FORM OF WATER THAT MAKES IT FROM THE SKY TO GROUND LEVEL. SNOW COUNTS, TOO, WITH THE FIGURES TRANSLATED INTO INCHES OF WATER TO CALCULATE ANNUAL PRECIPITATION AMOUNTS. THOSE NUMBERS CAN BE DECEPTIVE, THOUGH, BECAUSE IT TAKES SEVERAL INCHES OF SNOW TO EQUAL AN INCH OF RAIN. IF YOU'RE LOOKING FOR A NEW HOME WHERE YOU CAN COUNT ON USING YOUR CROSS-COUNTRY SKIS OR YOUR KIDS' SLEDS, IT'S A BETTER IDEA TO CONSULT A SNOWFALL MAP. THEN YOU CAN DECIDE WHETHER TO BRAVE IT IN MICHIGAN OR NEW ENGLAND, WITH MORE THAN 5 FEET OF WHITE STUFF A YEAR, OR TO HEAD FOR MISSOURI OR NEW JERSEY, WHERE YOU'LL ONLY HAVE TO KICK YOUR WAY THROUGH 1 TO 3 FEET A YEAR.

Sowing the Seeds of Condensation

Water vapor molecules in clouds need to stick themselves together around other particles, usually tiny bits of dust, smoke, or sand in the air. When many molecules congregate, they eventually form water droplets and possibly rain (or snow). To encourage precipitation, "cloud seeders" spray various substances from airplanes, such as silver iodide, to serve as the condensation nuclei around which water vapor molecules can coalesce, and thus form droplets of water heavy enough to fall from the sky. Interestingly, some cloud-seeding companies work winters as well as summers: They're hired by municipalities who need that winter mountain snowpack, which will melt and supply water in warmer months.

Rain on the Way

Creaky knees? Gray skies? Sure sounds like rain is on the way. Or maybe not! Rain is notoriously capricious, and just what makes that cloud dump its precious load of liquid is still somewhat of a scientific mystery.

The ancients offered rituals and dances to encourage the gods to bring much-needed rain. Even in recent times of severe drought, those with strong ties to traditional cultures may still perform rain dances and chants.

I follow my own superstitions: When my garden is looking parched and the sky is looking promising, I wash my car or plan a picnic with friends just to make sure the rain comes down. You'd be surprised how well it works!

Signs of Rain

These conditions are a clue that rain is a possibility, usually within the next 24 hours:

- Horizontal gray clouds low in the sky
- Ring around the moon
- Cumulus clouds beginning to build vertically
- Dark gray sky to the west
- Wind shifting from north or west to south
- Falling barometer

RAIN LINGO

Forecasters use their own nuances of language to describe rainy weather, from light drizzle to heavy rain. Those aren't merely subjective adjectives: Each variation is based on factors such as visibility, size of drops, and hourly accumulation. Drizzle, for example, consists of fine drops less than 0.02 inches in diameter, falling so close together they form a mistlike effect. To be called rain, the falling drops must be larger than 0.02 inches in diameter and be more scattered and separated than in a drizzle.

DESCRIPTION	WHAT IT MEANS	WHAT TO DO
Light drizzle	Visibility is greater than $5/8$ mile	Great gardening weather; wear a flannel shirt to catch the mist and shake off afterward
Moderate drizzle	Visibility between $5/8$ and $5/16$ mile	Still possible to garden; wear a water-repellent jacket and a hat with a brim to keep the drops off your neck
Heavy drizzle	Visibility less than $5/16$ mile	Perfect weather for transplanting; you'll need dry clothes and maybe a warm bath afterward
Light rain	Separated drops; accumulation $1/10$ inch or less per hour	Great gardening weather; wear a water-repellent sweater
Moderate rain	Continuous streams of rainfall with accumulation from just over $1/10$ inch to $3/10$ inch per hour	Pull on a slicker if you plan to be outside; avoid walking on bare soil, which will compact under your weight
Heavy rain	Driving sheets of rain that accumulate more than $3/10$ inch per hour	Visibility poor; stay inside and plan for tomorrow

Managing Rain in the Garden

Only another gardener understands that certain kinds of rainy weather are the best days for gardening. When I spot someone puttering around the yard in a hooded sweatshirt during a drizzle, I know that's an experienced gardener! With a few years of gardening under our belts, we quickly learn that rainy weather is perfect for sowing seeds, rearranging plants, and setting out new perennials. Many's the day that I've lifted a clump of Shasta daisies in full bloom and moved it just a few feet to the left, say, or hefted out a huge clump of deep red daylilies to jazz up a low-voltage bed of pastels, stopping only to wish for windshield wipers on my glasses. Sunny days are great for admiring the garden, but rainy days are my favorite because I can get so much done. And when a rainy day arrives after a spell of dry weather, it's a pleasure to stroll the yard and see what's coming up.

Rain brings the garden alive. Its moisture makes sleeping seeds germinate and gives a jolt of new growth to young plants. Colors look richer on rainy days, and foliage is fresh-washed and at its best.

Rain can also ruin a garden in short order. A deluge can wash out seedbeds, erode a hillside of newly planted groundcover, batter the tomatoes, topple tall perennials, and splash tasty herbs and salad greens with hard-to-wash-off mud. If rain is sustained at critical times of the gardening year, your strawberries may be watery-bland instead of sugar-sweet, your pumpkins may fail to pollinate, your silvery artemisias may melt into mush, and your lawn and flowers may suffer from fungal diseases.

Too little rain is just as bad as too much. Seeds that refuse to sprout, rock-hard soil, and withering plants can be the result. Although it may seem like

> "When in the zodiac, the fish wheel round; they loose the floods and irrigate the ground." —Edmund Spenser

PREVENTING RAIN PROBLEMS

Fond as we are of rainfall, there are times when those falling drops can spell trouble for our gardens. Use these simple moisture management techniques to keep rain on the good side in your garden.

PROBLEM	SOLUTION
Rain washes out just-planted seeds.	Transplant seedlings back into place. To prevent, mulch new seedbeds and rows with grass clippings or straw to break the force of the rain.
Rain washes away soil from plants on slope.	Build catch basins, using rocks or bricks if needed to hold soil at plant. Mulch bare soil.
Rain splashes mud onto herbs and vegetables.	Mulch with straw or other drop-busting organic material.
Rain runs off rapidly when soil is dry and hard on the surface.	Rough-textured organic mulches slow down runoff. They protect the soil from erosion and collect the rain, allowing it to filter through to the soil instead of flowing away.
Clay soil stays waterlogged after a heavy rain.	Choose appropriate plants that thrive in clay. Mulch to encourage the activity of worms and other critters, which will help aerate the soil.
Water stands in low areas during late fall and winter.	This is a natural occurrence because plant growth slows tremendously in the dormant season. Plant pussy willow (*Salix discolor*), cardinal flower (*Lobelia cardinalis*), Japanese iris (*Iris kaempferi* hybrids), or other moisture-tolerant plants in the area, and add stepping-stones if you need to cross it.

drought has a simple solution—simply haul out the hose—the reality is a little more complicated. There may be municipal ordinances against supplemental watering, prohibitive water-meter expense, or your own ethics about using water for nonessential purposes. Even if your community allows endless watering, the hours of labor needed to supply 1 inch of water to your entire yard can be hard to manage. You'll find tips on managing drought in Chapter 8. Meanwhile, here's what to do in case of rain.

A Moisture-Managing Trick

Your rain-management program will vary by the season and the soil. In summer, actively growing plants quickly absorb a downpour, and the full foliage of shade trees and shrubs deflects its sheer force. In late fall or early spring, a downpour may cause erosion or puddling because plant roots aren't as active; it may also wash out roots of plants growing on slopes. After a prolonged dry spell, a downpour will at first run off because the soil's surface takes a while to become moist and receptive. Your soil's natural makeup also affects the effects of rain: Lightweight, sandy soils dry out much faster than heavy clay.

WATER IS PRECIOUS, SO KEEP IT RIGHT OVER THE ROOT ZONE BY BUILDING A LOW BERM AROUND THE BASE OF A NEWLY INSTALLED PLANT.

The best long-term defense is the same, no matter what the season or the soil: Add organic matter to your garden. Think of the spongy texture of soil in the woods—that good loam is the result of centuries' worth of fallen leaves decaying back into soil. Organic matter in the soil doesn't just feel like a sponge, it works like one, too. It sops up extra water, releasing it to the surrounding soil particles as they dry out.

Many folks dig in wheelbarrow after wheelbarrow of compost and other materials to improve their soil, but I get good results by using the lazy-woman's approach—mulch. I layer chopped leaves, compost, grass clippings, pulled weeds, and anything else I can get my hands on directly into the garden, where they are worked into the soil with no effort on my part. Worms, beetles, and other organisms do the soil improvement all on their own, coming to the surface to feed. The mulch also protects the soil surface from drying out.

When I moved into a house with four old sugar maples shading the front yard, I at first resorted to growing only plants that thrived in dry shade. Then a "Eureka!" light bulb went off, and I realized that in the nearby woods, the ground beneath the sugar maples was moist and crumbly even during the dry stretches of summer. While my neighbors worked at laying drip irrigation and digging in bags of store-bought compost under their trees, I simply stopped raking the fall leaves in my front yard, letting them decompose in place. In 2 years, the soil was transformed into dark brown, fragrant, humusy perfection. The thick canopy of maple leaves still kept the soil from receiving as much rain as open areas, but the humus hung onto every precious drop. Dry shade no longer!

Water Conservation Methods

With 10 minutes' worth of work shaping a rim of soil, you can save hours of watering over the growing season. Whenever you plant a new shrub or tree— or even a good-size perennial—build a mounded wall of soil a few inches high around the planting hole. The rim will keep water over the plant's roots, preventing it from running off. Whenever you water the new plant, fill this reservoir to the brim; it will gradually soak in.

Catch basins are also useful on slopes, where water runs off quickly as it heads downhill, sometimes taking soil with it. In this case, build the mounded wall on the downward side of the plant. I usually add a few rocks or bricks to help keep the soil rim in place.

ANCHOR NEWLY PLANTED GROUNDCOVERS WITH A ROCK ON THE DOWN SIDE OF THE SLOPE TO
PREVENT SOIL FROM WASHING AWAY BEFORE THE PLANT GETS GROWING.

GROUNDCOVERS

Keep your soil in place during heavy rains by using groundcovers, which also
shade the soil to slow down evaporation due to sun and wind. Spreading plants
that root along their stems or through a network of underground stems are
best—the many roots form a vast network that keeps a good grip on the soil.
A slope is a great place to grow a garden of mints, those aromatic plants
renowned for their takeover personality. In as little as a year or two, a handful
of mint cuttings can fill into a solid plantation. Plenty for sparkling teas and
heavy-duty soil control, too—what a workhorse!

MULCHES

Like living plants, mulches shield bare soil from the brunt of driving rains.
They also keep the soil cool and conserve its moisture. A mulched bed stays
moist long after an unmulched bed is crying for a drink.

Planting by Rain Seasons

What's the first command a seed packet gives you, after planting depth and spacing? "Keep moist." Water in the soil softens the hard coat of a seed and wakes the sleeping sprout into growth. Continued moisture is just as vital as that initial dose. The developing roots are tiny compared to those of a mature plant, and if they can't find moisture, the seedling will rapidly keel over and die.

The Rainy-Day Logic of Bulbs

Spring-flowering bulbs are excellent choices for gardens that are hot and dry in summer and fall. Most of our classic spring performers—tulips, daffodils, crocuses, and hyacinths—hail from regions with long, hot summers. That's why the bulbs are adapted to shift into dormancy after blooming. Over the inhospitable hot season, they harden and ripen, going into an underground holding pattern until late winter rains call them forth again.

If your climate tends to run to extremes, investigate the world of bulbs for possible solutions. In steamy southern Indiana, it's impossible to grow tall delphiniums, which thrive in cooler, wetter climes. But in midspring, I found the wild woods filled with a diminutive version of the delphinium—that springs from a bulb. *Delphinium tricorne,* named for its three-corner-hat-shaped seedpods, shines deep blue but is only 10 inches

MARK SPRING BULBS FOR TRANSPLANTING IN FALL, WHEN THEY'RE DORMANT, OR MOVE THEM WHEN THE FIRST SHOOTS POKE UP IN SPRING.

tall; after blooming, it gracefully yields the field and dies back to the bulb for the long, hot summer, just like the Turkish tulips I grow it with.

Autumn is the time to plant spring bulbs, and it's also a good season to transplant established bulbs. Be sure to mark the clump at bloom time because no evidence of the plants will remain in fall.

> ## "When a spadeful of earth crumbles, the plows may be started, but not while the spade comes out of the ground smeared."
>
> —*John P. Morton & Co.'s Western Farmers' Almanac*, 1884

In bone-dry soil, seeds will wait to wake up. But most soil holds at least a bit of residual moisture, enough to start the process. Rain kicks germination into high gear, however, making seeds poke their heads above ground in as little as 2 or 3 days, depending on species.

The best time to sow seeds is before a rain. Then, the soil is dry enough to work: You can make furrows without clumping or easily crumble a handful to cover even the finest petunia seeds. You can also walk on bare soil when it's dry without compacting it as you would saturated soil.

I also sow certain seeds during a rain: big seeds, like nasturtiums and scarlet runner beans, which I can poke into the soil with my thumb exactly where I want them, and easy cottage-garden annuals like bachelor's buttons, annual baby's breath, cleomes, cosmos, and Shirley poppies, which I scatter on roughed-up ground and let the rain "plant."

If you garden in a wet season/dry season climate, there's no sense planting as the dry season begins unless you plan to water daily. Time your planting to the rainy season instead, just as the wildflowers in natural areas around you do.

Summer Planting

East of the Rockies, summer brings warm temperatures and sporadic rains, usually in thunderstorm form. Wet weather is interspersed with what can be long stretches of dry days. Still, the heat in the soil and in the air makes seeds spring to life quickly if they're given a boost of water.

When I wanted a burst of flowers for a butterfly garden I was making in early July one year, I planted zinnias, which bloom in just 8 to 10 weeks from seed—plenty of time to catch the last wave of swallowtails and monarchs. The thermometer was hovering at about 95 degrees when I planted the arrowhead-shaped seeds one afternoon, and towering cumulus clouds were building into thunderheads. I scratched up a patch of soil, sprinkled out a few packets of giant cactus flower mix, and hoped for the best. I was astonished to see the trademark paired leaves of zinnias poking up just 2 days later. Germination can be stunningly swift in summer. In my area, supplemental watering was available to anyone willing to pay the water bill, so I took advantage of the long growing season and sowed seeds right through August, watering my beds of seedlings when rain was sparse.

THE NURSERY BED

Established plants require less water than those that are just getting started. Keep your young'uns in a separate bed, and you'll be able to concentrate your watering efforts on those that need it most when rainfall and time are in short supply (most of the summer, for me).

A nursery bed for seedlings, cuttings, and first-year perennials isn't just convenient, it's also a guarantee that your babies won't get lost among established plants and miss out on the extra dose of TLC they need to help them flourish. There's nothing sadder than stumbling across a dried-out cutting of Grandma's prize dahlia that shriveled to its doom in an overlooked corner of the perennial garden.

Once I discovered how easy it was to grow perennials from seed, I was hooked. I loved the idea of having 20 to 50 plants for less than the price of a single potted store-bought one, but I wasn't so fond of the extra year it takes to grow them to blooming size. That's why I corral all my seed-grown perennials in their own bed: I can sow seeds of coral bells, columbines, and anything else that strikes my fancy in easy-care rows because it's convenience, not display, that matters that first year. Then, after they've been regularly watered

10 Easiest Plants to Root from Cuttings

Taking cuttings is one of the most gratifying tricks of gardening: It's truly something from nothing! If you're uncertain whether a plant will succeed from cuttings, try it anyway — nothing to lose but a few snippings. One rule of thumb I use is to look for plants with square stems: They are generally very easy to root from cuttings. Here are my top candidates for ease of rooting. No special treatment needed, just strip the lower leaves and stick them into moist soil.

1. Artemisias, any kind

2. Bee balms (*Monarda* spp.)

3. Butterfly bush (*Buddleia davidii* cvs.)

4. Cardinal flower (*Lobelia cardinalis*)

5. Threadleaf coreopsis (*Coreopsis verticillata*, including 'Moonbeam')

6. Dahlias, any kind

7. Forsythia

8. Great blue lobelia (*Lobelia syphilitica*)

9. Mint, any kind

10. Russian sage (*Perovskia atriplicifolia*)

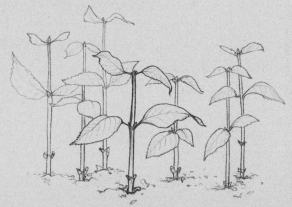

STARTING NEW PLANTS FROM CUTTINGS IS SO EASY, YOU CAN TAKE SNIPPETS FROM A SINGLE PLANT AND IN A SEASON OR TWO HAVE MORE BEE BALM, PHLOX, OR FORSYTHIA THAN YOUR GARDEN CAN HOLD.

and have flourished into full-size specimens, I can transplant them to places of honor the following spring (on a rainy day, natch).

Don't let the fancy name fool you—a "nursery bed" is simply any bit of empty ground you can rustle up. Dig it up as you would any bed, and use it to:

- Start seeds of perennials.

- Start seeds of biennials, and transplant to the garden in fall or spring.

- Start seeds of perennial herbs, such as lavender, sage, and thyme.

- Start seeds (and bulblets) of trumpet lilies and daylilies.

- Root cuttings of forsythia, weigela, kerria, butterfly bush, chaste tree, and other flowering shrubs.

- Root cuttings of arborvitae, privet, boxwood, and other evergreens.

- Root stem cuttings of *Coreopsis verticillata*, dahlias, artemisias, cardinal flower, Russian sage, salvias, and other perennials.

- Start root cuttings of Oriental poppies, balloon flower, and horseradish.

- Reinvigorate tired plants from window boxes and container gardens.

A drip hose connected to a timer makes watering a no-brainer. Or, if you prefer to hold the water source, as I do, invest a few dollars in a hose attachment that breaks the water stream into a fine spray.

Fall Planting

Fall rains signal the start of a different kind of gardening season. For those in cold-winter areas, fall is the time to plant shrubs and trees; their roots will have several weeks of good growing before the soil cools off to slow-down temperatures. In areas with milder winters, fall signals a rush almost as big as that of spring: Not only trees and shrubs, but also berry bushes, roses, perennials, and winter-blooming annuals are planted now, in time to benefit when the rains set in.

Turn a Perennial Bed into a Cottage Garden

Perennials are everybody's best friends, returning year after year as reliably as robins. But it can be tricky to get the timing of their bloom seasons right so that your garden is always overflowing with flowers. Annuals and biennials are ideal for disguising those off times of perennial bloom: I like to scatter seeds of these self-sowing "cottage garden" flowers among my perennials. They add a softening touch to the more stalwart shapes of established perennials, and they bloom in abundance. Better yet, once you plant them, you'll have them for years because the seeds drop for the following season's flowers.

Late summer through early fall is an ideal time to scatter seeds for a cottage garden, no matter where you live. Use a claw tool or hoe to scratch up the soil wherever there's a bit of sunny space among your perennials, and sprinkle out the seeds. Part of the fun of this style of gardening is its lack of exact planning: You never know exactly where the plants will spring up.

CORN COCKLE (*AGROSTEMMA GITHAGO*)

HOLLYHOCK (*ALCEA ROSEA*)

CALENDULA, POT MARIGOLD
  (*CALENDULA OFFICINALIS*)

BACHELOR'S BUTTONS
  (*CENTAUREA CYANUS*)

CLEOME, SPIDER FLOWER
  (*CLEOME HASSLERIANA*)

LARKSPUR (*CONSOLIDA AJACIS*)

COSMOS (*COSMOS* SPP.)

ROSE CAMPION (*LYCHNIS CORONARIA*)

ANNUAL MALLOW (*MALOPE TRIFIDA*)

LOVE-IN-A-MIST (*NIGELLA DAMASCENA*)

SHIRLEY POPPIES (*PAPAVER RHOEAS*
  SHIRLEY SERIES*)

ANNUAL POPPY
  (*PAPAVER SOMNIFERUM*)

FEVERFEW (*TANACETUM PARTHENIUM*)

Winter Planting

Those of you who see snow when you look out a winter window can skip this part, unless you want to entertain/torture yourself with the thought of how the other half lives. In cold, snowy regions, indoor planting is the only gardening you'll be doing because the ground outside is frozen rock-solid. Start your tomatoes under lights or on a sunny windowsill, bring in a bunch of forsythia to coax into bloom, and consider what you could be doing if you lived in California.

Mild-winter gardeners can engage in their favorite pastime year-round. Nurseries are refreshed with blooming plants in all seasons, allowing you to

> "A sort of frozen rain this afternoon . . . which stiffens your umbrella so that it cannot be shut. Will not the trees look fine in the morning?" —Henry David Thoreau

add or change the garden beds and containers whenever you like. Because winter is the rainy season in the West, plants will quickly become well rooted, and seeds will sprout lickety-split.

In areas of moderately cold winters, such as the Lower Midwest and Southeast, a surprising amount of winter gardening is still doable. You can plant cheerful pansies, hellebores, and other winter bloomers to enjoy a taste of springtime, as long as the soil is unfrozen. Avoid putting new perennials or shrubs into the ground, though, because a sudden cold snap can make things very inhospitable. Continue sowing seeds of cold-hardy annuals, like those mentioned above, for earliest bloom and to get a leap on spring gardening.

Snow

Forecasting snow is a funny science: Most old-timers will get a feel for the air, and then pronounce "Nope, too cold for snow." They have a valid point. When the air is frigidly cold, many of its water droplets are evaporated, turning back to water vapor without ever falling to earth. That "too cold" hunch may also be due to wind blowing: When a snowstorm settles in, it usually doesn't announce itself with a roar like a summer thunderstorm. Instead, the air feels heavy and still, and then the snow starts falling on its silent cat feet.

Plants to Match Your Moisture

Into every garden a little rain—or a lot—must fall: thank goodness for that. No matter when the showers sprinkle your site during the course of the year, there are plants that are well-suited to your area's rainfall patterns and amounts.

Find the heading that best describes your local rainfall, then brighten your garden with plants from the appropriate list.

PLANTS FOR DRY SUMMER, WET WINTER AREAS

PERUVIAN LILIES
   (*ALSTROEMERIA AUREA* CVS.)
ROCK PURSLANES (*CALANDRINIA* SPP.)
SUN ROSES (*CISTUS* SPP.)
LIVINGSTONE DAISY, ICE PLANT
   (*DOROTHEANTHUS BELLIDIFORMIS*)
CALIFORNIA POPPY
   (*ESCHSCHOLZIA CALIFORNICA*)
FENNEL (*FOENICULUM VULGARE*)
MEXICAN TULIP POPPY
   (*HUNNEMANNIA FUMARIIFOLIA*)
CANDYTUFTS (*IBERIS* SPP.)
LAVENDERS (*LAVANDULA* SPP. AND CVS.)
MOSS ROSES (*PORTULACA*
   GRANDIFLORA AND HYBRIDS)
ROSEMARY (*ROSMARINUS OFFICINALIS*)
SALVIAS (*SALVIA* SPP.)
HENS-AND-CHICKS (*SEMPERVIVUM* SPP.)

Snow forms more often in the clouds than it ever does on our gardens. Oddly, many raindrops begin as snow crystals because they form high up in supercooled clouds. When they hit the warm air above the earth, they rapidly melt and meet our heads as rain.

When the saturated air—what we now know is a cloud—is below the freezing point, and the air beneath the cloud is also below the freezing point, all systems are go for snow. If the ground the snow lands on is above the freezing point, the snow won't "stick" unless it falls fast and thick enough to outpace the melting.

PLANTS FOR AREAS WITH 4-SEASON MODERATE RAIN

YARROWS (*ACHILLEA* SPP.)

MONKSHOODS (*ACONITUM* SPP. AND CVS.)

BERGENIAS (*BERGENIA* HYBRIDS)

COREOPSIS (*COREOPSIS* SPP.)

DELPHINIUMS (*DELPHINIUM* HYBRIDS)

GLOBE THISTLE (*ECHINOPS RITRO*)

HARDY GERANIUMS (*GERANIUM* SPP.)

CORAL BELLS (*HEUCHERA* × *BRIZOIDES*)

JAPANESE IRIS (*IRIS KAEMPFERI*)

SHASTA DAISY
   (*LEUCANTHEMUM* × *SUPERBUM*)

BEE BALM (*MONARDA DIDYMA*)

ORIENTAL POPPY (*PAPAVER ORIENTALE*)

GARDEN PHLOX (*PHLOX PANICULATA*)

CLARY SAGE (*SALVIA VIRIDIS*)

PLANTS FOR AREAS OF LONG, COOL, RAINY SPRINGS

BERGENIAS (*BERGENIA* HYBRIDS)

CALENDULA, POT MARIGOLD
   (*CALENDULA OFFICINALIS*)

CARPATHIAN HAREBELLS
   (*CAMPANULA CARPATICA* AND CVS.)

BLEEDING HEARTS (*DICENTRA* SPP.)

CORAL BELLS (*HEUCHERA* × *BRIZOIDES*)

SIBERIAN IRIS (*IRIS SIBIRICA*)

SWEET PEA (*LATHYRUS ODORATUS*)

PRIMROSES (*PRIMULA* SPP.)

PULMONARIAS
   (*PULMONARIA SACCHARATA* AND CVS.)

FOAMFLOWERS
   (*TIARELLA CORDIFOLIA* AND CVS.)

PANSIES, VIOLETS, JOHNNY-JUMP-UPS
   (*VIOLA* SPP.)

A Close Look at a Snowflake

Snowflakes are so beautiful that they inspired at least one person, Wilson Bentley of snow-blessed Vermont, to spend his whole life trying to capture their images, first on paper and then with a camera. Most of us are content to marvel at them a few times a year, usually when the flakes are so big and lacy they can't escape our notice. Snowflakes are crystals, just like diamonds, amethyst, or grains of salt. They start as very simple shapes and gradually become more complex as they move through their mother cloud.

The traditional snowflake, like the kind you once cut out of folded paper, is just one type of snow crystal. Stand in snow with a dark sweater on and you may catch crystals that are thin and spiky like needles, in hollow columns, or flat plates that look something like itty-bitty stop signs. The ultimate shape of a snow crystal depends on how long it spent in the cloud, how many water molecules attached to it, and the temperature of the air that it came from.

The shape of a snow crystal tells you its history—the conditions when it formed. The fancier the crystal, the wetter and warmer the air was. Water molecules make the lacy arms on the otherwise simple start of a snowflake: If the cloud in which it forms holds an abundance of water, its arms grow longer with more branches as they become rimed with instantly freezing water droplets. Clumped-together flakes fell through warmer air on the way down, causing just enough melting to make the flakes stick together.

Snowflakes deserve a closer look anytime they're falling, and not so that you can check the theory about no two being alike. (For the record, two identical snow crystals have been recorded. But they were very simply shaped, not the intricate beauties we can still think of as infinite in their variety.)

> "Snow, blessed snow,
>
> comes out of the sky
>
> like bleached flies." —Anne Sexton

Birth of a Snowflake

The incredible beauty of snowflakes is due to the angular symmetry that is created when the crystals enlarge. Just like raindrops, snow starts in a cloud with water vapor molecules glomming onto a condensation nucleus, such as a speck of dust. In fact, all snowflakes begin their life as droplets of water:

1. Water-vapor molecules coalesce around a speck of soot or dust in the cloud, forming a teeny-tiny water droplet.
2. The droplet cools and freezes into a simple, six-sided ice crystal. (Water molecules always assume a hexagonal arrangement when they freeze.)

Windbreaks, Wyoming Style

Snow is serious out west, where the wind comes sweeping down the Plains. Many towns are marked at their terminus with unsettling signs that warn, "If this light is blinking, turn back." You won't see those lights blinking in summer, but in winter, this is serious snow country. Look beyond the sign pole in summer and you'll spot humongous rail fences, taller than two grown men standing on each other's shoulders. Bolstered by angled timber braces the size of utility poles, those 12-foot-high fences run for miles along the roads.

In winter, you're not likely to see the fences because they'll be buried under snowdrifts. The snow fences of the West work as windbreaks, breaking the force of the snow-carrying gusts that howl across the wide-open spaces. As the wind blows, it picks up more and more snow, waiting for a change in elevation (a house, a road cut) to drop it into giant, sculpted drifts. The snow fences break the wind, which dumps its snow against the fence. By controlling the placement of snowdrifts, westerners keep their roads and homes from being buried. Try it on a smaller scale in your yard!

3. More water molecules attach to the simple crystal, and it grows six branches, which themselves sprout symmetrical arms near the tips.
4. Water vapor continues condensing onto the crystal, enlarging it and adding more branches to the arms.
5. The crystal is now heavier, and it begins to fall through the cloud.
6. More water vapor condenses onto the crystal, changing its shape and size as it falls to earth.

Should the crystal meet warmer air, it begins to melt very slightly. When you see snowflakes that are made up of more than one flake stuck together, it's because the melting edges of a snow crystal have attached to other crystals that are also falling, forming a larger cluster of snowflakes.

Snow-to-Rain Conversion

Meteorologists take sophisticated measurements of the water in each snowfall so they can convert it to inches of precipitation to plug into data charts. But for the rest of us, our knowledge is mostly limited to the 10:1 theory we learned in school: 10 inches of snow is equivalent to 1 inch of rain.

Hate to knock your snowman down, but that's just not true. At least, not in all cases. Only very wet snow, the kind that gives you a backache before you've shoveled half the walk, fits the 10:1 ratio. The fluffier the snow, the more air it contains—and the less water. That dry powder that gets skiers so excited is at the other end of the snow-to-rain scale: 40 to 50 inches of that fluffy stuff in winter is equal to 1 inch of rain during the rest of the year.

Snow is highly variable in its lightness or wetness:

- Wet snow—the stuff that makes an instant snowball when you grab a handful—clocks in at 10:1.

- Moderately powdery snow—you have to pack it into snowball shape—falls in the 20:1 to 30:1 range.

- Very dry powder that's great for sledding but lousy for snowman construction may take 40 to 50 inches to equal 1 inch of rain.

Snow Is Good for the Garden

Snow is cold, below the freezing point, but it's the best blanket your garden could ask for. As those tiny snow crystals pile up, they trap plenty of air molecules among them. Like the feathers of a chickadee or the fluffy down comforter on your bed, the trapped air helps hold in heat and keep out cold. A blanket of snow protects the plants and roots below from the frigid blasts above the drifts.

Winter damage to plants is caused by three factors: desiccating wind, pure cold that freezes branches or the growing point (crown) of the plant, and roots heaved out of the soil as the ground freezes, thaws, and refreezes. An insulating layer of snow keeps the crowns of your plants bundled up against Old Man Winter and maintains a steady temperature at soil level.

Snow is a garden ally, but it can also be a bully. Heavy snow can pummel evergreens, especially those of columnar shape, such as arborvitae. Bare-branched deciduous trees are usually unharmed by the burden of snow resting on their limbs, but evergreens can collect amounts that are too much to bear. A heavy load of snow may snap branches from pines or hemlocks, or force open the branches of rhododendrons and other evergreen shrubs. You'll find suggestions for preventing such damage and applying first aid in Chapter 10, "Winter Weather", starting on page 237.

Sleet, Freezing Rain, and Other Slick Stuff

Our names for "water that falls from the sky" are pitifully few compared to the vocabulary of the Eskimos, who have dozens of terms to describe the nuances of snow alone. While they mutter "*Pukak!*," pointing out snow that can cause avalanches, or comment on the *Upsick* (snow that is heavily compacted), we talk about wet snow, powdery snow, and sleet.

And we can't even agree on what those words mean. In some parts of the country, "sleet" is white and pelletlike, like tiny bits of Styrofoam bouncing from the sky; in other areas, "sleet" describes a slanting rain that freezes as it hits the ground or the window.

Television meteorologists try to keep it simple for us laypeople by sticking to rain, snow, freezing rain, sleet, and hail (usually a summer phenomenon). That leaves out my personal favorite form of precipitation, the fairylike coating of heavy frost that's called "rime."

What we can agree on—and I bet the Eskimos would second the motion—is that freezing rain by any name is a mess. It makes walking darn near impossible and turns driving into a Firestone roller derby. And a heavy accumulation absolutely wreaks havoc in the garden, breaking major branches, toppling entire trees, and sending power lines crashing.

When water droplets cool to below the freezing point without forming crystals in the cloud or air (because of lack of nuclei to crystallize around), they are raindrops looking for trouble. Although they fall from the cloud in liquid form, they freeze as soon as they touch any surface, glazing plants, houses, roads, and your car's door locks with a sheet of ice.

It's a magical effect—but a dangerous and damaging one. Ice may look ethereal as it sparkles on every twig and pine needle, but it's incredibly heavy, especially when multiplied by the surface area of a tree. What looks like a delicate transparent glaze on your trees' branches can easily weigh enough to snap them like toothpicks. On more flexible stems of shrubs or hedges, the weight of the ice can bend them to the ground in an arching, frozen waterfall.

> "When the ice is covered with snow, I do not suspect the wealth under my feet; that there is as good as a mine under me wherever I go."
>
> —Henry David Thoreau

Sleet is usually less damaging than freezing rain because it's already frozen as it falls, so it doesn't stick like glue to every surface. Usually it piles up on the ground and other flat surfaces and is only a general annoyance rather than a crisis for the garden or gardener.

Get a Grip on the Ground

No matter what the slick stuff is named, there's only one garden-safe way to make it a walkable surface: Sand. Coarse builder's sand supplies grittiness to the slippery surface, and it's easy to sweep off into the neighboring lawn or flowerbeds after the season.

Cat litter made of clay granules will give you traction, but its distinctive look may cause visitors to wonder where you're emptying the litter box. It may also contain perfumes, dyes, or other chemicals that could be harmful to your garden.

Never use salt, the time-honored solution: It will kill off nearly all nearby plants. The only possible application for an economy-size saltshaker of ice-melting rock salt is a paved but unmortared patio area. The salt may inhibit the frustrating growth of weeds between the bricks or other pavers. On the other hand, it may also wash off into nearby garden beds or eventually into creeks. And it can cause deterioration to the paving itself, as highway crews have discovered over decades of spreading road salt.

CHAPTER 7

IF A ROBIN SINGS IN THE BUSH
THEN THE WEATHER WILL BE COARSE;
IF THE ROBIN SINGS ON THE BARN
THEN THE WEATHER WILL BE WARM.

Spring Weather

EVERYTHING SEEMS POSSIBLE IN SPRING. THIS IS THE TIME OF NEW BEGINNINGS, and it brims with all the pent-up hopes of the winter that went before. For once, you'll have the perfect garden. Every seed you drop into the soil holds a miracle in the making. Your flowers will be glorious, your strawberries plump and juicy, your vegetables will fill baskets and bins to overflowing—and, of course, pests, diseases, and weeds will never plague your days. Ah, spring! No wonder we love it.

Friends accuse me every year of announcing spring's arrival long before the calendar date. Not only that, but, "You say it's spring earlier and earlier every year," they comment, along about February. That's probably true—no time to waste, now that the years are flying by so fast—but my pronouncement of the season is always tied to natural signs. The vernal equinox may be weeks (okay, months) away, but in my heart, I know it's spring.

Heralding the News

You can feel spring in the air, but temperature alone isn't enough of a basis for announcing its arrival. Gardeners know the fickleness of spring. The season seems to move in, then retreat—over and over—until finally we can all breathe a sigh of delight and get to planting.

Nope, knowing spring is here is not a matter of looking at the calendar. The start of spring for me is when the season's "firsts"—the harbingers, both the famed and the hardly noticed—begin to pile up, reaching a point of critical mass at which I lift my head, sniff the air, and holler "Spring is here!"

10 Spring Harbingers to Look and Listen For

1. Changing color on distant trees: Maples acquire a red tinge as their buds swell; willows glow golden with brightening bark

2. Sap icicles or dripping sap where passing traffic has broken twigs of overhead trees

3. The first tentative notes of spring peepers or chorus frogs, sounding like sluggish crickets from a distance

4. Lady beetles and slow, buzzy flies that wintered in crevices of the house waking up and gathering at indoor windows

5. Turkey vultures in the air: big, dark birds noticeable from a distance and easily identified by the wide V-shape of their soaring wings

6. A group of robins or flickers on the lawn

7. Crocuses blooming

8. Tight-furled shoots of tulip leaves

9. The smell of humus on the air—a sign that soil is thawing

10. Spring beauties (*Claytonia* spp.) in bloom, the first of the coming wildflower extravaganza

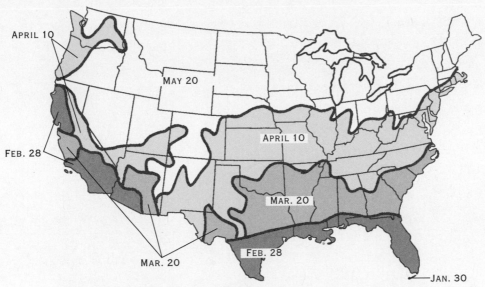

APRIL 10

MAY 20

FEB. 28

APRIL 10

MAR. 20

MAR. 20

FEB. 28

JAN. 30

AVERAGE LAST FROST DATES: PLANTING DATES SHOWN ON SOME SEED PACKETS MATCH THE
CALENDAR OF FROST-FREE SPRING PLANTING ACROSS THE COUNTRY. THEY'RE BASED ON THE
AVERAGE LAST SPRING FROST DATE—BUT WATCH OUT FOR RENEGADE COLD SNAPS!

Warming Air

Spring starts in the South, triggering bloom and birdsong beginning in early
February. Then the season begins advancing northward at a pace of about 15
miles a day. Mountains slow it down because the air cools as it climbs. Moving
1,000 feet up a mountain is like traveling 600 miles across flat land, which is
why spring comes later to higher elevations. Valleys and plains let the warm
air move faster (unless a cold front sweeps it temporarily aside).

Depending where you live, spring can be a slow and gentle warm-up, or a
sudden splash of balmy days that melt the last of the snow and stir frozen creeks
and rivers back into motion. While the pattern of the warming air varies from
place to place and from year to year, there's no mistaking the true spring thaw.

A few days of warmth may be enough to fool the mourning cloak butterflies and bring them out for a basking session, but I know better. What spring
giveth, spring taketh away. Capriciousness is the name of this season's game,
at least in the early stages. One fine day, you wake to delicious 50-degree

warmth and gentle sun. You play outside as much as you can manage, finally shedding at least the first layer of winter clothes. The next night, a blue norther roars down from Canada, and you're reaching for an extra blanket, hoping for the best for those peas you planted too soon, and yearning for the next warm, sunny day.

Making It Official

The vernal equinox, usually March 20 or 21, is based on the stars and the sun—and what do they care about gardeners? If you planted your garden on the first day of spring according to the calendar, you'd be waiting until you have summerlike heat in southern states, and facing the icy wrath of snow-covered soil in the North.

To gardeners in southern states, "spring" can start in January. To gardeners in the cold north and in mountain areas, "spring" may not arrive until May. We'll both be planting our spring crops when the season gets here, but we may be digging in the soil and thinking spring as much as 5 months apart from each other.

The calendar start of spring is more important to animals, including us, than it is to gardening. On this date, which has been calculated since the time of ancient astronomers, the rays of the sun fall straight down on the equator. On every single inch of the globe's surface, day and night are equal in length. From that day forward, hours of daylight lengthen day by day in the northern hemisphere and lessen in the southern, as the earth swings along on its 365-day orbit around the sun. The longer stretch of daylight kicks hormones into

"Beckoning from blue or stormy skies,

April smiles, and then April sighs."

—Louise Bates

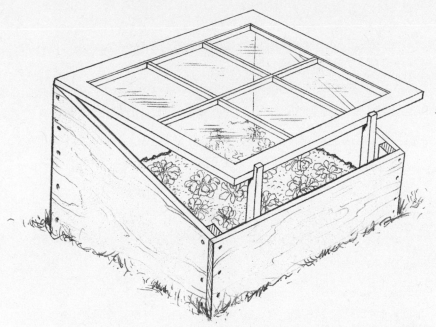

HEAT BUILDS UP QUICKLY IN A GLASS-TOPPED COLDFRAME, EVEN ON WINTER DAYS. ON VERY COLD BUT SUNNY DAYS, CRACK THE LID JUST A BIT TO LET THE EXTRA HEAT ESCAPE IN THE MIDDLE OF THE DAY; AS THE WEATHER GROWS MILDER, PROP THE GLASS PANE HIGHER.

gear in animals, sending birds to pack their bags for migration and putting love on the brain for courting animals. Seeds, too, get the signal to wake and grow, and suddenly you'll notice weeds sprouting everywhere.

Spring Sunshine

In our mid-latitudes location, relatively far from the Equator, sun is a welcome presence in spring. Our big flaming furnace is still shining from a relatively low angle in the sky, not near the zenith as it will be in summer, so the rays that reach us are less powerful. Be aware of the changes that the gradually increasing sunlight causes in your garden, and be prepared to adjust your gardening activities accordingly:

- Thousands of weed seedlings are one of the earliest signs of spring. Don't panic—many will be crowded out, and it's easy now to swipe off whole colonies at the roots with one stroke of the hoe.

- Notice the microclimates that heat-holding structures or sunny exposures create in your yard. Where do crocuses and daffodils bloom first? That's a hot spot, a good place to later plant surefire sun-loving perennials—or tomatoes, to win the race for the first ripe red one in the neighborhood!

- Heat can build up fast in a coldframe on a sunny day. Remember to crack the lid to let it escape, even if the temperature outside is still mighty shivery. Close the lid on chilly nights to keep the plants protected.

- Plant leaves soak up the sunshine, transforming it to food for the roots, which is why your seedlings seem to take off with a leap in sunny weather and go into slow motion during an extended spell of overcast skies.

- Honeybees and other pollinators are active in fair weather because sun encourages nectar production. Sometimes you may see a honeybee weeks before the flowers are blooming, when an unusual late-winter warm spell brings it back to life. Dab a few drops of honey on a plate to feed early-riser bees if you see them looking befuddled at the lack of blossoms.

- Move low-light houseplants a few inches away from windows to shield them as spring progresses and the sun's strength intensifies.

- Plan some basking time to boost a feeling of well-being in your own winter-weary brain.

The Early Bird Gets the Worm

Some robins live year-round in cold-winter regions, but most of them move south in fall and return to announce the arrival of the spring season. They're as reliable today as they were 200 years ago because their northward migration follows the line of advancing warm air. Of course, "warm" is relative.

To robins, it's 35°F (2°C), the temperature that means thawing soil and, as a result, worms. When you see a flock of robins in your neighborhood, go ahead and get ready for the early garden. Even if cold weather moves back in, sending the robins to huddle in the bushes, it won't stay for long.

Warming Soil

As the average daily temperature of the air begins to rise, the warming earth pulls slumbering animals back to the surface. Worms are migrants just like birds, but their path is a vertical one. In fall, they move downward as the soil cools. In spring, as the soil absorbs the warmth of the sun, they move up from their winter hideouts deep below frost level. When the soil reaches 35°F, (2°C), it's free of frost, and that's the signal worms are waiting for. Microscopic bacteria and other organisms come alive, too, and begin the eternal process of decay that makes soil a storehouse of nutrients for plant roots.

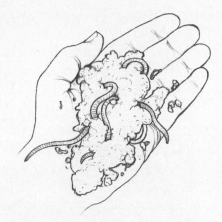

WIGGLY WORMS ARE JUST AS MUCH A HARBINGER OF SPRING AS ROBIN REDBREAST. EARTHWORMS MIGRATE UP FROM THE DEPTHS OF THE SOIL AS THE TOP LAYER OF EARTH GROWS WARMER.

As the soil community awakens, their activities release chemicals of decomposition and fermentation that create that signature scent of warming earth—a rich, heady perfume to any gardener who's been stuck in the winter

Worm Erosion Control

Organic matter in the soil attracts worms to feed, and that's good news for your spring garden. Without plants in active growth, the bare soil of spring is vulnerable to erosion in the downpours that are bound to come. The humble earthworm is a great ally in preventing such damage. The leavings from their digestive tract, known as castings, are deposited on the surface of the soil. Take a look and you'll easily spot these tiny piles and pellets. The castings are harder than the soil on which they lie, so they resist raindrops falling on their heads. When your healthy soil is teeming with earthworms, their multitude of castings creates a vital mulch on the soil surface, protecting it from eroding when rain arrives. As a bonus, the castings are also a gentle fertilizer for plant roots.

A Migrating Plant

One more group of "migrants" respond to warming temperatures, this time in water. These are the tiniest flowering plants in the world, and among the fastest reproducing: the itty-bitty duckweeds (*Wolffia* spp.). In summer you'll see floating sheets of *Wolffia* duckweeds and the related *Lemna* species of duckweeds forming a bright green film, made up of zillions of individual plants, on garden pools and ponds. In winter, the duckweeds disappear. They haven't died, they've merely switched to another stage of their life cycle. As autumn cools the water and shortens the days, the plants form winter buds that are heavy with starch to sustain the plant through the winter sleep and that lack the air spaces that keep the summer plants buoyant. The winter buds sink to the bottom of your garden pool to spend winter in the mud or debris. When spring warms the water, the buds begin to grow, producing air-filled structures that lift the new plants back to the surface. Although duckweed can quickly overgrow its welcome in a small pool, its reappearance is another indicator that says "Welcome, Spring!"

doldrums. Take a good, deep sniff whenever you step outside your house, and you'll soon become aware that spring, indeed, is in the air.

As the warmth increases and reaches deeper, frogs and toads wake up and struggle to their breeding ponds to sound the first plaintive "Anybody out there?" calls of their kind. The magic number for these spring singers is 50°F (10°C), which means you'll usually hear these harbingers a few weeks after the arrival of the early-bird robins. Turtles and snakes wake at the 50-degree mark, too, although they may make earlier forays to test the sun. Mostly these early risers do exactly what gardeners do in the early days of the season: They bask in the welcome warmth of the sun.

USE CAUTION TO AVOID COMPACTION

We gardeners leap from the gate in spring, champing at the bit to do any kind of pleasurable work that we can find. We riffle through our hoard of seed packets, feeling like Midas as we plan what and where to plant. But spring, despite its temptations, is also a time for restraint. Newly thawed soil is easily damaged by even something as innocuous as walking across it.

Spring soil is generally very full of moisture, and it will compress easily. Your footfalls will squeeze the air out of the soil, and it will dry into hard lumps. Even hoeing or spade work can pack the wet particles together, destroying that fluffy texture you need to grow a good garden. Sure, weeds can sprout even in a blacktop street, but more desirable plants' roots have a much easier time in loose soil.

The old-fashioned fistful-of-soil test is still the best gauge of when to work the soil. Scoop up a handful from the bed and give it a gentle squeeze, then open your hand. If the ball crumbles on its own or when you poke it with a finger, start digging. If you're left with a mud ball on your palm, stay out! Give the soil time to dry out a bit—unless you enjoy breaking up lumps of cement-hard soil and hauling wheelbarrows of compost to repair the damage you caused.

If you must cross bare soil in early spring, lay out boards or plywood scraps to distribute your weight over a larger area with each footstep.

Reading the Signs

Gardeners need no coaxing to spend every free moment outside in spring. Suddenly the fascinations of TV and the mall hold no attraction—not when robins are singing and the irises need dividing. As you stroll the yard to plan and plant, look around as often as you can. Look up and out as well as down. Stop in your tracks; look and listen. This is a great time to actually sit a spell on that garden bench you placed just so. But brief pauses during your meanderings are equally important because they get you in the habit of noticing your surroundings. Don't forget to come outside at night, too. Listen for migrating geese and songbirds overhead, look at the moon, check for clouds, listen for a far-off or nearby frog.

As your senses sharpen, you'll be stunned to see how much you've been missing. I'm always delighted when folks tell me they saw their first meadowlark, their first red-winged blackbird, their first whatever of their life: The next comment is always "That must be a rare one." Wonderful, I assure them, but really not rare—once you see your first redwing, you'll be noticing them everywhere. When you train yourself to notice things, you'll quickly discover the world is full of wonders.

The next step is to figure out what your sightings mean. Often the interpretation of seasonal signs is obvious, once you stop and think. But you can also enjoy building on old-time knowledge, wisdom that was second nature in country families, when survival was tied to the weather and not to the bank loan on the new combine.

The Sap Is Running

Got a big old shade tree in your yard or on your street? For 50 years, maybe 100, it has grown thousands of new leaves each spring. For a whole or half-century, those leaves—each one a little sugar factory—have manufactured the food needed to nourish the roots and keep the tree alive for another year.

In spring, sap begins to course upward from the roots, pumping out to each and every tiny twig. It's the same system that carries nutrients within a tomato plant or a petunia, and it's a wonder. Just consider the pressure that living pump produces. Scientists have figured out that the juice within a tomato plant's stems travels at up to 100 pounds of pressure per inch—no wonder sap can reach the tip-top of your maple or oak.

When a branch of a tree is broken in spring, the sap pumps out. Look up as you drive along tree-lined city streets, where tall trucks or SUVs brush against the branches. After a cold night, the leaking sap forms icicles dripping from every broken twig.

Lots of birds have a sweet tooth for sap. Sapsuckers, of course, are devoted to the stuff, but so are titmice, chickadees, and house finches, along with other occasional visitors. Even hummingbirds seek out sap to dip their long tongues into. Squirrels, too, enjoy these natural sweets. In early spring, before trees leaf out, keep an eye on maples and you may spot wildlife satisfying their thirst. Birds position themselves within reach of the tip of the sap icicle, where they can sip the sweet stuff. The golden-bellied fox squirrels in my neighborhood are daily visitors to the sugar maples in front of my house. If traffic hasn't broken the twigs, they'll do the job themselves, then return to lap up the results.

Smaller creatures also seek out sap. Look for butterflies in the daytime at a sap spill, and moths at night (their tiny eyes will glow red in the beam of a flashlight). The big, fearsome-looking beetle called the eyed elatior is also a sap aficionado, as are other interesting beetles.

Sapsuckers Anonymous

Sap has a relatively high sugar content, and that means it ferments quickly when exposed to the air. Leaking sap that collects in the bark of a tree or on a branch can become a neighborhood tavern for birds and other imbibers, who seem to enjoy alcoholic sap even more than the unfermented variety. Watch the behavior and departures of the customers and you may notice distinct signs of tipsiness: uneven flight, blundering into objects, staying put instead of flying off in the face of danger (that's you), or even unusually aggressive behavior. Luckily, "silly sap" is only a temporary offering; it soon dries up as spring progresses.

CHICKADEES AND OTHER BIRDS ARE QUICKLY ATTRACTED TO SAP LEAKING FROM BROKEN TWIGS IN LATE WINTER.

If you sample a sap icicle yourself, you may wonder what all the fuss is about. Unlike honeysuckle nectar, with its concentrated sweetness, maple sap is very diluted. I can detect only a faint tease of sugar, but I still like to suck on a sap icicle just for the fun of partaking in the bounty of spring.

Pruning Considerations

Maples and cherries produce copious amounts of sap, and lopping off a branch in spring when the sap is running is as bad as an amputation. Preserve your trees' strength by pruning them when they are completely dormant. Although the cuts may still exude some sap as spring arrives, the negative effects are greatly diminished.

Tree Leaf-and-Flower Timetable

All that pumping sap is for one purpose: plumping up the buds of a tree and awakening the growth of leaves and flowers. Sap runs are dependent on the weather, which means that you can gauge the progress of the season by the development of tree leaves and flowers. Only rarely will these signs steer you wrong, *as long as you follow the suggestions of native trees.* Imported ornamentals seem to get the timing wrong much more often than the natives. It's rare for, say, a redbud (*Cercis canadensis*) to have its flowers nipped in the bud, but the nonnative saucer magnolia (*Magnolia soulangiana*) is a victim of false starts in many springs, much to its hosts' dismay.

It's often a surprise to realize that trees are flowering plants, too. Most don't bear big, showy blossoms, but their flowers are perfectly adapted to their jobs. If you're unfamiliar with the flowers of your backyard trees, you'll enjoy putting a budding branch into a vase of water and watching what happens. Maple flowers, for instance, are as sweetly scented as lilacs—and they bloom two months earlier. Pussy willows are charming flowers, but so are the catkins of every other willow; some are long and skinny, some curled, some silvery, some green. One caveat: Most tree flowers produce huge amounts of pollen, so if you're allergy sensitive, admire them through the window instead of on the kitchen table.

PLANTING BY THE TREES

Native trees and shrubs can provide reasonably accurate guidance when it comes to spring planting. Try following these natural cues to know when to get your gardening show underway—it's fun to keep records from year to year to see how often the trees are right.

	LORE	EXPLANATION
	Plant peas when pussy willows bloom.	Unless your ground is still snow-covered, that is: Pussy willows bloom early, and peas are one of the first crops you can safely put into the soil.
	Plant onions when red maples bloom.	Red maples are another early bloomer, and onion sets can tolerate cool soil.
	Plant corn when oak leaves are the size of a squirrel's ear.	Oaks are one of the last trees to leaf out. By the time their leaves are about ½ inch in size, the soil has warmed enough to safely sow corn.
	Start seeds of herbs and tomatoes indoors when you notice willows turning brighter yellow.	Willow bark develops its brighter color as spring approaches. When the branches are noticeably yellow, you can bet it's only a few weeks until robins and daffodils appear.
	Plant impatiens, geraniums, and other tender flowers already in bloom when fruits form on mulberry trees and bramble bushes.	If you're a risk taker, you can put out tender flowers when fruit trees bloom. But waiting for these fruits will save you from those panicky nights of covering up tender plants to ward off a late spring frost.

Listen to the Birds

Spring not only smells different, it sounds different, too. Birds that have spent the winter with us begin singing songs to claim nesting territories and impress mates, and migrant birds begin sweeping back north, increasing the life and loudness of the backyard.

Arriving migrants are great weather forecasters. They often show up in advance of an approaching front, using the winds at the edge to make travel

PLANTING BY THE BIRD-RETURN CALENDAR

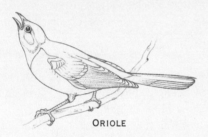

ORIOLE

The songbirds arriving in your backyard during spring migration, from February through June, are a good clue to timing the planting of your garden. They move northward along with the warming air, arriving according to a schedule they've maintained for millennia. Use their annual appearance as a reminder to get outside and plant seeds, but keep in mind that although this system is generally reliable, it's not perfect! Birds can be fooled by Mother Nature, too: Those who keep purple martin houses know the birds may arrive and then fall upon hard times should the weather turn too cold to support the insects they eat. Similarly,

ROSE-BREASTED GROSBEAK

hummingbirds have been known to move northward and then retreat in the face of a chilly cold front. Use your common sense along with this chart. If snow covers your garden when fox sparrows show up at your feeder, toss them some extra millet and settle back for another week of dreaming over seed catalogs.

SPARROW

faster. When spring storms threaten, they hunker down in backyard trees and shrubs, still in the loose groups that traveled together.

Most songbirds migrate at night to escape the eagle eye of hawks and other predators, which often migrate during the same time period but fly only in daytime hours. Step outside at night from February to April, and you may catch the faint chirps and cheeps of birds passing overhead. When dawn comes, the tired travelers drop out of the sky and set to feeding, to restore their bodies and stock up for the next leg of the long trip.

Bird(s)	What to Plant (if not specified, refers to seeds)
Fox sparrow, chipping sparrow	Cabbage and other cole crops; pansy plants
Goldfinch	Onion sets, peas
Robin, brown thrasher	Lettuce, radishes, carrots
House wren, gray catbird, swallow, purple martin	Bachelor's buttons, cosmos, Shirley poppies, California poppies, dill
Oriole, tanager, hummingbird	Annual or perennial flower seeds; bulbs of Asiatic lilies, gladiolus, cannas
Rose-breasted grosbeak	Corn, beans, tomatoes, squash, cucumbers, zucchini, herbs; tomato plants, peppers, geraniums, impatiens, and anything else at the garden center

Spring is so welcome, you may forget to tend to regular activities while you revel in it, "suffering" that curious condition called spring fever. Old societies recognized the need for celebration at spring's arrival and created ceremonies to welcome the season. "The aged feel a kind of youth," wrote one observer in the 17th century, "and the youthful cheeks are red as a cherry." Romans offered sacrifices to Venus, the goddess of love, and overindulged in food, drink, and Venus-inspired activities. The Welsh wore a daffodil on the first day of March. English milkmaids put daisies under their pillows to inspire dreams of their true loves, and on May Day in Tudor England of the late 1700s, people bathed their faces with the dew on the grass to "render them beautiful." Spring *is* the season of the optimist!

Along with giving you clues to the immediate weather, birds also reveal the progress of the season. Hummingbirds, which depend on flower nectar, follow closely behind the early-blooming plants that they favor. When they hit an unexpected cold snap, they retreat to lower elevations or slightly southward, where the blossoms are in bloom.

WILD COLUMBINES BLOOM AT EXACTLY THE RIGHT TIME IN SPRING TO NOURISH NEWLY ARRIVED HUMMINGBIRDS.

Insect-eating birds are one of the best seasonal prognosticators, though a late cold snap can catch them unawares just as it does gardeners. Insects become plentiful when temperatures reach about 50°F (10°C), so when that temperature settles in, you'll soon see thrushes, bluebirds, brown thrashers, wrens, flycatchers, purple martins, and other insect eaters arriving.

Awakening Weeds

Weeds are just as eager to get growing as the seeds you planted among them. In fact, thanks to their rugged habits, they can quickly sprint past desirable seedlings and turn your garden patch into a backyard weed observatory. Some weeds are even sneakier. Their seeds sprout in fall, grow over winter, and begin flowering in earliest spring (or even late winter), striving to set seed before you even notice them. Keep watch for these devious invaders—they're easiest to control early in the spring, when there are few other outdoor gardening tasks to distract you.

Risky Business

I don't know any gardener who isn't a gambler. We push the seasons, planting too early, growing perennials that survive winters a full zone warmer than our own, and setting out geraniums as soon as they crop up in garden centers, even if the official last spring frost date is weeks away. We're an impatient bunch, and sometimes it actually pays off. Every extra week we can eke out of the growing season is a bonus. Every too-tender plant that survives a winter is a triumph.

Garden suppliers know what we're like because they're gardeners, too. Shelves and catalogs are crammed with tempting gadgets and products to help us behave impulsively instead of cautiously. Insulating caps or walls for plants put out too soon are ever popular.

"It is the new-mown hay smell calling and the wind of the plain praying for them to come back and take hold of life again." —Carl Sandburg

PLANTING BY THE WEEDS

Early-blooming weeds are good news for small insects, which seek out their dependable flowers for nectar and, in exchange, perform the necessary service of pollination. Their blossoms can also give you clues about planting times. Add to the following suggestions by making your own observations as you plant. When you follow the seed packet advice to "Plant after April 15," for example, look around and see what weeds are blooming in your backyard. With experience, you'll be able to gauge whether planting time is ripe just by seeking the advice of your weeds.

WEED IN BLOOM	WHAT TO PLANT	COMMENTS
Common chickweed (*Stellaria media*)	Onions, peas	Chickweed blooms even in winter; be sure soil is workable and not too wet before planting.
Purple dead nettle (*Lamium purpureum*)	Peas, carrots, radishes	Both purple dead nettle and henbit are in peak bloom while spring is still cool enough for early crops, but soil is warm enough for mid-spring planting.
Henbit (*Lamium amplexicaule*)	Peas, radishes, carrots, scallions	Henbit is often in peak bloom at Easter.
Dandelion (*Taraxacum officinale*)	Carrots, strawberry plants	Dandelions can bloom year-round if weather is relatively mild; wait until you see lots of flowers to plant according to its appearance.

HENBIT

DANDELION

CHICKWEED

Weed in Bloom	What to Plant	Comments
Oxeye daisies (*Leucanthemum vulgare*)	Annual flowers	Late spring frost is no longer a threat.
Chicory (*Cichorium intybus*)	Tomatoes, eggplant, hot peppers, sweet peppers, melons	Soil and air are warm to stay.
Foxtails (*Setaria* spp.)	Summer planting of cole crops, perennial seeds, biennial seeds; bearded iris; daylilies	Arching green or yellow seedheads of foxtails are a noticeable presence in garden beds (gasp!) or along roadsides.
Pokeweed in ripe berry (*Phytolacca americana*)	Garlic, leeks; annual poppies, bachelor's buttons, spider flower, Klondike Series cosmos, love-in-a-mist; oriental poppy plants	Look up from your planting to watch for cedar waxwings, robins, or bluebirds eating the poke berries.

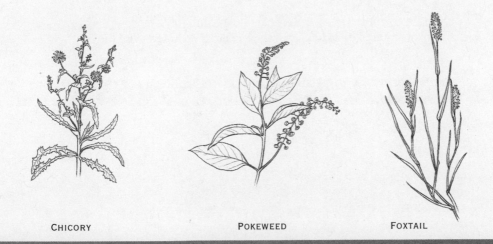

CHICORY   POKEWEED   FOXTAIL

Starting "Too Early"

Weather statistics, from which USDA plant hardiness zones and frost dates are derived, are based on averages of many measurements over many years. The weather doesn't always pay attention to these limits! As weather records have accumulated in our relatively young country, it's easy to see that swings and cycles are hardly predictable. An early spring is a possibility in any year. So is a late spring, or an evil late-spring cold snap that sneaks in and wreaks havoc with our early garden start.

LAST SPRING FROST DATE

A 5-minute phone call to your county extension agent will give you the date of the last expected spring frost, a number that remains constant from year to year. In my area of southern Indiana, it's April 29. Good gracious! By then, my peas are already in bud and my annuals sown from seed are well on their way. Most years, the tomatoes are already out in the garden and impatiens is already in the shady beds. Only once in my decade of gardening here have I been punished for my eager-beaver ways. One memorable April morning, I awoke to find that the gentle rain that had been falling for a couple of days had suddenly changed to snow, thanks to a stiff wind out of Canada. The thermometer sank and sank, despite all my efforts at positive thinking, and by nightfall, every plant in my yard was suffering. Most recovered quickly, even if they had to grow anew from the roots.

Will There Be Frost?

Look for these signs to gauge the likelihood of frost:

- No clouds at sunset

- Clear, starry sky

- Lack of wind

- No frogs singing

- Noticeable drop in temperature after sunset; air feels "nippy"

- Moon near full

- No ring around the moon

Backtracking in a Hurry

Always take the prediction of a late-spring frost seriously. It takes only a little time to cover plants so that you don't lose days or weeks of growing time from frost damage. Meteorologists know how important our gardens are to us, so you'll often read or hear warnings a day or two ahead of the event. I still gripe when removing covers after no frost fell, but I'd rather be safe than sorry.

When you have warning of a possible late frost, patrol your garden to inventory which plants will need protection. Frost occurs on a clear, still night, which makes it easy to shield plants with a light fabric sheet or spun covering. I keep a stack of old bed sheets on my side porch, at the ready in case of danger. One sheet covers a lot of plants.

Because frost forms in the wee hours of the night, you have plenty of time to get protection in place, even if it's already dark when you begin. By the way, don't fret too much over making sure you covered every last susceptible plant; you're guaranteed to overlook a few. Should frost hit, compare the effects and

Annuals That Can Take the Cold

These plants, grown from seed sown in fall or early spring, will barely blink should a late frost or cold snap strike the garden. Generally, any tender new growth will weaken and lie on the ground, but the plants will soon recover and stand up straight.

BACHELOR'S BUTTONS (*CENTAUREA CYANUS*)

SENSATION SERIES COSMOS (*COSMOS BIPINNATUS* SENSATION SERIES)

CALIFORNIA POPPY (*ESCHSCHOLZIA CALIFORNICA*)

LOVE-IN-A-MIST (*NIGELLA DAMASCENA*)

CORN POPPY, FLANDERS POPPY, SHIRLEY POPPY (*PAPAVER RHOEAS*)

VIOLAS (*VIOLA CORNUTA*), STARTED FROM SEED OR PLANTS

PANSIES (*VIOLA* × *WITTROCKIANA*), STARTED FROM SEED OR PLANTS

A FEW MINUTES OF PROTECTIVE ACTION KEEPS SENSITIVE ASIATIC AND HYBRID LILY SHOOTS SAFE FROM FROSTY FINGERS, WHICH CAN STEAL A SUMMER'S WORTH OF BLOOM OVERNIGHT.

eventual growth of both frost-nipped and protected plants of the same kind. I've noticed that, except for hybrid lilies (which never grow much taller once kissed by frost) and tender flowers such as impatiens and geraniums, nearly all frost-damaged plants quickly catch up to their unharmed cohorts. Conduct your own observations, and maybe you will be using those sheets to tie up tomatoes instead of to cover them.

Plants to Protect

Native-plant gardeners generally have little to fear from a late frost or cold snap. Regionally adapted plants are genetically attuned to time their growth to the local weather and are rarely damaged by an unexpected turn of events. But most of our gardens include plants that hail from exotic locales as well as close to home. Even if they can take the usual climatic conditions and seasonal

Shielding Flowering Shrubs

You've waited all winter for the show of azaleas, so don't take chances when frost threatens. Throw a bed sheet over all flowering shrubs in bud or in bloom—and over roses—and you'll preserve the show for milder days to come. No need to tuck in the edges of the sheet; it should stay in place without any anchoring. In the morning, after the sun is warm, flip off the sheets and restore your garden of ghostly figures to its glory. Hang the sheets to dry on a clothesline, then fold them and keep them in a handy place for future use.

Perennials to Protect

If a late spring frost threatens your garden, here are some perennials that will benefit from a bit of protection.

DELPHINIUMS (*DELPHINIUM* SPP.)

FUCHSIAS (*FUCHSIA* HYBRIDS)

CHINESE HIBISCUS (*HIBISCUS ROSA-SINENSIS*)

HOSTAS (*HOSTA* SPP. AND CVS.)

LAVATERA (*LAVATERA TRIMESTRIS*)

HYBRID LILIES (*LILIUM* HYBRIDS)

ANNUAL MALLOW (*MALOPE TRIFIDA*)

VIRGINIA BLUEBELLS (*MERTENSIA VIRGINIANA*)

GARDEN PHLOX (*PHLOX PANICULATA*)

BALLOON FLOWER (*PLATYCODON GRANDIFLORA*)

changes, they are likely to be ill equipped to come through capricious weather absolutely unscathed.

Learn, by observation, which of your plants suffer in unusual spring weather. If you can protect them without going to great effort, or if the plant is near and dear to you for whatever reason, keep it. If the plant is not a sentimental favorite and is frequently affected by vagaries of weather, consider replacing it with a more suitable garden citizen. Some gardeners would rather chainsaw an established magnolia than see one more spring show of frost-browned blossoms. Others would settle for 1 good year out of 5. It's your garden; you get to decide!

CHAPTER 8

Summer Weather

SUMMER IS A TIME OF INCREASING WARMTH. AS THE MILD DAYS OF MAY STRETCH into balmy June, we welcome the sun on our shoulders and the longer hours of daylight. Now the sun doesn't set until well after dinner, so we can make the garden rounds almost until bedtime! Even the nights are inviting, the perfect time to welcome friends for an alfresco dinner (and a chance to subtly show off the garden).

Perennials are at their peak in summer, and harvest season begins for herbs and those veggies we've nurtured for months. Strawberries usher in the season, crowning a supper accompanied by just-picked greens, tender young peas, and eventually that first ripe tomato of the year.

Summer also ushers in some of the most challenging gardening weather of the year. Balmy June turns into hotter-than-heck July, followed by the doldrums of August, when even dogs are too hot to do much more than feebly wag their tails during their namesake days. Increasing heat is often accompanied by periods of drought, a major frustration for those of us tending summer flowers, checking the ripening raspberries, and monitoring the swelling ears of corn.

Strong winds, hail, and torrential thunderstorms blow up quickly. Dry spells may lengthen into bona fide droughts. In the West the rains are long gone, and the adaptable survivors carry the garden through the dry days.

Birds and insects, our garden allies and occasional foes, are at the height of activity. Butterflies swirl over the flowers, songbirds scour plants for morsels to feed their young, and if we're lucky, a praying mantis takes up residence in a likely spot. The wild creatures provide lots of hints—if we hear them—about the weather to come.

Summer is a time for celebrations. Put a fresh-picked blossom in your buttonhole, brew a pitcher of apple mint leaves for iced tea, and host a solstice party to welcome the season.

Spinning Makes a Summer

Like other seasons, summer seems to pay little attention to the calendar, which marks its official start around June 21. In northern regions, summer comes weeks later than to southern areas, where April may well herald the first 90-degree days. Yearly differences in the weather make the start of summer an iffy proposition, too: You may still be wearing a sweater in a colder-than-usual year, or swatting summer's official ambassador—the mosquito—for weeks before that day rolls around.

Sun Safety

All those extra rays should sound a warning as well as a whoopee—when the sun is strong, as it is in summer, it's doubly important to make sure your skin is protected against potentially problem-causing sunburn. That red flush on your overexposed skin is really a mild radiation burn, and repeated sunburns can cause changes in cells that lead to skin cancer. Keep a tube of sunscreen handy and don lightweight long sleeves to work outside safely.

THE SUMMER SOLSTICE WAS THE FOCUS OF MANY RITUALS IN FOLKLORE: ONE INVOLVED LIGHTING A TORCH FROM A COMMUNAL BONFIRE AND BLOWING THE SMOKE OVER YOUR GARDEN TO PROTECT IT FROM PROBLEMS.

The solstice date is still a red-letter day, though, no matter how far off the season seems to be, weatherwise. On the instant of the summer solstice, the sun is as far north as it will get all year, directly over the Tropic of Cancer. It's time for the Northern Hemisphere to bask in the brightness, while the underhalf of the globe leans away from the light (and begins their winter season of short days and long nights).

The official start of summer, like that of spring, fall, and winter, has nothing to do with swimming suits and school's-out. Instead, it is determined by the tilting, sweeping spin of the earth. Our home planet has poor posture: It leans at an angle of 23½ degrees away from vertical, which means sometimes it leans toward the smiling face of the sun, and sometimes it tilts away.

The summer solstice is the longest day of the year, so go ahead and garden from sunup to sundown if you have the stamina! In northern latitudes, this is the time for the fabled "midnight sun," when fishermen row out onto lakes as if it were late afternoon instead of time for the late-night news. In mid-latitudes, kids ride their bikes and sprinklers hiss until twilight falls at 9 P.M. or later, and even early birds wake up to brightening skies.

Get Ready for Summer Sun

Sunny summer days are just right for picnics, baseball games, and trips to the beach or pool. But hot summer sun can take its toll on you—and your garden—if you're not prepared for it. A cloudless sky in summer can quickly reveal misplaced plants in your garden plan. Plants that thrive in partial shade will soon show signs of distress in all-day sun. With the sun as close to directly overhead as it will get, its light is intense and evaporation is extremely rapid. Water plants appropriately, and take these steps as needed to keep your garden at its best throughout the summer:

- Germination is faster in warm weather. Be sure to keep seedbeds watered so the emerging roots can easily find moisture to match the speedy topgrowth that will soon be showing.

- Impatiens and other shade-suited plants that may have blossomed happily in full sun in spring now look peaked until the sun sinks in the late afternoon sky. Soak their roots well in the morning before things heat up.

- Even plants labeled for full sun may become distressed in the lower half of North America when the sun shines without a break all day long. Some catalogs now note levels of hardiness "in the South" for such susceptible plants. Give any wilted specimens a spritz with the hose and a good soaking at the roots until cloudier, wetter transplanting weather arrives.

- Provide temporary shade for garden crops that suffer in heat, particularly leafy salad greens. An aluminum lawn chair makes instant shade for a small summer patch of lettuce or spinach.

- Restrict weeding chores to morning, when the soil is likely to have some moisture and the temperature is more comfortable. Or weed in the early evening after the sun goes down.

LIGHTWEIGHT LAWN FURNITURE MAY NOT BE AS PRETTY AS TEAK, BUT ON A JULY AFTERNOON, YOUR GARDEN GREENS WILL APPRECIATE THE INSTANT RESPITE OF SHADE POPPED OVER THEIR HEADS.

- Mulch to keep roots insulated from the sun's heat and prevent evaporation of soil moisture.

- Move houseplants outside for a growth-stimulating vacation, but keep them in full shade until they're used to the stronger light outdoors. Because the rays aren't filtered by window glass, even complete shade is stronger in intensity than indoor light.

- Hot weather speeds up decomposition, so turn your compost pile frequently to take maximum advantage of the organisms hard at work within. Douse with a spray from the hose as needed to keep the pile moist (but not wet).

The Stormy Season

Summer flips a switch on the giant blast furnace in the sky. Because we are tilting toward the tremendous heat of the sun, the air is much warmer than at other seasons.

Swirl that overheated air with the cooling breezes streaming from the poles, and what you get is an electrified brew of strong winds and sudden weather changes as air masses fight it out overhead. Warm air streams up from the Gulf of Mexico, cold fronts blast down from Canada, and there you have it: ringside seats at the duel of the Titans.

The Year without a Summer

Scientists are still arguing over how much and how fast our climate is changing, but weather extremes are nothing new. Ancient catfish bones left at Indian ruins in Peru show the effects of the warm ocean current called El Niño, and in more recent times, newspaper archives document dramatic shifts from the norm.

When you're tempted to mutter about the summer heat, think about 1816, "The Year without a Summer," according to the *Indianapolis Star*. In the second week of the month of June, about the time we're lounging at patio tables and wiping perspiration from our brows, blizzards swept across North America. Fifteen of the then-19 states and most of the territories were buried under drifts. All plant growth was killed, and so were many head of livestock.

That was only the crescendo— snow and ice had already battered the country beginning in late April and continuing through May. Fourth of July celebrations were held in bitter cold, and August brought repeated and widespread frosts across the northeastern states. No crops at all were harvested north of the Ohio and Potomac rivers that year, and very few even in the South. After repeated attempts at planting the fields, even seed was in short supply across the nation. In the spring of 1817, seed corn was selling for an astronomical $5 to $10 per bushel.

The awful year of 1816 was the bitter end of a 5-year period of abnormally cold weather, shifting winds, and dust storms. Folks reported a reddish aura around the sun, a clue that suggests a volcanic eruption was to blame for the weather's emphatic reminder of just who's boss. Interrupt the warming rays of the sun with a cloud of volcanic ash, and every one of us may be shivering through the summer.

Short notice, soon to pass;
Long notice, long will last.
—Folk saying

Even at the local level, weather is more intense because of the added heat. In the Rockies, mountain air clashes with warmer air rising from the lowlands, making afternoon thunderstorms an almost daily occurrence.

When summer storms descend upon your garden, will it take them in stride or suffer serious damage? What makes the difference? Like the Boy Scouts tell us, being prepared is half the battle.

Just 2 or 3 days of notice before an approaching summer storm is enough time for crisis management, but to prevent your garden from looking like a flattened wheat field, the preparation process begins at planting time.

Practical Plant Selection

Start by choosing plants that will flourish in the worst weather extremes of summers in your area. By planting for the worst-case scenario, you can save yourself hours of hand wringing and hasty plant protection when nasty weather arrives.

Think about your typical summer weather when you select plants. Is humidity a major player? How about hail or high wind? Long dry spells? Broiling temperatures? Fog may even be a factor in coastal areas along the Pacific, where cool ocean water creates blankets of sun-blocking fog clouds and, thus, cooler temperatures.

Consider the worst, and then plant garden citizens that will bounce back or shrug off the worst Mother Nature can throw at them. Use common sense, and read catalog and label descriptions to choose cultivars that will thrive in the trials of your summer weather.

Humidity. Silvery, woolly-leaved plants, including many artemisias and some salvias, generally do best in drier climates. Where humidity and rainfall are typically low, their light-colored foliage is a survival adaptation designed to deflect sun and trap any bit of moisture. Plants prone to fungal problems, such as bee balms (*Monarda* spp.), tall garden phlox (*Phlox paniculata*), zinnias, bottle-brush buckeye (*Aesculus parviflora*), and roses, are likely to become disfigured as moist air encourages the growth of mildew and other fungal diseases.

Hail. Large, tender leaves will shred easily under a barrage of hail, so choose plants with small leaves and wiry stems. Many fine branches are better than a few main stems, which may snap from the force of the ice pellets. Plants that produce showpiece blossoms of large size and small number will be a big disappointment if hail hits when they're at their peak; look for those that offer an abundance of flowers and weeks of new buds instead.

Plants to Shield from Hail

Plants grown for bold foliage, plus all types of lilies, need protection from a barrage of hail. Big leaves are easily ripped, shredded, or bruised by the pelting ice pellets, and the stems of lily buds can snap right off, leaving a summer's worth of flowers in the dirt. If your area is hail-prone, plant these specimens only in well-protected sites:

BERGENIAS (*BERGENIA* HYBRIDS)

CANNAS (*CANNA* HYBRIDS)

ELEPHANT EARS (*COLOCASIA ESCULENTA*)

DAYLILIES (*HEMEROCALLIS* SPP. AND CVS.)

HOSTAS (*HOSTA* SPP. AND CVS.)

HYBRID LILIES (*LILIUM* HYBRIDS)

ASIATIC LILIES (*LILIUM ASIATICA* SPP. AND CVS.)

BANANAS (*MUSA* SPP.*)*

FERNS

High winds. Another case where using your head will result in a better garden! Wind-catchers are not what you need when high winds whip through your yard. Instead, select plants of shorter stature, with strong-but-flexible, nonbrittle stems and smaller flowers that won't lose their petals in a gust.

Drought. Whether it's a regular dry season or an unexpected prolonged dry spell, lack of rain can be frustrating if your garden depends on thirsty plants. Include a good number of things that flourish in dry conditions, and you won't have to worry about your greenscape going brown in the height of summer. Plant portulaca and other flowers with succulent, water-storing leaves; look for plants with water-conserving silvery or furry leaves, such as mulleins and lamb's-ears (*Stachys byzantina* cvs.); and explore the world of desert denizens. You can go native and use plants typical of the wild areas nearby, or go loco and make a mixed planting from the great deserts of the world, with African daisies rubbing shoulders with Indian marigolds.

Fog. Low clouds of moisture can encourage fungal problems similar to those caused by high humidity, but the generally cooler temperatures of foggy weather may counteract the effect. Regular fog is actually an extra dose of moisture for plants, so that even in drought periods they are not as dry as those in clear-skies gardens. Luxuriate in the Mediterranean herbs—lavender, rosemary, oregano, and thymes—and be sure to include plenty of bright colors to make the garden look cheery on gray days.

Protecting Plants

No gardener worth the name ever sticks to plants that make sense. We're forever trying to test the limits, and summer gardening is no exception. That's why practicing plant protection is as much a part of our routine as selecting the right candidates to start with. There'll always be a few plants that are too tall, too big, or otherwise unsuited for the extremes of summer weather. That doesn't mean you can't have them—they'll just need a little extra care.

Layered Planting

One of the best ways to protect plants is to use other plants as a physical shield. Where hail is a fact of life, you can still enjoy your hostas and bergenias if you grow them beneath shrubs or trees that take the brunt of the storm. Say "sayonara" to that banana tree out in the middle of the wide-open lawn, though!

IF HAIL IS A POTENTIAL THREAT IN YOUR AREA, GROW HOSTAS AND OTHER LARGE-LEAVED PLANTS BENEATH THE PROTECTIVE BRANCHES OF "BIG-BROTHER" SHRUBS.

Layer your garden beds wherever possible, and the lowest plants will usually come through relatively unscathed. Insert flowering crab apples and other decorative small trees into your beds of perennials, grow annuals at the foot of overarching flowering shrubs, and offer your prized miniature columbines and other delicacies the protection of big buddies, such as dwarf azaleas or midsize roses.

Physical Barriers

Your house, garage, and garden shed are solid allies against summer storms. Plants on the lee side will be protected from driving rains and wind by the bulk of the building, which deflects the full force of the storm. Reserve the sheltered side for beds of less hearty plants—and for your vegetable garden, which deserves all the help it can get.

Depend on windbreaks, either living or constructed, to filter the force of strong summer gales. A wall or sturdy trellis provides shelter from the storm for lower-growing plants. For more details on using windbreaks, see Chapter 5, "Winds, Fronts, and Storms."

Help a Feathered Friend

Birds are great pest controllers because they eat thousands of insects a day. Keep your hard-working crew growing by extending a helping hand to bird families in trouble after summer storms. Strong wind and rain frequently knock down nests or dash baby birds to the ground, leaving them generally unharmed but highly vulnerable.

You may have heard that the scent of a human hand will cause the parents to reject the foundling, but that's not true. The unfortunate fact is that the human smell may cause a predator to take interest in the nest, endangering the rest of the family. The nest is also likely to be out of your reach.

If the parent birds are behaving in an agitated way, calling or fluttering around the fallen offspring, it's worth a try at fashioning a makeshift nest from a wicker basket or plastic strawberry basket, with a few tissues or soft dried grass for a lining. Wire or tie the substitute "nest" to a branch and hope for the best. If the parents haven't reclaimed the youngster within a couple of hours, contact a wildlife rehabilitator. If the bird is a starling, house sparrow, or pigeon, you can try raising it yourself (an exhausting but gratifying project!); songbirds are protected from ordinary well-meaning folks by federal law.

Early Harvest

You've nurtured your vegetable patch or your rows of berry bushes for months, and all your efforts are almost ready to pay off. Then summer strikes with a vengeance: Drought lingers in your region, or hail threatens the crop. What's a gardener to do?

First, protect what you can. Water whatever is feasible, and conserve moisture with mulch and sensible watering methods. Rig shelters to counteract hailstorms from boxes, benches, or other lawn furniture.

If you must leave some plants to the mercy of the weather, consider harvesting early. Baby squash, zucchini, string beans, sweet corn, and eggplants are just as tasty as—and much more tender than—their mature kin. Fried green tomatoes are delicious, and so are green-tomato relish and pickles.

> ## It is the year which bears,
> ## and not the field.
> — Ancient Greek saying

Full-size tomatoes that haven't colored up will continue to ripen even when plucked from the vine. Their flavor won't be as intense as their vine-ripened siblings, but at least your total crop won't be pocked by hail. Slice off lettuce and other greens and extend their life in the refrigerator with special produce-storage bags, available at supermarkets and in catalogs. The roots in the soil will soon push up new leaves for a later crop.

First Aid after Summer Storms

You can always tell when a significant storm has blown through a neighborhood: Everybody comes outside when it's over and looks for signs of destruction! Neighbor helping neighbor is a wonderful thing when storm damage is severe. Shared chain saws and other tools, shared muscle, and shared experience foster goodwill that lasts long after the winds have died down.

After the storm, it's time for triage to determine which patients receive first aid first:

1. Assess the damage. Walk around your yard and see exactly what the storm hath wrought. Depending on the severity of the storm, limbs may be down, trees may have toppled, perennials may be plastered, and twigs may litter the lawn.
2. If wires are down, call the utility company and stay safely away.
3. Replant uprooted plants. If the roots are whole and not snapped off, the plant may take hold again if given some TLC. Stand it back up, and cover the roots with soil. Firm the soil with your feet, and add a sturdy

support. Treat the plant as you would a new transplant, keeping it well watered until it's reestablished.

4. Look for downed branches, fallen shingles, windblown lawn furniture, or other items that are weighing down relatively undamaged plants or lawn grass. Pick up debris so the plants beneath can spring back.

5. Prop up plants. Tall-stemmed perennials and vegetable plants that have bent without breaking will probably recover if given some support to help them hold their heads up. Quick action means faster recovery, so get busy with stakes and wire supports.

6. Prune damaged plants. Snip or saw back branches to an outward-facing twig or bud, instead of leaving a splintered stub.

7. Clip off battered blossoms and bent stalks that can't be propped back into position.

8. Collect the storm trash of blown-off leaves and dropped twigs. Toss green things and small twigs on the compost pile, and add larger twigs and branches to the brush pile or process in a chipper machine.

9. Cover any eroded areas with soil that has washed away or with fresh topsoil. Mulch and consider planting groundcover to ward off future erosion.

10. Replace eroded mulch.

The after-storm adrenaline rush can be deceptively invigorating. Avoid overexertion, and call in help if the work is more than you can easily handle by yourself. Enlist family members, neighbors, or hired help to assist in cleanup if needed.

Heat and Humidity

Plants wilt under the strong rays of the summer sun, and so do those who tend them. Sun evaporates moisture, drying out soil and skin alike. Sweating is our natural response to keep our bodies cool, but plants don't have this defense. When they are stressed by high heat, they may stop producing buds or fruit, or droop and wilt.

Humidity, or air that is saturated with moisture, prevents rapid evaporation, which is why it's so tiring to work outdoors on a muggy day. Many plants thrive in the moist air of a humid spell, but some are adapted to dry conditions, and they show signs of distress. Unable to release excess moisture through their leaves, these plants may respond by "melting," collapsing into a heap that looks just as tuckered out as we do after a day of gardening in high humidity.

Shade by Degrees

Part shade, full shade, dense shade, light shade, dappled shade—garden catalogs and reference books use a varied and sometimes confusing vocabulary to talk about areas that are shielded from full-force sun. Fortunately, plants handle shade much more readily than garden writers. Unless you're growing some really finicky specimens, of which there are few, you don't need to spend much time worrying about the fine points. In case you're a worrier by nature, though, here are some general guidelines:

- Shade is any area of your yard that is protected from direct sun most of the day. If you live in a mild-winter area, you need to consider deciduous trees' leaf loss when you decide where to plant shade lovers like hostas and some ferns. Cold-winter gardeners needn't bother: When the leaves are down, the plants under the trees are usually sleeping.

- Part shade means some sun, some shade. The changing angle of the sun usually accounts for this common condition. As the sun rises in the morning or sinks in the afternoon, the lower rays sneak under tree branches to give a dose of light to plants.

- Sun means just that: a site that gets no shadow, or very little, cast across it during the course of the day. That's the theory. In practice, unless your beds are far away from any taller neighbors, such as trees or buildings, the shifting position of the sun on a daily and seasonal basis often sends some shadows falling across the site. Not to worry: Plants adapt. A little shade doesn't damage sun-loving specimens.

Blessed Shade

When I moved to serious farm country in the Midwest, where the fields take half an hour to walk across and much longer to plow, I wondered why a single old tree sometimes stood all alone out in the middle of a huge field, surrounded by acres of tilled land. A retired farmer finally satisfied my curiosity. In the old days, he told me, the farmer—and the team, in the really old days— needed a respite from the sun. The tree provided an oasis of welcome shade in which to enjoy a cool drink, a packed lunch, or a brief break when the sun just got to be too much.

A mature tree in your yard is a treasure to treat with respect. Not only does it give you a great place to sling your hammock, it also helps keep your house cool. Every autumn, I mutter about the painfully spiny balls a big old Chinese chestnut tree drops all over my yard. Every summer, when the thermometer settles at 95°F (35°C) for weeks on end, I'm grateful for its aid (in the form of shade on my roof) in keeping my air-conditioning bills at a less than astronomical height.

It takes decades for a tree to reach its potential, and lots of homeowners are tempted to take a shortcut. They plant trees touted as fast-growing, in hopes of adding shade in a hurry. Unfortunately, superspeedy growth also creates weak wood. Usually the tree topples before its time, or else it eventually outstrips the roofline, creating an out-of-proportion anomaly. Silver maples are probably the most popular trees for providing fast shade, and also among the worst choices for a house on a typical lot. Willows, Siberian elms, and catalpas are also fast-growing—and fast to fall when a blustery wind challenges them.

Select a shade tree by its strength of character as well as by how fast it grows. Trees native to your area are usually the best choices when you're shopping because they've had generations to become adapted to the conditions. Don't forget to consider the ultimate height of your new tree. Twenty years may sound like a long time, but those seasons have a way of speeding by. Stick to small or medium-height trees if your house or lot isn't sized for a 100-foot oak.

Homemade Shade

A lean-to provides a hospitable nook for potted plants, houseplants, orchids, and seedlings that would suffer in full summer sun. You can also include a nursery bed inside for divisions of hostas, cuttings of coleus or begonias, and other sun-susceptible plants.

A shade-providing lean-to can be as simple as a temporary roof that blocks most of the summer sun, or as elaborate as a three-sided lattice structure. Your aim is to filter the sun so it doesn't fall full-strength on the plants within, not to block it entirely.

- If you're handy with carpentry, make walls and a roof out of 2 × 4s and prefabricated lattice (plastic or wood).

- If hammering is not your forte, use tall shepherd's crooks as corners on which to tie the ends of wide roll-up shades attached by eyehooks to the side of an existing building, and fashion a roof-only version.

- Another possibility includes walls of wire fencing, and a roof of roll-up shades. Plant scarlet runner beans or other annual vines along the fence to make it look prettier and to block more sun.

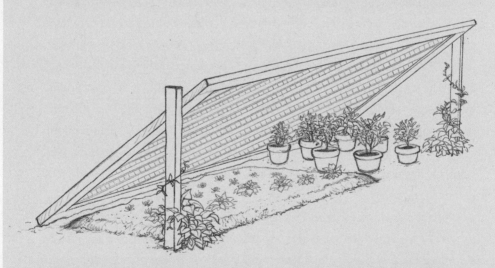

USE PREFABRICATED LATTICE AND STAKES TO CREATE A SHADY SPOT WHERE HOUSEPLANTS CAN SPEND THE SUMMER OUTDOORS WITHOUT RISKING SEVERE SUNBURN. DIVISIONS OF HOSTAS WILL ALSO THRIVE BENEATH SUCH A SHELTER. GROW SCARLET RUNNER BEANS OR HYACINTH BEANS OVER THE LATTICE TO DRESS UP YOUR SHADE HOUSE AND TO FURTHER MODERATE THE SUN'S RAYS.

Creating Shade

Now that gardeners have been educated about the dangers of sun exposure, it's our plants rather than our skins that are more likely to show signs of sunburn. When we stretch the limits by putting shade-loving plants in a "mostly sun" spot, susceptible specimens may become scorched by the intensity of the light. Hostas and coleus are common victims. Although both will grow in nearly full sun, they may become discolored or faded-looking. Southern gardeners should particularly beware because their plants face the biggest risk of overexposure. If your plants start showing signs of sunscorch, the easiest permanent solution is to transplant them to a more appropriate site. The sooner you move them, the better: It takes time for new growth to take the place of the damaged leaves.

You can also erect your own shade. Trellises take less than an hour to set in place—or as little as 5 minutes if you use a plastic fan that simply pokes into the ground. Sections of privacy fence or prefabricated lattice will work well to block lower-angle sun, like the afternoon rays that can suck moisture from shady plants in marginal settings. Cannas, sunflowers, ornamental grasses, and other fast-growing plants that reach significant height also supply shade in a relatively short time.

I also use container gardens to provide portable shade. A giant-size pot, planted with tall, fast-growing sunflowers (*Helianthus annuus* cvs.), creates a decent shadow. Line up three or four of them and you have an instant wall of respite for at least several hours a day. Only for a few hours around high noon, when the sun is nearly overhead, will nearby plants feel the full force of Old Sol.

Help for Humidity

If your garden is filled with plants selected for your summer extremes, you'll have nothing to worry about. Plant suppliers have recently begun recommending summer limits as well as winter hardiness, so pay attention to labels and descriptions. But chances are your yard includes some garden citizens that don't take kindly to heat and humidity. Here are some tricks to make them more comfortable.

BETTER CIRCULATION

Race car drivers powder themselves with talc or cornstarch before they zip up their suits because fungal problems thrive in damp, warm conditions. Moving air in the garden reduces fungal diseases that thrive in the dim light and humidity of crowded conditions, just like athlete's foot fungus or diaper rash. Give your plants room to breathe, and you'll have a healthier garden. Judicious pruning and cutting back—and transplanting, if necessary—will open up space around existing plants so that air can circulate.

Fading Colors

Long before the weathered look became fashionable, my own clothes showed the effects of time spent outdoors. I didn't own a clothes dryer until I was 45 years old, so I've learned plenty about colors fading in the sun. Dark hues and reds were the first to go; even a single afternoon of drying on the sunny clothesline was enough to lighten them by a full shade (and leave a dark mark on the hem where the clothespins held them in place).

Certain plants are also notorious for fading in strong sunlight, even if their growth flourishes in full sun. Spring, early summer, and fall bloomers are usually not at risk because the sun's rays are less intense. But those that show off in the height of summer may not be such crowd pleasers.

Daylily blossoms are notorious for their reaction to strong sun. They may pale quickly to lighter hues or may even change color entirely: Many soft pink daylilies turn to glaring gaudy orange in strong sun.

Foliage, too, can show the effects. Old-fashioned coleus is enjoying a modern heyday thanks to its beautiful colored foliage, but it can suffer in sunlight in the lower half of the country. Although the plants show no signs of wilting or other heat stress, the maroon, pink, salmon, or near-black foliage may begin to look washed-out and eventually acquire an unappealing bleached look.

Extra water won't slow the process or restore the fading colors. The only cure is to provide shade or transplant the susceptible plants to a less sunny spot.

Pruning is a paradox because it stimulates future growth while removing current excess. Examine each stem before you snip, and always clip just above a bud that faces to the outside of the plant. Then, when new growth emerges, it won't clutter the interior. For a plant that has several stems arising from the soil, you can safely snip out as much as one-third of the stems without threatening the plant's survival. Cut them back to ground level.

Drought or Dry Spell?

Dry spells are a normal part of most climates. When they last longer than a few weeks without being relieved by rain and you are not in a naturally dry area, consider it a drought. Managers of water supplies keep a close eye on average rainfall amounts, both by monthly and yearly increments. Severe droughts occur when those figures remain well below the norm.

The effects of water deprivation vary a lot, depending on what's growing in your garden and what the plants are accustomed to. In subtropical areas where annual rainfall is abundant—such as Florida, which gets about 60 inches of rain per year—the lush, large leaves of garden plants will rapidly show signs of stress after a week or so without a drink. In the naturally parched summer conditions of Arizona, dry-land plants will keep blooming during dry spells because they're adapted to those conditions. Even lawn grass varies in its response to water deprivation: Cultivars bred for drought tolerance will stay green much longer than those that depend on a weekly watering.

Managing Dry Spells

When your plants are under water stress, you'll know it. Seedlings and recent transplants will look droopy, and their leaves will wilt. Eventually, buds and leaves will yellow and drop, a sign that intervention is needed immediately to prevent potential loss of the plant.

Generally speaking, a period of 2 weeks without rain poses a threat to vegetable gardens and shallow-rooted ornamentals. Unless plants have adaptations such as woolly leaves, silvery foliage, or succulent leaves that help them withstand low levels of water, they're apt to keel over quickly when water is withheld. Established shrubs and trees have larger root systems, so they can withstand a longer dry period without permanent damage.

The Danger of Drought

Droughts can last for years, and that's when real trouble occurs. We now know that weather follows cyclical patterns, and that year-to-year rainfall amounts can vary wildly. Annual rainfall averages can be thrown way out of whack when a period of unusually wet years is followed by a span of dry years, as happened during the time we remember as the Dust Bowl. Average the rainfall figures over 20 or so years, and you'll get a respectable number of inches of rainfall per year. But put the 5 years of wet next to the 5 years of dry, and it's easy to see why the Okies left Muskogee.

Taproots Can Take It

The first victims of dry spells are plants with lush topgrowth and shallow, fibrous roots. Because the top few inches of soil dry out quickly, these plants are soon left high and dry. Like plants growing in a container, their roots have no hope of finding water within the limited area they explore.

Deep-rooted plants have a better survival rate during lean periods. They draw water from lower soil levels where residual moisture is still present. Deep roots are usually connected to a thick central core that augers down through soil like a drill. This arrangement is called a taproot because it "taps" water and nutrients from deep in the earth.

Taproots can burrow to incredible depths. When I attempted to transplant a 2-year-old clump of cup plant (*Silphium perfoliatum*) that I started from seed, I was astonished to discover that its taproots penetrated to a depth of more than 5 feet! No wonder the big, stout plant kept looking good when the more traditional "English border" perennials around it were withering in dry-soil distress.

No one can predict droughts. Even when they're happening, there's no way to tell when they will end. A second Plains dust bowl that occurred during the drought years of 1934 to 1941 was the impetus for the construction of many of the major dams in the West. With water held in huge reservoirs, residents and farmers at least had a hope of getting through times of trouble.

In the face of major sustained drought, there's nothing a gardener can do—other than to hope for reprieve. Water conservation measures don't help when there's no water to conserve. Supplemental watering is one of the first uses to be banned as nonessential. If you garden in an area that is historically susceptible to prolonged drought, it's vital to plant appropriately. Make sure your garden includes tough characters, such as deep-rooted prairie grasses and wildflowers, that can eke out survival when water is scarce. Get creative about recycling household water. The cooled cooking water from a pot of pasta, for instance, can make a lifesaving drink for a parched plant.

Miracle Mulch

You've heard it over and over, but all the hype is actually true: Mulch is a miracle. The mechanics are as simple as it gets. By applying a layer of material over the soil, you immediately slow down evaporation from the earth that holds the roots of your plants.

Mulch has other benefits, including improved soil texture, thanks to the workings of organisms that feed upon it; increased soil fertility, as organic matter gets distributed through the soil; erosion control; and last—but definitely not least—decreased and easier weeding! Here are a few tips on mulch use:

- For water conservation purposes alone, both organic mulches (which decompose) and inorganic mulches (which stay in place forever) will do the job.

- Unless you want the mulch to serve a decorative purpose—white gravel to highlight a formal bed, for instance—it makes sense to take advantage of all

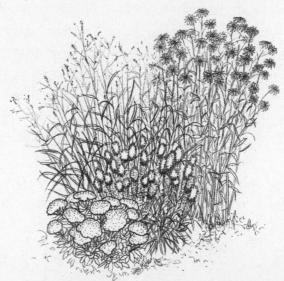

GROW PLANTS OF SIMILAR WATER NEEDS TOGETHER. A COMBINATION OF MAXIMILIAN SUN-FLOWERS (*HELIANTHUS MAXIMILIANI*), SWITCH GRASS (*PANICUM VIRGATUM*), BLAZING STAR (*LIATRIS SPICATA*), AND 'AUTUMN JOY' SEDUM MAKES A SHOWY DISPLAY THAT WILL TOLERATE DRY SOIL.

Dust Bowl Days

In 1862, the all-too-tempting Homestead Act was passed, giving free land to any settler who lived on and cultivated 160 acres for 5 years. The Great Plains were quickly grabbed in the decades-long rush that followed.

Unfortunately, that area had been enjoying a period of unusually generous rainfall during the 1860s and 1870s. Not long after the humble houses were built and the plows turned to the earth, drought came knocking on the door.

From 1887 to 1896, the region saw barely a drop of rain. Crops and home gardens dried up, and the rich soil turned to dust.

More than a million families were affected. Desperately, they searched the skies for rain clouds, and in despair watched their dreams blow away. By 1890, more than half had given up and returned to the East or struck out toward the new promised land of California in the West.

the benefits mulch has to offer and use organic mulch that will add to the goodness of your soil.

- A solid sheet of cardboard, recycled carpet, or plastic holds the most water in the soil.

- Finer mulches break down more rapidly than coarse chunks, but their light weight is ideal for mulching seedlings. Capture the clippings from your lawn mower to take advantage of one of the best sources of fine-textured mulch.

- Check with your local solid-waste agency to see if your town offers compost for the taking; this often makes a fine mulch as well.

- Most yards have a terrific source of free mulch: shade trees. Compost the leaves or chop them with your lawn mower for a freebie mulch that looks great.

- If you must buy mulch, straw is inexpensive and surprisingly good-looking when it weathers to an unobtrusive gray-tan shade.

Lay that hose below your maples and rhododendrons after you're done watering your vegetables and flowerbeds. Trees and shrubs are slow to show signs of water deprivation, such as wilting, but with that large canopy of foliage to support, they also suffer in sustained drought. Often, the effects of a season of drought aren't visible until the following year, when the tree or shrub is full of dead twigs and branches. If supplemental watering is part of your program, give the older residents a good drink, too, even if they're not visibly begging for it. A thorough watering this summer may mean the difference between a live or dead dogwood next spring.

If you have nut trees, you may notice an odd side effect of prolonged drought. In an apparent last-ditch effort to continue the species, pecans, walnuts, oaks, beeches, and other nut trees often produce a bumper crop. Enjoy the pickings, but reward the tree for its outstanding effort, too, and water it deeply in hope of future harvests.

The Big Question

When you're worried about drought, scanning the sky for rain clouds becomes part of the routine. It's not easy to know when the clouds are a teasing promise or a guarantee, so look for other signs that indicate rain may be coming soon. Here are some folklore aids—and accompanying modern assessments—to help you get your hopes up:

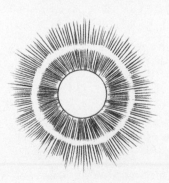

- Watch the night sky for a ring around the moon: the wider the ring, the sooner the rain. (With any luck, those clouds the moonlight is reflecting through will drop some rain the next day.)

- Dew in morning light, no rain before the night. (Dew forms when the air is clear and cool—no rain clouds in sight.)

- Birds fly low before a storm. (True, but they also fly low when the humidity is high.)

- When the catalpas bloom, it will rain for a week. (Not always.)

- When earthworms come to the surface, rain is on the way. (More likely, it already is raining! Worms can suffocate in saturated soil, so they move upward.)

- Tree frogs croak before a rain. (Often they do; they also croak when humidity is high.)

- When leaves look silver, rain is on the way. (Could be true. Watch silver maples and autumn olives; when the wind picks up, as it often does before a rain, their undersides will flash.)

- Mountains in the morning, fountains in the evening. (Tall billows of cumulus clouds may develop into thunderheads.)

Water Gardens

When heat settles in to stay for a few months, nothing is as refreshing as water. I have a feeling that's why so many gardeners love to water—the spray rejuvenates the plants, but playing with water also boosts our own mood.

The simplest "water feature" you can add is a low-cost sprinkler. Even well past chronological kid age, many of us giggle with delight when the oscillator unexpectedly swings our way. And who doesn't like to watch the rainbows in the shower of spray?

Sprinklers have fallen out of favor in recent years because other forms of watering are much more efficient. Drip hoses and irrigation systems concentrate the water at root level, so little is lost to evaporation in the air or "wasted" on the foliage. But if your water meter allows, a sprinkler is plenty of spirit-refreshing fun for very little money.

Fancier water features such as pools and fountains provide the cooling look and sometimes sound of water, too, and they are big business as people seek ways to make their home landscapes more soothing and enjoyable. They're not low-maintenance gardens, either, because water plants grow fast and need frequent management, and the water itself requires attention to maintain clarity and not become a swamp. Think of a garden pool as a new flowerbed, and you won't be taken by surprise by the amount of time it requires to keep it looking good.

Easy Water Gardening

The first rule of water gardening is: Make it bigger. Almost everyone who installs a garden pool soon wishes for one twice the size. Water opens a whole new world of plants for us to experiment with, and naturally we want to try them all. You may start with a single water lily and think that will be plenty, but I'll bet that soon you'll be lusting after a dozen others. It's as delightfully addictive as any other kind of collecting!

Years ago, a water setup required days of digging, pouring concrete or laying unwieldy liners, and the side effects of an aching back and emptied pockets. Today, you can buy a prefab pool for about $30 and install it in an hour or so.

Adding a pump and plants will boost the budget, of course, but it's still possible to make a small oasis of cooling water for less than the cost of dinner for two at a fine restaurant. If your heart desires a larger water feature, get educated before you buy. Many garden centers display sample setups, and books are filled with practical help. Be sure to explore water garden forums on the Internet, too, where you'll find many firsthand stories of common dilemmas and how to solve them—which aren't necessarily featured in those mouthwatering books. Troubleshooting is part of water gardening because you are creating an artificial environment. In nature, lakes and ponds are subject to the cycles of the weather and many wild creatures big and small; in the garden, the pool is maintained by you instead of Mother Nature.

THE SOUND OF COOL

A good way to get your feet wet with water gardening is to start small, with a containerized planting. A big oriental "fishbowl" made of ceramic—or any good-size decorative container—will do for starters, and it will make a pretty conversation piece in the garden. Mount it on a sturdy pedestal for extra oomph and to bring unusual plants closer to eye level.

A small recirculating pump is the heart of the fountain because it provides that trickling water music we all love. You can buy one at garden centers for about $20.

Put your summer water garden where you can hear it burble—a corner of the patio, in front of the garden bench, or anywhere else you can linger to enjoy it.

1. Place the empty pot into position. A shady location is best because it discourages algae growth.

2. Put the pump into the pot, arranging the outlet of the fountain a couple of inches below the rim.

3. Fill the pot with water.

4. Plug the pump into an outside outlet. Adjust the fountain outlet height until you're pleased with the sound it creates.

5. Add plants without dislodging the pump. Be sparing: One dramatic accent plant and a few sprigs of floating plants for extra texture may be all you need.

6. Maintain your water garden by keeping plants in check so that about one-third of the water surface is visible.

7. Invite friends to share the cooling sound of your new water garden.

CHAPTER 9

THREE MONTHS AFTER THE FIRST KATYDID CALLS, THE KILLING FROST WILL COME.

Fall Weather

FALL ARRIVES LIKE A SIGH OF RELIEF, USHERING IN COOLER TEMPERATURES, RAPIDLY falling humidity, and a switch from punishing storms to steady rains. In the early part of the season, we're still busy bringing in the sheaves—and the last flush of late tomatoes, humongous zucchinis, and the rest of the summer vegetables that most of us have seen enough of by now. As the season deepens, we pick pumpkins, crisp apples, and tangy fall raspberries.

In the flower garden, annuals are still going strong, with many putting forth a new burst of effort now that they're getting a reprieve from summer's heat, humidity, and drought. Late-season asters, mums, perennial sunflowers, and anemones fill the borders with seasonally appropriate hues of purple, red, and gold, playing off the changing foliage of nearby trees and shrubs around them. Conditions are ideal for planting new shrubs and trees, and maybe just another dozen daffodils.

The autumn sky turns impossibly blue, the clouds are soft and wispy, and morning fogs become a routine event as the warm earth meets cooler night air. Soon we'll be scurrying to squeeze out a few extra weeks of the season with frost protection and coldframes, eventually relinquishing the last big burst of the garden year.

Day Length

The autumnal equinox occurs on or around September 21, marking the hour that days and nights are equal in length as the earth begins its annual tilt away from the sun in the Northern Hemisphere. With each passing day of the season, the nights grow longer by several minutes, and the hours of daylight shorten correspondingly.

Make the Most of Sunny Days

Fair weather in fall is the perfect time to enjoy the garden tasks that would have made you sweat in summer. Continue garden maintenance as needed, deadheading and cutting back, to keep flowers blooming longer. Also:

- If soil is moist, weed as needed.

- Renew mulch that decomposed over the summer.

- Cut flowers for indoor bouquets.

- Shake seeds from ripe seedheads into paper bags for next year, or snip mature but unripe seedheads for further drying on trays.

- Harvest fruits and vegetables.

- Clean and sharpen garden tools.

- Get the coldframe ready for extended-season gardening.

- Disconnect, drain, and store garden hoses.

Lengthening Shadows

Horses spook more easily in fall—partly because they're feeling frisky in the cooler weather, but also because shadows are changing. Just like in an old horror movie, those spooky dark shapes reach out across pathways, moving unexpectedly as the breeze blows the trees that are casting the shade.

When you notice a shift in shade after autumn arrives, you'll want to keep hold of the reins in the garden, too. Because the sun rises to a lower angle than it did in high summer, shadows are lengthened, even at noon.

Perhaps your deck on the north side of the house now lingers in shade until well after noon—that's because the house now blocks the rays of the lower morning sun.

Those suddenly shady spots are the first places where early frosts will settle because the soil and surfaces are cooler there than in more exposed areas. Take note of susceptible plants that fall beneath autumn's lengthening shadows, and tuck them under a protective cover when frost is in the forecast.

IN FALL, THE EARTH BEGINS TO LEAN AWAY FROM THE SUN, AND FOR US EARTHLINGS, DAYS ARE SHORTER AND NIGHTS GROW EVER LONGER. SHADOWS LENGTHEN BECAUSE THE SUN IS LOWER IN OUR SKY, CASTING MORE OF OUR YARDS INTO SHADE.

Plant Response to Day Length

Fall is a lot like spring in terms of day length and light intensity, which is what causes some bizarre happenings in the garden. When a period of cool weather occurs in early fall, followed by a warming trend (as often happens), forsythia, flowering cherries, and rhododendrons may undergo a second youth, flowering gaily alongside mums and goldenrod. They've been tricked by the tilt of the earth into behaving as if it were spring.

The internal clock of a plant also affects its earliest beginnings: as a seed. Somehow, through a complex interaction of hormones, seeds are timed to sprout only at certain seasons of the year, no matter how tempting the conditions are at the "wrong" times. This biochemical "safeguard" is what enables plants to self-sow by dropping their seeds in late summer or fall to have them begin growing the following spring. Likewise, gardeners can take advantage of seeds' internal clocks by sowing next summer's flowers this fall.

FLOWERING TIME

Nobody knows for sure how the biochemical systems of a plant prepare it for flowering, so just enjoy the unscheduled phenomenon of out-of-season flowers should it occur in your yard. There will still be plenty of forsythia buds left for next spring, even if fall brings a flash of unexpected gold.

The "discovery" of plants responding to day length was first noted in the annals of science fairly recently—in 1920, to be exact, when botanists W. W. Garner and H. A. Allard described the response they named *photoperiodism*. Gardeners and gatherers of wild foods no doubt noticed the way things work much earlier because plants behave differently at different seasons.

Those first theories, and the vocabulary that describes them, are actually 180 degrees off base. It's not day length that plants respond to, but night length, or the number of hours of darkness. Fortunately, we can leave the technicalities to the experts. It's enough to know that plants flower in response to light (or dark!) in three main ways:

Short-day plants bloom only when nights are long, as happens in spring and fall. Many spring and fall bloomers fall into this category, including strawberries, poinsettias, violets, and chrysanthemums. Calendula and sweet peas will only stagger along through summer, but as soon as the nights begin to lengthen, they go into a fresh round of bloom.

Long-day plants need extra-short nights (extra-long days) to burst into bloom. You can plant seeds of baby's breath in early spring, but you'll never see flowers until the days are at least 16 hours long. Dill, sedums, and spinach are also long-day plants. That's why you can plant a late crop of spinach in fall and enjoy it for months without it bolting into flowering stems.

Day-neutral plants are unaffected by day length; they grow to a certain maturity and then flower no matter how many hours a day the sun shines. Plant zinnia seeds in May, for instance, and they will bloom in about 10 weeks, weather permitting; plant them in July, and you'll wait a similar length of time for flowers to appear.

Scientists are still working to crack the code of hormones that governs blooming, but they have learned that it can be manipulated—an important factor for the florist trade. Those shelves brimming with blooming fall mums, or the Christmas displays of luscious poinsettias and Christmas cactuses we take for granted, owe their existence to fooling Mother Nature. Greenhouses equipped with shades put them in blackout mode for the necessary hours (poinsettias, more than 11½ hours of "night;" mums, more than 9 hours), so that the plants will form buds on cue.

> ## "Season of mists
> ## and mellow fruitfulness!"
> —Keats, "To Autumn"

Seed Responses

Spend a few seasons weeding your patch, and you'll quickly realize that you see chickweed sprouting by the millions in spring and fall, but nary a seedling in the summer. Like bloom time, seed germination is also dictated by seasonal timing—or appears to be. Like many botany puzzles, this one is still being worked out. We on the front lines, however, can draw from our own battle experiences.

Fall is prime time for many weeds—particularly those classified as winter annuals—plus a host of others that sprout when the soil cools. You may be

10 Winter Weeds to Head Off at the Pass

Learn to recognize seedlings of fall-sprouting weeds and weeds that regain strength in cool weather, and hoe them off, pull them out, or bury them under mulch. Here are some of the most common offenders you'll see cropping up.

ANNUAL SEEDLINGS

HERB ROBERT (*GERANIUM ROBERTIANUM*)

HENBIT (*LAMIUM AMPLEXICAULE*)

PURPLE DEAD NETTLE (*LAMIUM PURPUREA*)

CHICKWEED (*STELLARIA MEDIA*)

SPEEDWELL (*VERONICA ARVENSIS*)

PERENNIAL PESTS

WILD GARLIC (*ALLIUM VINEALE*)

CANADA THISTLE (*CIRSIUM ARVENSE*)

GROUND IVY (*GLECHOMA HEDERACEA*)

WHITE CLOVER (*MELILOTUS ALBA*)

BROADLEAF PLANTAIN (*PLANTAGO MAJOR*)

CHICKWEED

BROADLEAF PLANTAIN

GROUND IVY

ready to put the garden to bed for the year, but it pays to spend at least some time in fall working on weed control. As usual, mulch is the easiest solution. Dump a layer on the heads of emerging weed seedlings, and your problems will be much lessened in spring.

Fall Color Signals Maturity

Ever notice that the same colors that tell us fruit is ready for plucking are evident in leaves at the end of their road in autumn? A red apple, a cluster of purple grapes, an orange persimmon or pumpkin are painted with the same palette as the red leaves of oaks, the purple of ash trees, and the orange of sugar maples. When the green of growing chlorophyll disappears from fruit or foliage, yellow, orange, and red pigments surge to fill the color void.

In our garden fruits and veggies—as well as in wild fruits and berries—another change also takes place. Bitter tannins are what make animals (including two-legged green-apple robbers) curl their lips at the astringent taste, and thus protect the maturing seeds from being plucked before they're ripe for growing. In autumn, those tannins yield to developing sugars, the temptation offered to seed-dispersing fruit eaters.

The exterior color change of a ripening fruit or vegetable is the final stage of the coming-of-age process. Inside, the seeds have grown to full size and readiness for maturation. From the outside, we recognize the state of perfect ripeness by the color change.

The trigger is twofold: seasonal changes in temperature, plus a shift in hours of light and darkness. These external cues send plant hormones and other chemicals into maturity mode, so that the crisp apple or other fruit is just right to carry on the seeds for another generation. That same trigger is the start of leaf maturation, when the thousands of chlorophyll factories attached to a plant's stems and branches start shutting down, revealing the bright red, orange, and yellow pigments remaining, and preparing to jettison the leaves for the dormant season.

Flowers for Fall Foliage

Trees are rightly famous for their fall colors, something to keep in mind when you're choosing a new shade tree for your yard. But many smaller plants also blaze with color in fall and are much easier than shade trees to snuggle into a garden bed. Most gardeners focus on flowers when selecting late-season plants because we want to extend both the beauty of the garden and the fun of anticipating the next plant to bloom. You can make plenty of fall-hued combinations with late-blooming flowers, but look beyond the flowers and you'll discover foliage that adds even more zing.

Use leaves to boost the color quotient of your autumn yard. And don't overlook the potential of your other garden occupants: silver or gray foliage, like that of artemisias; evergreen foliage; ornamental grasses in gold, beige, rusty orange, or gray; and even the eventual yellow and tan of many garden plants. All these colors work together in the fall palette.

RED FOLIAGE
ANNUALS
- CELOSIAS AND COCKSCOMBS (*CELOSIA* AND *AMARANTHUS* SPP. AND CVS.)
- FALSE CYPRESS (*KOCHIA SCOPARIA*)

PERENNIALS
- 'AUTUMN JOY' SEDUM (SEEDHEADS)
- BERGENIA
- LEADWORT, PLUMBAGO (*CERATOSTIGMA PLUMBAGINOIDES*)
- WILD GERANIUM (*GERANIUM MACULATUM*)

MAROON FOLIAGE
PERENNIALS
- JAPANESE ANEMONE (*ANEMONE × JAPONICA*)
- HARDY GERANIUMS (*GERANIUM* SPP. AND CVS.)

YELLOW FOLIAGE
PERENNIALS
- AMSONIAS (*AMSONIA HUBRECTII*, *A. TABERNAEMONTANA*)
- FALSE INDIGO (*BAPTISIA AUSTRALIS*)
- LILY-OF-THE-VALLEY (*CONVALLARIA BIFLORUM*)
- SIBERIAN IRIS (*IRIS SIBIRICA*)
- SOLOMON'S SEAL (*POLYGANATUM BIFLORUM*)

BLACK FOLIAGE
IF YOUR TASTES LEAN TOWARD THE DRAMATIC, FERRET OUT BLACK-FLOWERED PANSIES (*VIOLA × WITTROCKIANA* 'BLACK PANSY') AND WILD INDIGO (*BAPTISIA TINCTORIA*), WHOSE FOLIAGE ALMOST INSTANTLY TURNS BLACK (BUT REMAINS ORNAMENTAL) AT THE FIRST TOUCH OF FROST. EITHER MAKES AN INTERESTING PARTNER FOR BRIGHT REDS OR YELLOWS.

DESIGNING WITH FALL COLOR

We gardeners seem programmed to satisfy our plant-acquisition needs in the springtime, when fall color is only a distant memory. In spring, we look for bright flowers, bold foliage, or dynamic size and shape. Then, when October rolls around, we often wish that we had chosen something with more fall flair than that undistinguished green blob of forsythia in the corner, which at best will mellow to a quiet yellow.

No matter when you shop for plants, considering what their fall color will be makes a lot of sense. The rich hues of fall foliage help to keep your garden looking good until the last leaves drop, and shorten the bare months of winter when there seems to be little else to look at in the garden. But choosing plants

Top 10 Plants for Flaming Foliage

These shrubs and small trees are well sized for a garden bed or lawn, and they offer attractive garden attributes at other seasons too: attractive flowers, good form, and an interesting winter silhouette. Try one or more:

1. Serviceberries (*Amelanchier alnifolia, A. canadensis*)

2. Chocolate shrub or Virginia allspice (*Calycanthus floridus*)

3. Smoke tree (*Cotinus coggygria*)

4. Witch hazels (*Hamemalis vernalis, H. × intermedia*)

5. Oakleaf hydrangea (*Hydrangea quercifolia*)

6. Heavenly bamboo (*Nandina domestica*)

7. Virginia creeper vine (*Parthenocissus quinquefolia*)

8. Deciduous azaleas (*Rhododendron* cvs.)

9. Shining sumac (*Rhus copallina*)

10. Mountain ash (*Sorbus aucuparia*)

for their fall color isn't as straightforward as selecting flowers in just the right shade to match the trim on your house:

- Unless a plant has been cloned (reproduced vegetatively rather than from seed), its fall display may not be as flashy as the best members of its kind.

- Fall color varies from year to year depending on the weather. Crisp, cool nights and sunny days generate the most striking hues. Mild weather, prolonged rainy periods, or drought keep the colors muted.

The first problem is an easy one to overcome: Simply visit a nursery and choose your plants in person—when the foliage is in fall color. That way, you'll be sure of getting a brilliant red maple or a burning bush that ignites the whole yard.

The solution to the second concern is a familiar and comforting truism among gardeners: There's always next year.

Harvesting Seeds

You'll be amazed by how much seed a single blossom can produce. A dandelion—not that you need any more of them—may mature thousands of potential offspring from each yellow puff. A zinnia can hold 50 seeds at the ready; a bean, a half-dozen; a sunflower, hundreds. Multiply the seeds in each seedhead times the number of flowers borne by a plant, and you may never visit a seed rack again!

Not all seed will yield children that resemble the parents. The seed of breeder-selected cultivars and cloned plants may produce a throwback to some homely ancestor—or to some beauty lurking in the background. I myself much prefer the "wild" progeny of hybrid petunias; their seed produces tough, sprawling plants with smaller blossoms in pure white, cool lavender, pale pink, and screaming magenta.

CONEFLOWERS AND ZINNIAS PRODUCE HUNDREDS OF SEEDS PER BLOSSOM, SUPPLYING ENOUGH TO COLLECT FOR NEXT YEAR'S PLANTING AND TO PROVIDE AN ON-THE-PLANT BIRDFEEDER FOR GOLDFINCHES AND OTHER SEED EATERS.

Seed collecting is an easy skill to learn. All it takes to be an expert is to watch your plants. As flowers die, the seedheads that replace them swell and grow. When the seed is ready, the receptacle will be brown and dry.

The trick is catching the seeds before Mother Nature shakes them loose—or before someone eats them. Many plants drop their seeds as soon as they're ripe. If you have other plans or want to spread the plants to other parts of the garden, you'll need to be ready to seize the moment.

It doesn't hurt to snip off seedheads before they are thoroughly dry. Spread them in a layer on a cardboard tray, and they will soon finish drying so that you can shake the seeds loose. Store dry seeds in small paper envelopes, or in sealed, letter-size white envelopes. Keep away from moisture and excessive heat.

Collect seeds in mid-afternoon during dry weather, when pods and seedheads are free of excess moisture.

Seed Savers' Top 10

Penny-pinchers love seed collecting in fall. For a few minutes of time, you can fill envelopes with the start of next year's garden without spending a penny. These annuals and perennials will yield hundreds of seeds that are easy to collect. Store them in a dry place, and shake out seeds or crumble seedheads for planting in spring.

1. Bachelor's buttons (*Centurea cyanus*)
2. Painted daisy (*Chrysanthemum carinatum*)
3. Spiderflower (*Cleome hassleriana*)
4. Cosmos, any kind (*Cosmos bipinnatus, C. sulphureus*)
5. Purple coneflower (*Echinacea purpurea* cvs.; caution: Seedheads are prickly!)
6. Annual poppy (*Papaver somniferum*)
7. Gloriosa daisies (*Rudbeckia* spp. and cvs.)
8. Marigolds (*Tagetes* spp.)
9. Mexican sunflower (*Tithonia rotundifolia*)
10. Zinnias (*Zinnia* spp.)

Fall Rains

Those folks who live in wet season/dry season regions get ready for gardening in earnest when fall rains arrive. As soon as the weather changes, it's perfect planting time for perennials, roses, shrubs, and just about anything else that can go into the soil.

In four-season climates, fall rains also signal the start of planting season, although the choices are more limited because roots must have time to settle in before the ground freezes. You'll want to avoid planting

FALL PLANTING CALENDAR

"Fall planting" is a category with wide boundaries. It includes crops sown in summer for fall harvest, as well as plants put into the ground after the autumnal equinox. Here are some hints to help you get the timing right.

MONTH	WHAT TO PLANT
JULY	Sow seeds or set out seedlings of cole crops for fall harvest, including broccoli, kohlrabi, turnips, collards, and mustard.
AUGUST	Sow spinach, lettuces, arugula, and other greens for fall picking even after frost. Plant bulbs of fall-blooming crocuses and colchicums. Plant daylilies and bearded iris. Plant container-grown roses and shrubs.
SEPTEMBER	Sow cottage-garden annuals, including poppies, love-in-a-mist, cleome, bachelor's buttons, and California poppies. Plant daylilies and perennials in all zones south of Zone 5. Plant shrubs, trees, and evergreens. Sow grass seed to fill in bare spots in the lawn.
OCTOBER	Plant spring-blooming bulbs. Continue sowing annuals. Plant shrubs, trees, and evergreens.
NOVEMBER	Continue planting bulbs, shrubs, and trees as long as the soil remains unfrozen.

shallow-rooted perennials now because they will be vulnerable to root stress. Of course, if you're a gambler (and who isn't?), you can try the trick of blanketing newly planted perennials with a thick layer of mulch for extra insulation.

In all regions, fall is also the season for planting spring-blooming bulbs. Tucked safely in the soil, they will put out roots and get ready to make a show of themselves when spring arrives.

Falling Leaves

Americans are a funny bunch. We assiduously rake or blow every leaf away from our yards in fall, typically to be hauled away by municipal trucks. Then in spring we haul home bags of compost to spread over our garden beds.

Save yourself time and trouble by letting the process happen right in place. Explain to your neighbors what you're doing so that you don't become the black sheep on the block for going against traditional tidiness standards.

- Instead of raking, wait for the wind to nestle leaves around your shrubs and beds. If your lawn adjoins another property, you may want to temporarily erect a fence of garden netting stapled to tomato stakes so your leaves don't blow into your neighbor's yard.

- When they are securely in place, usually after fall rains, then remove the excess from lawn areas by chopping them up with the lawn mower.

- Dump the bagged chopped leaves from your mower over the blown-in leaves, and spread out as mulch. Or use the chopped leaves to cover your bare vegetable plot for the winter.

By spring, the leaves will have weathered and be on their way to decomposing into a new layer of humus. Plants will push their way up through the layer with no problem. Should you want to plant seeds, it's an easy job to pull the leaf mulch aside with a hoe to expose the soil.

Plant Protection

The growing point from which a plant produces new stems is particularly vulnerable to cold—and to those nasty shifts from warm spells back to bitter cold. A fluffy blanket of leaves traps insulating air, moderating the temperature extremes and protecting that vital crown of perennials, roses, and other plants.

Plants to Protect

An extra layer of fall leaves can mean the difference between life and death for perennials that are particularly sensitive to swings in temperature. I pile the leaves on extra-thick, at least 8 inches deep, directly on top of the crowns and roots of these plants:

BALLOON FLOWER
  (*PLATYCODON GRANDIFLORA*)
CANNAS
COLUMBINES (*AQUILEGIA* SPP.)
CORAL BELLS (*HEUCHERA SANGUINEA*)
CULINARY SAGE (*SALVIA OFFICINALE*):
  CUT BACK TO NEAR GROUND LEVEL

DELPHINIUMS
FRINGECUPS
GLADIOLUS
MONTBRETIA

One caveat before you get too frisky with those leaves: Plants whose foliage persists in winter resent being buried completely. Instead of covering over lamb's ears, artemisias, lavender, rosemary, and evergreens, for example, nestle the leaves around them so that the foliage can still see the sun.

THOSE DRATTED FALL LEAVES, NESTLED AROUND YOUR SPINACH AND OTHER GREENS INSTEAD OF BAGGED AT THE CURB, PROVIDE INSULATION TO HELP YOU HARVEST SALAD GREENS WELL INTO WINTER.

Bird Benefit

A layer of leaves is good protection for plants in more than just the physical sense. Leaves attract a horde of beetles and other insects—harmless to garden plants but highly desirable to birds. As birds discover that your yard is a welcoming banquet of their favorite foods, they will increase their visits. That means more pleasure for you, and more aid to the garden as the feathered crew downs pests along with other prey.

As an added precaution, I avoid cutting back most of my garden plants until spring so that the dead stems can act as effective catchalls for blowing leaves, just as they do in nature. The extra insulation also lets me experiment with plants that are not supposed to be cold-hardy in my area. For many years, I have routinely nurtured Zone 7 plants in Zone 6 gardens, with great success. Only in brutally cold winters, which don't happen every year, do my garden experiments freeze to death.

Frost

The very word "frost" sends a chill up the spine of all self-respecting gardeners. Our mission is to keep plants growing, and frost is the death knell of the season. No wonder we strive so hard to shield our precious plants from its effects!

A light sheet or strip of floating row cover will protect plants from the first brush with frost, but as cold air gets more serious, eventually there's no delaying the inevitable. Most of us are ready by then to say goodnight to the garden. When the killing frost moves in, turning pepper plants and tender cannas into limp black hulks, we switch gears into fall cleanup—and getting ready for next year.

Understanding Frost

Frost doesn't "fall." (And neither does dew.) Both are forms of condensation—the natural reaction of a warm object coming in contact with cool air (or vice versa). The sheen of moisture that glazes your iced tea glass is condensation

CELEBRATED FOR CENTURIES, THE HARVEST MOON OF AUTUMN SIGNALS THE TIME FOR BRINGING IN THE SHEAVES. WHEN IT SHINES BRIGHT AND CLEAR, BE ON GUARD AGAINST FROST—THERE'S NO BLANKET OF CLOUDS TO KEEP THINGS WARM OVERNIGHT.

caused by the cold tumbler touching the warm air. The icy crystals of frost on your windshield or your lawn are condensation caused by moist air touching colder surfaces—and freezing.

Liquid dew does not freeze into frost. The lovely ice crystals of frost are created when water vapor goes directly from its normal gaseous state to a solid (ice).

During the day, plants soak up heat from the sun. At night, they release their heat into the chillier air. On a cloudless night, heat loss is especially rapid. Clear nights are definitely a danger signal for possible frost.

When air temperatures dip to 32°F (0°C), frost forms on plant leaves and other surfaces. That's a light frost, and damage will be minimal. Should the air be even colder, the water within plant stems and tissues also freezes. Goodbye, garden!

Many plants can withstand a light frost. Colder temperatures, however, will do them in. Although their foliage may not blacken, it will remain limp, unable to recover from the cold damage.

Forecasting Frost

Dew point is the magic number that will alert you to a coming frost the scientific way. That measurement is the temperature at which dew will form—and if it's below 32°F (0°C), the "dew" will be in the form of frost. If you want to extend the life of your fall garden, it pays to listen to TV meteorologists and have a healthy respect for the dew point.

Fall Mums

Who doesn't fall in love with fall mums? Seems like there's always a new color to add to the border or nestle beside the front step. And mums are so tempting: For a few dollars, you can pick up a plastic potful for a big dab of instant color.

It seems a shame not to put that great plant into a permanent position, but many fall-planted mums never make a return appearance. Planted so late in the season, their shallow roots can't get a grip before the soil freezes stiff.

I've experimented with various solutions for keeping fall mums alive. Conventional wisdom recommends mulching the new plants deeply and hoping for the best. Here are a few other tricks I've tried:

- Take cuttings and keep them in a jar of water on the windowsill. They'll look ratty as winter progresses and may become infested with spider mites. Make sure there's always some water in the jar; otherwise, ignore them. When spring rolls around, snip off the tender top few inches of each cutting and stick them in moist garden soil. They will thank you for your efforts by growing into blooming-size plants by the following fall.

- Save the plastic pots, and when the flowers fade, pull the plant out of the garden and pop it back into the pot. Funnel in soil if needed to fill the pot, water well, and keep in a cool but bright room over winter. Park the pots in the kitchen sink about once a week and spray with the sink hose to discourage spider mites. When spring comes, pop them back in the ground.

- My favorite technique is to bury the plants alive. This sounds drastic, but it works better than mulch alone (with which your chances of survival are still iffy) and requires no maintenance over the winter. When the weather turns seriously cold, cut back the topgrowth to about 4 inches from soil level. Then mound loose soil or compost over the plant until it's entirely buried. Do not pat it down. Cover with an additional layer of leaves or straw. In spring, use your hands to unearth the mum, being careful not to rock the plant and disturb the roots.

BUTTON

DAISY

DECORATIVE

POMPON

SPIDER

Folklore has a few tips for forecasting frost, too. The most widespread ones are based on reading the weather—and they actually work, at least some of the time.

- Ring around the moon, no frost. Could be true, because a ring indicates the presence of clouds, which will help keep temperatures from dipping too sharply.

- Clear sky, frost tonight. The inverse of the first, and just as likely to hold true, as long as the temperature falls to near the freezing point.

Frost Protection

There's one very good reason not to yield to the first frost: It often is followed by a period of frost-free weather. If you can baby your plants through that first frost, you may get to enjoy them for weeks more.

The milk jugs, glass cloches, and Wallo'Waters you used in spring aren't very handy in fall because plants are much bigger than those tender spring seedlings. Now your main arsenal consists of bed sheets and similar light-weight coverings, as well as your garden hose.

- Water the garden before nightfall, spraying both soil and plants. That extra moisture will keep the air around the plants slightly warmer, perhaps enough to prevent the formation of frost. You may have seen this technique in the media; it's sometimes used by owners of citrus groves.

- Cover plants before dusk. Heat is rapidly lost as soon as the sun sinks, so the earlier you get your plants under cover, the better.

- Spread a bed sheet, lightweight plastic dropcloth, or floating row cover over vulnerable plants. The covering will help prevent loss of heat from the plants, thus hindering the formation of frost.

- For a modern innovation, try bubble-wrapping your prized plants—it works great in spring, too!

- If you run short of coverings, newspaper will work.

- To protect low-growing plants such as spinach and lettuce from frost, cover them loosely with fall leaves.

Remove the coverings after the sun is up and the air has warmed above 32°F (0°C) the next morning.

Frost is said to sweeten the flavor of Brussels sprouts and persimmons, which are allegedly too astringent to eat unless they've been touched by a hard frost. I don't know about Brussels sprouts, but I've found American persimmons taste just as sweet when they ripen for an extended time without frost. In that case, I suspect the reputation occurred because the fruit turns orange and looks ripe long before its flesh turns sweet. I wait until persimmons fall from the tree all on their own to gather them; frost or no, they're delicious.

Frost-Tolerant Flowers

Some plants are remarkably well adapted to withstand cold—and even freezing. While watery stems of impatiens and tender heliotrope topple at the first cold breath, the following fall-blooming flowers will keep going through much colder weather.

ASTERS, MANY NATIVE SPECIES AND HYBRIDS

CHRYSANTHEMUMS

DANDELIONS

GOLDENRODS (*SOLIDAGO* SPP.)

MARIGOLDS (FOLIAGE FREEZES SOONER THAN
   FLOWERS)

ROSES

SWEET ALYSSUM

ENJOY AS MANY WEEKS OF BLOOM AS YOU
CAN BY PLANTING FLOWERS SUCH AS ASTERS
AND GOLDENRODS THAT KEEP FLOWERING
EVEN AFTER FROST.

CHAPTER 10

"IT IS A PLEASURE TO THE REAL LOVER OF NATURE TO GIVE
WINTER ALL THE GLORY HE CAN, FOR SUMMER WILL MAKE ITS OWN
WAY, AND SPEAK ITS OWN PRAISES."

—DOROTHY WORDSWORTH, 1802

Winter Weather

WINTER IS OUR LAST SEASON IN THE CYCLE OF THE YEAR—OR IS IT THE FIRST?
The answer, of course, is neither. Winter is only another link in the rhythm of
the garden, even if you're stepping through snow rather than hoeing weeds.

For gardeners in northern climes, winter is a restful break in the gardening
year, a time to contemplate last season and make plans for the growing season
to come. Seed and plant catalogs start piling up beside your favorite chair, and
you begin compiling wish lists in anticipation of spring's eventual arrival.

But winter isn't only for dreaming, so don't put away your pruners and
loppers! This is peak season for shaping the trees and shrubs in your yard. It's
also time for preventive maintenance to stave off damage from snow and ice
storms or from sudden shifts in temperature.

Gardening moves indoors, too, as we rediscover houseplants and make
room for starting seeds.

In mild-winter regions where plants never sleep, gardeners don't either:
There's still planting, transplanting, seeding, and tending to be done.

237

Cold Weather

Forget about snow, or ice storms, or those windy gusts that rip right through the warmest sweater: It's cold alone that has the biggest effect on the survival of our garden plants.

We're so accustomed to looking for our "zone" on plant labels or catalog descriptions that it's easy to forget what that designation really means. The system, developed by the USDA, is very simple: It divides North

10 To-Dos for Sunny Winter Days

1. *Water* trees and shrubs (if the ground's not frozen).

2. *Fill* bird feeders.

3. *Repair* wooden trellisies and arbors.

4. *Tie* snow-bent evergreens back into shape.

5. *Evaluate* deciduous shrubs or hedges for aesthetic pruning later.

6. *Hoe off* topgrowth of clumps of chickweed.

7. *Sow* perennial seeds in the coldframe.

8. *Check* for waterlogged areas where plants are turning into mush.

9. *Cut back* winter-battered ornamental grasses.

10. *Look* for snowdrops or crocuses in sheltered nooks.

Unless you live on top of the Equator, you share one aspect of winter with every other gardener in the Northern Hemisphere, no matter how many blankets are piled on your bed: Days are shorter and nights are longer.

We're tilted away from the light-giving, heat-giving sun now, with the North Pole tipped as far from the sun as it gets. Those warming rays reach us for a much shorter time each day than in lovely long-lighted summer. The farther north you live, the less sunlight you'll see, and the colder your temperatures. (It's interesting to note that the length of day and night in winter is exactly reversed from what those figures are in summer, 6 months earlier. For example, a December 10th day with 7 hours of sunlight and 17 hours of darkness corresponds to a June 10th day, with 7 hours of dark and 17 of light.)

The official start of winter is the winter solstice, on December 21. But snow may fall long before then—or long after. I look forward to the solstice because, in one important way, it means the "end" of winter: After that date, we begin turning toward the sun, and the days begin to lengthen.

In the mid-latitudes, the sun may drop out of sight as early as 4 P.M. on the date that winter is ushered in; but every sunset afterward will be a little later, and every sunrise a little earlier. To a gardener as well as to someone susceptible to the light-deprivation depression called Seasonal Affective Disorder, the winter solstice is a great reason to celebrate.

TAKE A MOMENT DURING THE RUSH OF HOLIDAY FESTIVITIES TO NOTE THE WINTER SOLSTICE, THE TURNING POINT OF THE SEASON. AFTER DECEMBER 21, EACH DAY IS A FEW MINUTES LONGER.

America into 11 areas based entirely on the lowest reading of the thermometer in winter. The temperatures in Zone 4 gardens bottom out at around -45°F (-43°C); in Zone 6, -5°F (-20°C); and in lucky Zone 8, 15°F (-9°C) is the average low.

Plants are assigned to hardiness zones based on how much cold they can tolerate. Your beautiful impatiens will turn to mush in your Zone 6 garden at the touch of 32°F (0°C), but in Zone 10 it will live for years if its other needs are satisfied.

Unless a record-breaking cold snap blows in, that is. Then all bets are off. That's why citrus growers and other agricultural enterprises go into crisis mode at the first prediction of abnormal cold.

Our income may not depend on keeping our garden alive, but to lose months or years of growing time is heartbreaking, too. Paying attention to forecasts of coming cold fronts will give you enough time to try a few preventive measures for marginal plants in your yard. Here are some helpers in case of cold:

Snow. If you have it, use it. Snow is a terrific insulator, trapping billions of air molecules between the flakes. Shovel it gently onto beds, avoid compressing the snow, and you've just added several degrees of cold protection.

Mulch. Just as an extra blanket keeps you cozy, a fluffy layer that traps insulating air can help sensitive plants survive. Rake a layer of fluffy dead leaves (oak leaves are ideal) around and over the plant, or surround it with crumpled newspaper covered by lightweight fabric or a cardboard box weighted with a rock to hold it in place.

Rocks. Before winter sets in, consider using the thermal mass of rocks as a natural protection for cold-sensitive plants. Rock and masonry heat up in sunshine, then release the heat during the cold hours of night. That's why crocuses and other plants growing next to your foundation or other walls are first to bloom: They get a head start from the extra warmth.

Signs of Cold

Before you bundle up to head outdoors, take a quick glance out the window and you may spot signs that will help you gauge the temperature—without checking the thermometer! Here are a few common ones:

- Rhododendron leaves curl up to limit the surface area exposed to cold air. The tighter the curl, the colder the air.

- Birds fluff their feathers to keep warm. Look at your chickadees and other feathered friends: Are they fat balls of loose feathers instead of their usual sleek selves? That's a clue for you to add more layers, too.

BRRR, IT'S COLD OUTSIDE, AND RHODODENDRONS WILL TELL YOU JUST HOW BITTER THAT COLD IS. WHEN THEIR LEAVES ARE MOSTLY FLAT, NORMAL WINTER DUDS WILL DO THE TRICK. BUT IF THEY CURL UP LIKE A TIGHTLY ROLLED NEWSPAPER, MAKE SURE EVERY INCH OF SKIN IS COVERED BEFORE YOU VENTURE OUT.

- Birds protect their feet and legs by drawing them up into their feathers to keep warm. If your backyard birds take on a one-legged appearance—or if doves and other ground-feeders crouch low and hide their feet—baby, it's cold outside.

- A clear sky means a colder day because there's no layer of clouds to block escaping heat from the earth.

Frost/Thaw Cycles

Cold air alone isn't always the cause of demise for favorite plants. An even more common culprit is root heave, which is caused by the soil thawing and refreezing.

Those who garden in stony soil know well that alternating freezes and thaws will mean a great harvest of rocks the following spring. The stones are squeezed upward as the soil contracts.

Rock farmer or not, you may have to deal with the aftermath of that action when freezing follows a partial thaw. Roots may be shoved upward, sometimes to such an extent that bare roots are exposed. Shallow-rooted plants are especially vulnerable. Here are some to watch:

- Coral bells (*Heuchera* spp. and hybrids), asters, mums, catmints (*Nepeta* spp.), and other fibrous-rooted perennials or herbs

- Groundcovers such as foamflower (*Tiarella* spp. and hybrids)

- Azaleas, blueberries, and other shallow-rooted shrubs

- Newly planted trees

PREVENTION AND FIRST AID

In winter, frozen is good. Frozen soil that stays frozen will not lift plant roots upward. A thick layer of organic or inorganic mulch, at least 2 inches deep, is the best preventive for soil heaving because it helps the soil maintain an even temperature no matter what the weather. Wait until the soil freezes to apply the extra layer of protection so that the plant's roots can slow down naturally. When a mild spell settles in, a thickly mulched bed will remain frozen much longer than unmulched soil that can freely absorb the sun's heat.

Your boot heel is the simplest first-aid solution for plants that have heaved their roots out of the soil. Press moderately firmly to restore contact with soil, but don't stomp so hard that you force all the air out of the soil. Cover the root area with 1 to 2 inches of compost, then apply a few inches of mulch around the plant to ward off future problems.

If you don't discover damaged plants until spring, the victims will likely be suffering from exposure and lack of water over the winter. Press unearthed plants back into place, give them a good soaking, add soil or compost over the roots if necessary, and hope for the best.

Winter Storms

Changing skies are your clue to a winter storm on the horizon. Notice when the wind picks up or shifts to a different direction: The change heralds an approaching front that may bring snow, ice, or just plain cold. Increasing clouds or clouds that change from white to gray may signal snow.

Lightning and thunder are rare in winter because the air isn't as heated as in summer, and so the contrast in temperatures between air masses is much less. Without those extremes, the electrical charge that becomes lightning is not created.

The guiding forces behind our winter weather are the polar air masses. Their wintry breath surges across North America, bringing cold temperatures and changing the precipitation pattern from liquid rain to icy sleet and snow.

- The maritime polar air mass moves into the West Coast from the ocean side, picking up plenty of moisture as it travels. This brings the welcome winter rainy season to the Pacific coast and desert Southwest.

FEEDERS ARE LIFESAVERS TO BIRDS IN WINTER WEATHER. FILLING THEIR BELLIES AT YOUR BACKYARD SEED TRAY HELPS YOUR GARDEN ALLIES CONSERVE THE CALORIES THEY'LL NEED TO KEEP THEM WARM DURING THE LONG, COLD NIGHT AHEAD.

- The continental polar air mass is the father of the famous blue norther (also known as Canadian clipper, Alaskan blast, or any other name you want to bestow on the extremely cold wintry weather that flows from the North Pole). Passing over the Great Lakes, these air masses pick up even more moisture to dump as snow.

Reading the Signs

Look at the sky and "feel" the air in winter, and your skills at weather prediction will soon improve, just as they will in any other season. Although you may not recognize snow clouds right away, if you take note of the clouds frequently and then link them to the weather that follows within a day or less, you'll soon become a backyard expert at putting two and two together. Animal behavior, too, can give you valuable warning of what's to come. Here are some clues to watch for:

- Moist air signals snow; a clear, dry day is unlikely to yield any white stuff.

- Air must be below the freezing point for snow.

- Layered gray clouds often signal snow.

- Birds are notorious for getting busy before a snow- or ice storm. When you see a bigger number of birds than usual at the feeder, you can bet heavy weather is on the way.

> "There's a certain slant of light,
> On winter afternoons,
> That oppresses, like the weight
> of cathedral tunes." —Emily Dickinson

Old-timers who have weathered many a winter storm often note, "It's too cold for snow." You may also hear someone say, "It has to warm up before it snows."

These observations are more likely based on the humidity, not the temperature. When air is heavy with humidity and thus more likely to dump snow, it feels warmer to us. Also, as the clouds neces-sary for snow move in, the air often does warm a few degrees, thanks to the clouds' insulating effect in the atmosphere.

On the other hand, extremely cold air is likely to be dry (and cloudless) air; thus, it *is* too cold for snow. But ask any polar bear or penguin—or Minnesota gardener—and they'll tell you that it can still snow even at very low temps.

Snow and Its Benefits

Snow that covers the yard most of the winter is a blessing to the garden—and to the gardener. A layer of snow insulates ground and plants, adds moisture to the soil, and even lightly fertilizes your garden and yard.

Snow as Insulation

Snow has tremendous insulating ability. This fluffy white stuff is even better than two down quilts on the bed: In one test, the air temperature was 50 degrees colder than the temperature below a 7-inch layer of new snow! Snow compacts the longer it stays on the ground, but it still retains enough air to insulate. Here are a few of its benefits:

- Snow protects stems and buds from cold air and desiccation. This is good news for marginally hardy plants, as well as for those that hold their leaves all winter, such as boxwood.

- Snow shields plant roots and growing points from shifts in air temperature. Roses and perennials need no extra cover when snow blankets their crowns.

- Snow extends the harvest of spinach, kale, and other cold-hardy greens, which will stay fresh under their white blanket. Brush the snow aside and pick yourself a salad.

- Snow keeps the ground frozen, preventing the heaving of roots from the soil during alternating frosts and thaws.

Where snow cover is not continuous, plants may be damaged when their buds begin to push out tender new growth during a deceptive warm spell in winter, only to be shocked by the following blast of frigid air. A thick layer of mulch can help safeguard a plant's crown in such situations, but it's difficult to prevent injury to buds that open too early. Early-blooming shrubs and trees, such as star magnolia (*Magnolia stellata*), are most susceptible.

If you've paid heed to choosing regionally appropriate plants, your garden will come through a normal winter in fine shape. But winters aren't always normal. Those that bring unusually cold air are not good news for plants. Even more dangerous are those years when winter is capricious. When warmth lingers long into late fall, plants may not be sufficiently prepared—via a process known as hardening off—by the time the first cold wave sweeps in. Even worse, from a garden viewpoint, are those winters when an extended period—at least 3 days—of unusually mild temperatures occurs between periods of intense cold.

Snow can be a lifesaver—or garden-saver—in weird winters. One year, a mild spell moved in shortly after a blizzard in my area. My forsythias, with their cascading branches to the ground, were buried knee-deep in snow—which led to an odd sight in spring. The buds above the snow line responded

"We shall know it all again, and in seeing renew the old familiar pleasure."

—W. H. Hudson, in *Nature in Downland*

to the balmy air like racehorses that had slipped the bit—they were off and running, turning yellow as I watched with dismay. After 2 days of warm air, the cold returned with a vengeance, turning the upper buds to frozen mush.

In March, when the forsythias bloomed at their usual time, only the bottom 2 feet of the arching branches, where the buds had stayed tight and brown under snow, bore flowers. From a distance, it looked like I'd discovered a new ground-hugging variety. The effect may have been odd, but I was happy to have any flowers at all.

Snow as Antidesiccant

Winter air can be brutally dry, with humidity levels so low your lips chap quickly as the moisture is snatched from them into the air. Plants can't use lip balm, but manufacturers have formulated products that you can spray them with to prevent this drying out, or desiccation.

All plants that hold their leaves in winter are susceptible to desiccation, but those most severely affected are broad-leaved evergreens. Boxwood is notorious for suffering damage from winter dryness, but azaleas, privet, viburnums, and other evergreens may also be damaged. Often, the signs aren't apparent until springtime, when the affected leaves turn yellow or brown and drop off.

To stave off the effects of drying winter weather, make sure your plants are watered deeply in late fall so their foliage and stems have plenty of fluid. Snow is also an ally in this battle. If your snowfall is deep and stays on the ground most of the winter, dwarf evergreens in knot gardens or specimen collections will be safely insulated.

Snow as Fertilizer

You have to hand it to those old wives—their tales hold plenty of truth. One elderly gardener I learned from, who'd emigrated from Europe way back in 1910, used to say that snow was better than manure; so good, in fact, that he'd shovel it onto his plants from the neighbor's yard. Sure, his garden always looked great, but I have to admit I didn't believe the snow story until I saw "scientific" research.

It makes perfect sense, of course. As snow falls through the skies, it picks up tiny bits of everything else that's floating around up there. In fact, snow needs these particulates to adhere to in order to start the formation of the crystal.

I've always enjoyed eating snow, even though my mother warned me not to. The only time I listened to her advice was during the fallout scare of the late 1950s, when the snow was said to be contaminated with the radioactive after-dust of nuclear testing. I still enjoy a taste or two of snow every year. What does it taste like? Well, like snow.

Before you go scoop up a handful, though, you'd be wise to consider what could be in the stuff. The old wives were right: It's a chemical warehouse, including fertilizer! Nitrates, sulfur compounds, potassium, and calcium are the major pollutants of snow, picked up in the atmospheric dust created by industries and agriculture. Other not-so-nice things may also lurk in that snow, depending what's in the air in which it forms.

Pure as the driven snow? Not hardly. But generally, still beneficial to your garden.

The Wonders of Snowflakes

People who live in places that see a lot of snow have a vocabulary that includes words to exactly designate each type of snow: In Finland, for example, "qali" is snow that clings to branches, while the delightfully onomatopoeic "detthlok" is snow so deep it calls for snowshoes.

Vermont gets its fair share of snow, too, which was the beginning of a magnificent obsession for W. A. Bentley, who dedicated his life to photographing its marvels. *Snow Crystals*, his master work, includes more than 2,400 photos of snowflakes—along with several gorgeous shots of frost swirls and other icy formations. All are featured page after page on a simple black background with no words to detract from the beauty before you. The book

GET A SEMI-SCIENTIFIC MEASURE OF HOW DEEP YOUR DRIFTS ARE WITH A SNOW GAUGE. POSITION THE POLE—BEFORE THE SNOW STARTS TO FALLS—IN A LOCATION THAT YOU CAN SEE FROM INSIDE YOUR HOUSE.

is out of print, but it's worth tracking down in used-book stores or on the Web—at the least, it will inspire you to catch a few flakes again, as you did when you were a child.

Most of us have admired these wonders of winter falling on a dark coat sleeve. Millions upon millions, every one different, and every one beautiful, whether it's a simple six-sided disk or an intricate lacy star.

The geometry of snowflakes depends on the amount of moisture, the temperature of the air and the cloud, and other variables; the slightest variation is enough to change the final shape of the crystal. I keep a piece of black cloth in my freezer, in a moisture-proof plastic zip-top bag, so that when snowflakes start falling, I can catch them and get a good look before they begin to melt. I also keep Bentley's book on my bedside table, where its pages of thousands of snow crystal photos are in easy reach when I want to calm my mind before sleep.

Damaging Snow and Ice

Feel those aching arms and back after a half-hour of shoveling? Clearing a sidewalk is hard work because snow is heavy. It may feel like fluff, but snow packs on the weight quickly as it begins to pile up.

WHEN SNOW SWAMPS YOUR CONIFERS, USE A BROOM TO GENTLY KNOCK OFF THE EXCESS. RESHAPE THE PLANT IF NECESSARY BY WRAPPING IT WITH TWINE.

A wet snow can split apart your arborvitae or cause your pine tree to crack. It can disfigure young trees and shrubs by bending their branches to the ground and holding them there long enough to acquire a permanent crook. Late snows can break the necks of daffodils and other top-heavy spring bloomers.

To prevent snow damage, give your susceptible plants some support—or a shield if necessary. Here are a few quick-and-easy suggestions:

- A spool of green garden twine makes a quick wrap for conical conifers or other evergreens that could become deformed. Wrap them loosely before the snowstorms arrive.

- Foundation plantings are vulnerable to the heavy blow of snow sliding off the roof. Make a note to move any that are in harm's way next spring, and meanwhile place a temporary shield overhead. Plastic or wooden lawn furniture will work fine as a quickly placed snow catcher.

- After a snow, use a broom to sweep extra accumulation from plants that can't bear the load. Look for bending branches or swaybacked saplings, and gently sweep them free of the weight.

Ice Storms

Stunning beauty and the potential for stunning damage: An ice storm is gorgeous to gaze upon, but not nearly so benign when the layer of frozen water is heavy enough to take down power lines and trees. Not to mention making it darned slippery for a gardener out checking the damage!

> ## "I love snow, and all the forms
> ## Of the radiant frost.
>
> —Percy Bysshe Shelley

You can find inexpensive cleats and nonslip rubberized grids to attach to your shoes so that you can more surefootedly survey the damage after an ice storm, but there's not much you can do ahead of time to help your garden weather an ice storm. Low-growing plants won't be irreparably harmed, and preventive maintenance is impossible for large trees and shrubs. Unless you intend to box your plants in plywood, there's little you can do to keep tree limbs from cracking or dogwoods from snapping.

Predicting ice storms is extremely difficult because tiny changes in the moisture level or the air temperature can switch ice to snow, sleet, or rain. When rain falls from clouds and meets freezing air, it falls as sleet. When snow falling from clouds meets warm air above the earth's surface, it melts and falls as rain. If there is a narrow layer of below-freezing air underneath that warm air, the raindrops will become "supercooled" but remain liquid—until they hit something. Then they instantly turn to ice, glazing any surface they touch that is cooled below the freezing point.

Should you experience an ice storm, approach damage control and cleanup as you would the aftermath of a summer storm:

- Wait until the ice melts to go outside. Walking will be treacherous, and limbs and trees may snap without warning.

- Be on the lookout for fallen utility wires. Report them and avoid them.

- Keep looking up as you walk your yard. Avoid standing or walking beneath damaged branches or ice-covered trees.

- If you're not a chain-saw expert, hire an arborist to remove the damage and reshape the tree if needed.

Birds and Storms

Helping birds weather winter storms is a great investment in your garden because birds are the natural caretakers of plants. Also, life would be pretty dull in the winter garden without birdsong and motion to enjoy.

In cold-winter areas, the birds that linger year-round are those that eat seeds and berries. Insect eaters depart before the first frost because they would soon starve without their major food source.

Birds and animals can dig or burrow through snow to reach food, but a layer of ice can be impenetrable. Ice storms have historically decimated bird populations in some areas. Birds have been reported with their feet frozen to branches, or unable to fly because of iced feathers. Grouse, which typically shelter under snow, may be unable to break free from their roosting spots when an icy crust forms over the snow.

During snow and ice storms, be generous at the feeding station and cast plenty of seed on the ground so there's lots of room for all customers. Provide high-fat suet, doughnuts, meat scraps, peanut butter, and other foods with hefty calories to keep birds warm during the cold nights to come.

In extreme weather situations, every little bit of help can make a big difference to our wild friends.

Put your birds on a high-fat diet when winter arrives. Extra helpings of fat in the form of suet or doughnuts will let them pack in more calories in less time.

BIRD ROOSTING BOX

Bird houses do double duty in wintertime by serving as shelter on cold nights. If you find a bluebird box in your Christmas stocking, there's no need to wait until spring to put it up. Mount it now, and you may save a wintering bluebird's life.

Titmice, chickadees, and woodpeckers also seek bird houses for shelter. The birds often gang up inside, cramming in until the box is packed. You can find plans or buy "roosting boxes" that accommodate a number of overnight guests, but an ordinary bird house will also do the trick—and give you the pleasure of watching nesting tenants come spring.

Avoid the temptation to sneak a peek at nightfall. Instead, watch for evidence of use by checking the tails of your feeder birds. If the feathers are curved, they were probably pressed against the wall of a sheltering box in your yard last night.

Meet the Snowbird

One of the most beloved and most common visitors at the winter feeding station is the junco, a sparrow-size bird often called the snowbird. You'll usually spot this little bird on the ground beneath feeders, where it shows up in small groups of juncos and sparrows, picking up dropped millet and other small seeds.

Several races of juncos populate the continent, but the classic snowbird is the slate-colored junco. This wintertime bird, which arrives in mid- to late fall and disappears with spring to seek nest sites in the north and in mountains, gets its nickname from its color as well as its seasonal reappearance. Its back is gray, like a sky filled with snow clouds, and its belly is as white as freshly fallen flakes.

Winter Bloom

What is so rare as a rose in June?, asked 19th-century poet James Russell Lowell. How about a rose in January? Okay, What we know as the "Christmas rose" is not really a rose but a hellebore, a perennial that brings forth its liberal and lovely flowers at Christmastime in many zones. Few flower-hungry gardeners are interested in

EASTERN SKUNK CABBAGE IS A WELCOME—
IF ODORIFEROUS—WINTER BLOOMER.

Beat the Light-Deprivation Blues

The short days of winter, coupled with many days of overcast skies, can make you feel like you're living in a fog. Our brains need light to keep up the production of serotonin, and when winter light levels fall too low, a well-defined medical condition can result from the shortage. SAD (Seasonal Affective Disorder) makes sufferers feel just like the name says: They're weepy, irritable, lethargic, and just not happy.

To beat the blues, exchange a light bulb or two near your usual sitting spots with a full-spectrum bulb. For severe cases, catalogs offer full-spectrum lights in various devices, such as an alarm clock that gradually brightens like the rising sun peeping into your window. Other activities can also help elevate your mood. Here are some that work for me:

■ Visit a greenhouse. A nearby botanic garden or conservatory is ideal, but even a commercial operation will kick in the pleasure for a gardener as soon as you smell the humus and feel the warmth.

■ Arrange a scrapbook or photo album. Looking at pictures of your garden in its glory is great therapy, and it can help you plan for the coming spring, too.

■ Start an indoor garden of houseplants or soup beans.

■ Get outside. Take a daily walk, even if the skies are gray. Moving makes you feel better, and your brain will soak up whatever light is out there.

quibbling over such minor issues of nomenclature when Christmas roses are the only flowers in sight.

Skunk cabbage (*Symplocarpus foetidus*) blooms even before the hellebores, thanks to the snow-melting heat generated by its rapidly expanding flower bud. Unfortunately, its aroma keeps it from being a popular choice in backyard gardens, even though the mottled purplish brown hooded flowers are fascinatingly weird—and early.

Plants for Winter Flowers

These better-scented winter bloomers will also supply a flower fix in mid- to late winter when it's most appreciated.

WINTER HAZELS (*CORYLOPSIS* SPP.)

CROCUSES (*CROCUS CHRYSANTHUS*, OTHER SPECIES AND HYBRIDS)

WINTER ACONITE (*ERANTHIS HYEMALIS*)

SNOWDROPS (*GALANTHUS* SPP.)

WITCH HAZELS (*HAMAMELIS* SPP.)

CHRISTMAS ROSE, OTHER HELLEBORES (*HELLEBORUS* × *HYBRIDUS*, *HELLEBORUS* SPP.)

WINTER JASMINE (*JASMINUM NUDIFLORUM*)

AUTUMN-FLOWERING CHERRY (*PRUNUS SUBHIRTELLA*)

SNOWDROPS

WITCH HAZEL

HELLEBORE

Forcing Flowering Branches

Whether you call it forcing or coaxing, the trick of nudging flowering branches into bloom ahead of their season is a gratifying one. You can find all kinds of fussy instructions, but I keep it fast and simple, with good results every time. Just cut a few branches and stick them in a vase of warm water. It may take a week or more before the buds open, but they will.

Forsythia and pussy willow are the easiest, and they take the least amount of time to bloom. But others are fun to try, too—have fun experimenting with any spring-flowering shrubs or trees in your yard. The earlier they bloom outdoors, the more success you will have tricking them into bloom inside.

Plants to Force for Winter Color

RED MAPLE (*ACER RUBRUM*)

SILVER MAPLE (*ACER SACCHARINUM*)

REDBUDS (*CERCIS* SPP. AND CVS.)

FLOWERING QUINCES
(*CHAENOMELES* SPP. AND CVS.)

FORSYTHIAS (*FORSYTHIA* SPP.
AND CVS.)

APPLES (*MALUS* SPP. AND CVS.)

PEARS (*PYRUS* SPP. AND CVS.)

PUSSY WILLOW (*SALIX DISCOLOR*)

LILACS (*SYRINGA* SPP. AND CVS.)

A FEW GARDEN BRANCHES IN BLOOM ARE A TREASURE IN WINTER. COAX THEM INTO OPENING EARLY IN A VASE OF WATER INDOORS.

The End of Winter

Winter loses its grip in subtle ways at first. Seen from a distance, far-off woods begin to soften with red, yellow, and purple tones as buds begin to swell. Birdsong begins, with courting winter residents bursting into phrases of song now and then and showing interest in the opposite sex.

Even in the kitchen, you can tell the long months of winter are almost at an end. Potatoes and onions are hard to keep, and their shoots can turn into tentacles in the bags before you notice them. If you miss the natural signs, you're bound to spy the first signs of winter's end at the garden center: Seed racks and potting supplies sprout in the aisles.

Outside, the biggest change is happening out of sight. Within every tree, the sap is rising. Keep your eyes open when you see maple trees near roadways; if an icicle forms when a twig is broken by passing traffic, winter is on the way out.

The Sap Is Rising

Maple syrup is a delight for the sweet-toothed, whether they have two legs or four. I often spot tufted titmice and chickadees sipping sap from the ends of maple icicles, and I've watched squirrels break them off to eat like Popsicles.

If you're a fan of maple syrup, why not try tapping your own backyard trees? It's easy if you have a flat-topped woodburning stove where you can keep a pot at low simmer for days. Spouts and the "spile" to drive them into the trunk are inexpensive; check the Internet for sources. You can tap any kind of maple, though sugar maples have the sweetest sap; even the related box elder (*Acer negundo*) yields a sap good enough to boil down for pancakes.

Native Americans and the European colonists they instructed in the art of sap collecting knew that the flow depends on the weather. Sunny days and cold nights are the key to a strong flow. On such a day, put your ear against a maple, and you can hear the heartbeat of the tree. A stethoscope is even better, especially if traffic or other noise interferes. Listen carefully, and you can hear winter saying goodbye for another year.

CHAPTER 11

"THE WOOL OF THE SHEEP, THE FUR OF THE ANIMALS, THE
FEATHERS OF THE FOWLS, THE HUSKS OF THE MAIZE, WHY ARE
THEY THICKER SOME SEASONS THAN OTHERS...? DOES IT INDICATE
A SEVERE WINTER APPROACHING? ONLY OBSERVATIONS EXTENDING
OVER A SERIES OF YEARS COULD DETERMINE THE POINT."

—JOHN BURROUGHS

Animal Clues to Weather

INTUITION IS AN INTERESTING THING. "GONNA BE A HOT ONE," I SOMETIMES SAY
to my neighbors on a summer morning, or, "Nope, it's not going to rain
today." Although I'd like to take credit for some supernatural abilities to discern the weather, I know that my assertions are based on nothing more than
experience and awareness. Sure, after years of being outside, I no longer have
to spell it out to my own mind—it's become as automatic as, say, reading—but
if called upon, I could detail just what led me to make each forecast.

A cloudless sky, birds leaving the feeders by early morning, and butterflies
flying about the garden by 8 A.M. might have been the signs that told me a hot
day lay ahead. No rain? Again, I've taken a look at the clouds and combined
that information with the sight of a big yellow-and-black garden spider
working on a new web and the baby robins still snug in their nest—all clues
that rain isn't in the cards that day.

Understanding Animal Behavior

Every gardener soon learns that a garden isn't only about plants. The first awakening may happen when you brush aside the strawberry leaves and find a delicate cupped sparrow's nest hiding a treasure of two perfect eggs—or, less pleasantly, when the Japanese beetles descend upon your favorite roses.

We stewards of the backyard share our space with all kinds of living creatures, from the unseen underground multitudes that keep our soil healthy to the songbirds that delight our ears and the insects that live out their eat-or-be-eaten lives all around us.

All that lively activity contributes to the pleasures we enjoy when we spend time in our gardens. Watching the squirrels, toads, and other yard dwellers can also give us clues about the weather. As you learn to decipher the animal behavior you observe, you'll find that the creatures that share your garden can do more than emerge in February to look at their shadows. And, like other methods of predicting the weather, these animal clues were a part of a previous generation's system for taking cues from nature's forecasters.

Peel away the layers of civilization, and humans have the same basic goals as animals: food, water, shelter, and raising our young. In the garden and in the wild, those pursuits are on full display, whether the animal is a spider, an earthworm, a butterfly, or the squirrel at your bird feeder.

As you spend time watching the animals in your yard and in the sky overhead, you'll soon start to notice the cycles of natural life and how they are timed to or affected by the weather.

Furred Friends (and Foes)

Punxsutawney Phil may be the poster boy of springtime forecasting, but groundhogs can be the bane of a garden—at least from the gardener's viewpoint. Thanks to their appetite for juicy ripe tomatoes and lush marigolds and other flowers, they can mow through plantings like a mini reaping machine, practically inhaling their (and our) favorite foods.

Most furred backyard animals fall into the same category of cute but pesky, usually during certain seasons or when weather causes them to seek easier pickings than in the wild.

- Rabbits and deer are great garden appreciators, but they're more interested in edible plantings than in aesthetics. In spring and summer, succulent foliage is first choice. In winter, they may scour the backyard for tasty twigs or bark.

- Raccoons and opossums may sample the garden produce, but they generally leave ornamentals alone. In summer, 'coons may bring their young ones for fishing lessons at your garden pool. In winter, watch for 'possums and 'coons at your bird feeders.

- Skunks aren't interested in plants, but they do like insects and can cause digging damage to lawns and gardens as they unearth their prey. In fall, they dig up ground-nesting yellowjacket or wasp nests to eat the inhabitants, a favor for which gardeners can be grateful.

- Gophers, moles, and ground squirrels can make it tricky to walk about the lawn, thanks to the tunnels they dig with amazing speed, especially when the soil is moist.

- Ground squirrels, a problem mostly in the West, eat seeds, fruit, and plants, and can be pests in fall when their appetites increase as they fatten up for hibernation.

THE STOUT CLAWS ON SKUNK FEET ARE DESIGNED FOR RAPID BURROWING AND CLAWING— BEHAVIORS THAT CAN PUT THIS NOCTURNAL CREATURE AT ODDS WITH LAWN LOVERS.

- Mice—and the similar but larger voles—are small but mighty: Their incisors are all business, and they can girdle our favorite shrubs and young trees in winter by chewing off any bit of bark they can reach.

- As suburban sprawl meets wild places, coyotes and foxes may adapt to living in the midst of humanity. These wild visitors won't bother your garden plants, and they'll help keep rodents in check, but they can pose a threat to household pets. For safety's sake, keep Kitty and Little Rover inside at night, especially in winter, when wild food is scarce.

BRIGHT-EYED CHIPMUNKS AND OTHER GROUND SQUIRRELS ARE DOWNRIGHT CUTE WHEN THEY'RE NOT TUNNELING THROUGH YOUR GARDEN BEDS.

About the only furry creature that rarely causes a gardener headaches is the chipmunk, who's happy to make a snug home in a rocky niche, from which he can entertain us with chirring calls and capers. Also on the plus side are bats, one of the most interesting and most threatened animals in America. These nocturnal creatures are interested only in the insects in your garden. Look for them swooping about at dusk throughout the summer, gobbling up mosquitoes and other insect pests. You may see them visiting night-blooming flowers, not to sip nectar but to scoop up night-flying moths.

If you want to observe your animal neighbors without sacrificing your garden, your best defense is to barricade those areas you want to protect from pest animals. Secure wire fences are pricey, but they're the best long-term investment. Dogs are a good deterrent, too. Cats will keep down the mice, but they also discourage desirable visitors such as songbirds and butterflies.

Animal populations tend to run in cycles, with rodent numbers increasing gradually over 6 or 7 years until they reach a level that territory or food supplies can't sustain. In the wild, the "excess" animals would likely disperse to new territories or fall prey to disease or starvation. In the unnatural environs of a

Fat-Burner Deluxe

Sometimes heard, rarely seen, the shrew is one of the hungriest citizens of the garden. This tiny rodent looks like a stub-tailed mouse minus the ears, and its metabolism is legendary. A shrew's body operates at the fastest speed known on earth—so rapid-fire that scientists rank the metabolism of one species of shrew above the perpetual motion of a hummingbird.

To fuel that fire, shrews need to eat. A lot. Primarily insectivores, they're so voracious that "bloodthirsty" is a commonly applied epithet. But shrews are only doing what comes naturally. That can be good news in a garden because insects are tops on the menu. Shrews pounce on tons of grubs, beetles, caterpillars, ants, flies, snails, grasshoppers—and mice.

Listen for shrews' high-pitched squeaking, especially on humid days when rain isn't far off.

THE FASTEST METABOLISM ON THE PLANET BELONGS TO SHREWS, WHICH EAT VORACIOUSLY ALL THEIR WAKING HOURS. THEY'RE OFTEN ESPECIALLY ACTIVE ON HUMID OR RAINY DAYS.

garden, predators often help maintain the balance. Neighborhood cats, hawks, and owls will keep your home grounds from being overrun by furry critters.

While you erect your fences or hang your fake-snake scares, look and learn from your garden animals. They hold many hints as to what the weather's going to bring.

Animal Weather Forecasting

No self-respecting furred animal likes to get soaked to the skin in a rainy deluge, so animals seek shelter before bad weather. A fine drizzle may find bunnies nibbling on your clover, but when the wind and rain arrive in earnest, the cottontails move out in a hurry to seek shelter under a dense shrub or beneath your garden shed.

Winter weather drives animal behavior, too, at least for those that don't sleep away the cold months. Like birds, animals are especially active before a storm, bulking up on extra calories. You'll also see more evidence of activity immediately after the storm is over, when fresh snowfall is marked by tracks long before you get your own boots buckled.

Bad Winter Ahead?

People have credited animals with weather forecasting abilities for centuries. In particular, many animals supposedly provide clues as to the severity of the winter ahead. It's fun to follow the folklore and to keep track of how often it proves true. Here are some hints to help you separate the myths from the facts of forecasting by the critters:

GROUNDHOGS LOVE TO BASK IN EARLY SPRING SUN- SHINE AS MUCH AS WE DO, WHETHER OR NOT THEIR SHADOW ACCOMPANIES THEM.

If the groundhog sees his shadow, 6 more weeks of winter. If the groundhog sees no shadow, an early spring.

MYTH. Groundhog Day is February 2, which as any gardener knows is peak season for wishful thinking. We're so ready for winter to be over that we'll find our hopes rising right along with Punxsutawney Phil, even if his forecast is based on nothing more than hopeful anticipation.

When animals grow thick coats of fur, the winter will be a bad one.

MYTH? So say the experts, reasoning that animals grow luxuriant coats after they've had a summer of abundance, not because they can foretell the winter weather. You can make your own decision based on your own observations. My own eyes tell me that the raccoons at the feeder seem to be especially furry during the same winters that my heating bill is sky-high.

Squirrels have bushy tails when the winter will be severe.

MYTH? That's the fun of animal lore forecasting—you can doubt the experts. The fox squirrels in my neighborhood are well furred in severe winters, which makes me smile when I think of them tucking that furry stole around their cold noses.

A BUSHY TAIL COULD MEAN A WELL-NOURISHED SQUIRREL, OR MAYBE A HARD WINTER TO COME.

Squirrels gather nuts early if the winter will be a bad one.

MYTH. Squirrels gather nuts early when the nuts ripen early. They're always industrious about laying in a good supply of food to get them through the winter months. Even in the middle of abundant wild and backyard nut trees (pecans, oaks, walnuts, hickories), it's always a race between me and the squirrels to see who gets the first harvest.

Groundhogs get extra fat before a hard winter.

MYTH. Groundhogs double their weight every fall, packing on the pounds for the hibernation period when their body will sustain itself on the stored fat. Like other wild creatures, they'll be busy carrying out their task of fattening up, no matter how long or short the Indian summer before they head underground.

Wolves come into the village during a hard winter.

ONCE TRUE. But change that to coyotes, since forest wolves are a little scarce these days, and there's plenty of wild food to sustain them—unlike in long-ago Europe where this lore originated. Don't panic, though—coyotes are interested in your trash cans, not your children.

Who Goes There?

I look forward to a fresh snow because it's such a wonder to read the story of who lives in or visits my yard. Animals are adept at keeping out of sight, especially the little guys like mice, voles, and shrews, so it's hard to get a handle on just who lives in my garden. But after a snow, there are no secrets: Animal trails cross and crisscross the yard, sometimes spelling out dramas of life and death.

Checking the tracks will tell you not only who is visiting your yard but also how many. You may want to note your findings so that you can compare populations from year to year.

Copy the paw marks of common animals from a field guide, and you'll have a quick reference to tuck in your pocket on a winter morning's detective jaunt. While you puzzle over figuring out who goes there, take a look at just where those trails lead, too. You're likely to find mice paths heading to any standing seedheads in your flower garden, and rabbits shuttling under bramble bushes or the privet hedge to travel out of sight of owl eyes. Watch for the soft sweep of feathers traced in the snow, where a bird has taken flight or swooped low enough to snatch a meal. The story is written on the snow.

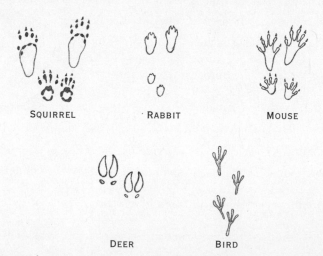

SQUIRREL RABBIT MOUSE

DEER BIRD

READ THE NEWS IN FRESH SNOW, AND YOU'LL FIND OUT WHO MAKES YOUR GARDEN A HOME OR A HUNTING GROUND. LOTS OF MICE TRACKS? MAKE SURE THE TEMPTING BARK OF YOUNG FRUIT TREES IS PROTECTED.

Hibernation

As the days begin to shorten in autumn, animals get really busy. Squirrels scamper around, burying nuts and making food caches in trees. Mice do the same, setting up storehouses in bird boxes, bird nests, and other handy hiding places where their seeds and berries will be ready and waiting in the lean days ahead.

Eating is the order of the season for animals that do the long sleep called hibernation. Groundhogs, skunks, chipmunks, opossums, and some ground squirrels put their extra food reserves right into their bodies, cramming themselves from sunup to sundown (or all night long, in the case of nocturnal opossums).

Hibernation is a peculiar survival adaptation in which the body slows way, way down. The animal slumbers away the cold months, snug in a burrow or den. Then they emerge, slow and groggy—and ready to start eating again.

Some hibernators, including possums, are light sleepers; in some years they're out and about all winter. Others may come above ground during warm spells in the winter, but most stay sound asleep until springtime resets their clock.

The reappearance of hibernators in spring is a lot easier to notice than their disappearance in fall. One harbinger of spring for me—which usually

THE OPOSSUM IS THE MOST UNUSUAL ANIMAL YOU'LL ENCOUNTER IN YOUR YARD. OUR ONLY MARSUPIAL, IT HAS FASCINATING HABITS AND IS RARELY A PEST. LOOK FOR ITS UNIQUE STAR-SHAPED TRACKS IN THE SNOW BENEATH YOUR BIRD FEEDERS.

occurs in late January or early February—is the unfortunate increase in road-killed skunks. Spotting a furry black-and-white-striped victim along the road is not quite as uplifting an event as the arrival of the first robin, but it's just as sure an indicator that spring's on the way.

Groundhogs have been reliable indicators of gardening seasons for me: When I spot that first lumbering brown body or hear the shrill loud whistle,

Timed by the Trees

Squirrels are the reforesters of America (with a little assistance from jays). Many of the nuts they bury in the soil aren't eaten over winter; they survive intact to sprout into young trees. My large pots, left filled with loose potting mix over winter, are a favorite nut-hiding place for my backyard squirrels—and a great cue for planting. When I see walnut or pecan seedlings sprouting to a few inches high in my flowerpots, I take it as a sign that the cold weather is over, and it's safe to refill the containers with geraniums. So far, the squirrels haven't let me down.

LEAVE SOIL IN YOUR OUTDOOR POTS, AND A SQUIRREL MAY BURY A NUT FOR SAFEKEEPING. MANY SQUIRREL CACHES AREN'T EATEN OVER WINTER, LEAVING THE SEEDS TO SPROUT COME SPRING.

I know it's time to get busy planting radishes, carrots, peas, and onions; rearranging the perennial beds; and planting out the packs of sweet alyssum. Chances are, though, with my bad habit of rushing the season, the garden is likely to already be well on the way when Mr. Groundhog emerges.

Spring Harbingers

Everybody loves to hear the confirmation that (hurrah!) spring is finally here. You won't need to wait until the vernal equinox to declare the season if you keep watch and listen to the goings-on outdoors. Cold-blooded animals are some of the best weather predictors and season announcers you'll find because their bodies respond to the outside temperature. When the thermometer is below 40°F (4°C), you won't see frogs, toads, or turtles. But the warmer the sun and air, the more active they get. Here's what to watch—and listen—for:

Frog chorus. Listen for the love song of Froggy as he and his relatives go a-courtin' beginning in late winter, as soon as the first weak rays of sun draw them from the mud. As the season progresses the chorus gets louder, with each species chiming in at its appointed turn. In the East, the frog symphony begins with spring peepers, tiny fingertip-size animals with huge voices; the similar chorus frogs are the harbinger in the Midwest and West. Wherever you live, there's a signature frog song for the season.

SPRING PEEPERS ARE MORE OFTEN HEARD THAN SEEN. ALTHOUGH THEY'RE TINY, THEY WELCOME SPRING WITH SURPRISINGLY BIG VOICES.

Frog and toad dispersal. On mild, rainy nights, frogs and toads are plentiful on roads as they head to or return from breeding ponds.

Baby toads. When you see itty-bitty toads hopping about your yard, spring is in full sway. I interpret the sighting as the green light for planting tender flowers and veggies, and for bringing my houseplants outdoors.

Turtles. Turtles are a territorial lot and often use the same paths they have for decades to reach a mate and then return to their own stomping ground. Look for box turtles and other backyard types trundling through in mid-spring, about the time of bearded iris and the earliest roses. Humid and lightly rainy weather seem to be the peak times for turtle traveling—and that's a good time for transplanting and dividing in the garden.

Snakes. No matter what your appreciation level of snakes, it's good to know that garter snakes are one of the earliest types to emerge in spring. Horizontal stripes indicate one of these nonpoisonous garden allies, who will be a great aid in keeping mice and voles in balance.

Summer Animal Activity

No matter how big a war you have going with their parents, there's simply no way to avoid being charmed by baby animals in the garden. Fawns, bunnies, and even pudgy baby groundhogs are so cute, a year's worth of garden

BUNNIES ARE CUTE—BUT ONLY WHEN THEY'RE NOT DEVASTATING YOUR GARDEN. A STURDY WIRE FENCE WITH ITS BOTTOM EDGE BURIED SEVERAL INCHES INTO THE GROUND HELPS TO KEEP RABBITS ON THE GOOD SIDE (THAT IS, THE OUTSIDE) OF YOUR GARDEN.

> **"If there is one way better than another it is the way of nature."**
>
> —Aristotle

depredation is all but forgiven in an instant when the parents bring the babies around.

Before you set out special food treats for your visitors, remember that these early summer babies will be big hungry adults by fall. Luring them to your yard is probably not a good idea, even if they are adorable. The appearance of young animals is a cue to get defenses in place. Check the fencing around your vegetable patch unless you plan to share the summer's harvest with all comers. If you want your entire yard protected, check that fencing or thorny hedges are in place to keep critters out.

Dry conditions cause animals to travel long distances to seek moisture. I offer several low pans of water at different places in the yard to refresh any creatures that need a drink and to prevent the squirrels and raccoons from toppling my ornamental pedestal birdbath. During a drought, animals may munch succulent leaves of sedums and other juicy plants to slake their thirst.

CHAPTER 12

"I HEARD A BIRD AT DAWN
SINGING SWEETLY ON A TREE,
THAT THE DEW WAS ON THE LAWN,
AND THE WIND WAS ON THE LEA."

—JAMES STEPHENS

Birds, Bugs, and Butterflies

IN THE DAYS WHEN GARDENING SUCCESS MEANT THE DIFFERENCE BETWEEN A well-stocked larder for winter and a table surrounded by empty bellies, weather-related sayings were abundant and served as the foundation of the planting season. Our great-grandparents would have known how big the oak leaves were when they planted their corn (compared to the size of a squirrel's ear), but nowadays we rely on calendars and on meteorologists' frost predictions rather than our own observations of the world around us.

Yet a few pieces of weather folklore still survive, even in the midst of our electronic-dependent culture. "Birds fly low before a storm" is something that's still lodged in our brains, along with the supposed ability of woolly worm caterpillars to foretell the severity of the coming winter.

"Talk to the animals!" urged Dr. Dolittle, but "watch and listen to the animals" is better advice for anyone wanting to know more about the weather. Birds, butterflies, and other insects in our gardens hold plenty of clues to what the day will bring. All we have to do is open our eyes.

Learning from Birds

Birds are the greatest allies a gardener can have because their role in life is to eat insects. Every day, thousands of bugs get snapped up by the busy beaks in your garden, especially in spring and summer, when demanding nestlings need constant feeding. Even "pest" birds earn their place now, with starlings stabbing Japanese beetle larvae from the soil and house sparrows gulping down the fat-bodied adults.

The life that birds bring to the yard is another big reason to encourage them. A cardinal on a bare winter branch, a bunch of squabbling house sparrows, or a confiding chickadee swinging overhead are fun to watch, especially when you lure them into easy viewing distance with a tempting feeder.

Bird behavior varies with the weather, another good reason to get to know the life cycles and behavior of your feathered backyard friends. Their activities will tell you when a storm is coming, as well as when the worst of severe weather is over. Here's how to interpret what you see:

INSECT-EATING WRENS ARE SOME OF THE BEST BUDDIES A GARDENER CAN HAVE, THANKS TO ALL THOSE CRITTERS THAT GO DOWN THE HATCH. THEIR HAPPY, BUBBLING SONG IS ANOTHER BENEFIT.

- Birds fly closer to the ground when winds are ushering in a possible storm. Higher-level winds make it difficult for birds to fly with minimum effort, so they shift to a lower flight pattern. Look up now and then to get accustomed to the heights at which birds travel the air in various weather. On calm days, crows, hawks, and swallows are likely flying high; lower flight should alert you to incoming bad weather.

AS SWALLOWS SWOOP AND DIVE ABOVE THE GARDEN, THEY SNAP UP COUNTLESS GARDEN
PESTS—PLUS MOSQUITOES, GNATS, AND FLIES THAT WOULD OTHERWISE PLAGUE THE GARDENER.

- Insects flying low means the air is heavy with moisture, and the swallows, swifts, and other birds that feed on them will also alter their flight in response. When you see such birds flying not far above rooftop height, add that data to your observations of the sky and clouds, and you can make an educated guess as to whether the elevated humidity will be bringing rain.

- A big increase in the number of customers at your feeders will precede approaching snow and ice storms.. If you hear the forecast before the crowds gather, be sure to lay in an extra sack of seed so you're ready for the rush.

Birdsong and Weather

In spring and early summer, birdsong is one of the pleasures of the garden. Birds sing most in the morning, with various species beginning at particular levels of light. Robins, which have a lovely fluting voice that tells of their Thrush family heritage, are among the very first to awake and greet the day with song. Birds stop singing in the heat of the day, as well as when breeding season is on the wane in late summer. Only a very few species, including the stunning indigo bunting, sing in the heat of a summer day. Here are a few telltale birdsong facts:

- Robins usually sing in chorus in the dim light of dawn and dusk. When the sky darkens before a storm, the diminished light may once again bring on a swell of robin song around the neighborhood.

- When you hear geese honking but can't see them flying, it's a good day to stay inside and keep cool. Migrating geese honk as they fly, and their voices carry much farther in humid air. If you step outside at night during spring and fall migration—even in the dark—you'll be able to get a feel for the moisture in the air when you hear their voices. Like a lonesome train whistle, the honking carries far when the air is heavy with humidity or clouds.

- If it's only 9 A.M. and the birds are mostly silent, expect a scorcher. Birds stop the choir activity early on the hottest days.

- In winter, birds are tucked into snug roosting places by late afternoon. Wonder where your feathered guests are resting on cold nights? Listen near a blue spruce or other dense evergreen and you're likely to hear their quiet goodnight cheeps and chirps.

- If birds linger at the feeder in winter after their usual bedtime, you can bet that bad weather is on the way. The birds are trying to stock up on calories in case snow or ice covers the food supply during the night.

> "O birds, your perfect virtues bring,
>
> Your song, your forms,
>
> your rhythmic flight."
>
> —Ralph Waldo Emerson

Summer Bird Behavior

Winter is the busy season for the bird feeder, but summer brings its own charming guests to the feeder and the garden. Their activity will give you many clues about the changing season and the weather. Continue feeding and providing water for birds, and mount wren boxes or other bird houses throughout your yard: Birds are great allies in the garden because they devour millions of insects.

- Birdsong begins extra early as the days lengthen in early summer. As breeding season wanes in late summer, singing decreases dramatically. A few robins may still greet the dawn, but the crescendo dies down by late July.

- When a storm approaches, birds take shelter. Listen for them announcing the "All clear" afterward with chirps and songs.

- Although you'll have less traffic at the feeders in summer, you're likely to spot youngsters as parent birds bring the family for easy pickings. Suet is a favorite of chickadee, woodpecker, nuthatch, and titmouse families. By keeping your feeders stocked through the summer, you'll encourage nesting birds to stay through the growing season; in exchange, they'll patrol your garden for insects to feed their hungry young.

- Notice that birds often bring their youngsters out of the nest just before a gentle rain. (My theory is that they know that cats and other predators are less likely to be on the prowl during wet weather.)

- Keep the birdbath filled. It will get lots of use during hot days, and it's a lifesaver in a drought.

Bird Forecasters

Birds change their outfit along with the seasons. During courtship and breeding season, males are eye-catching in their brightest plumage of the year. After the young are on their own, birds molt their breeding or nuptial plumage, and young birds begin to acquire some of the coloration of their parents. Migrants and residents in early spring may have a blotchy look, with some new feathers grown in among the drab remains of off-season color. Not only feathers change color: Beaks, too, take on new tones as hormones kick into gear. Watch for these changes in your common backyard birds:

- Goldfinches are one of the best barometers of the season. Males are olive drab in winter and change back to snazzy yellow and black in early spring, about the time the pussy willows bloom.

- Starlings are shining iridescent black in spring and summer, with a bright yellow beak. In fall, they change to a wardrobe of non-iridescent dark brown feathers spotted with starry white tips, and their bills pale to grayish tan.

- Male cardinals brighten from a dull, drab reddish hue to an almost neon red in spring.

- Scarlet tanagers replace red summer feathers with green for fall and winter.

THE DRAB STARLINGS THAT PIG OUT AT YOUR BIRD FEEDERS IN THE WINTER CHANGE INTO GLOSSY IRIDESCENT PLUMAGE FOR THE SUMMER MONTHS, WHEN THEY'LL PATROL YOUR LAWN IN SEARCH OF GRUBS.

Bird behavior can also tell you what time it is, seasonally speaking, unless you live in a mild winter area where birds nest year-round. In most regions, birds pal around in groups during fall and winter; in spring they pair up to raise their families. Feeder birds that formerly fed amicably side by side may become aggressively territorial, driving away other males of their species. Or you may get a peek at courtship or mating behavior at the feeder, as mourning doves, for instance, bill and coo.

Summer Hummers

Peak season for powerhouse hummingbirds is late spring to late summer, but in some lucky areas where flowers bloom all year, the little birds may be a constant presence in the yard. In cold-winter regions, it's summer gardens that may be filled with an audible—what else?—*hummmm* as the little birds zip from flower to flower. Unlike songbirds, hummingbirds don't seem to mind the heat. You may spot them foraging at any time of day. These little birds remain active even during showers, but they seek shelter in heavier rain.

A BATH IS MUCH APPRECIATED BY HUMMINGBIRDS, WHICH PLAY IN A FINE SPRAY LIKE KIDS AT A FIRE HYDRANT. ATTACH A MISTER TO YOUR BIRDBATH, OR KEEP AN EYE ON THE SPRAY OF YOUR SPRINKLER AND YOU MAY SEE THEM DASHING THROUGH.

The so-called raincrow is one of the most fascinating bird forecasters. You may hear it on a muggy summer afternoon, when showers or thunderstorms are in the offing. The call begins with a quiet chugging "coo coo coo" then picks up speed. That's the black-billed cuckoo you're listening to, a slim, sinuous, long-tailed brown bird about the size of a mockingbird. You're most apt to hear the cuckoo's raincrow call if you live near woods or large shade trees, the habitat this bird prefers. Black-billed cuckoos are fond of fuzzy caterpillars, a menu item most birds avoid; if gypsy moths plague your area, you're likely to see or hear this bird.

Insects

The lives of six-legged creatures are just as fascinating as the behavior of bigger, prettier songbirds. Examine your plants and you'll be surprised at what you see—and learn. Insect activity reaches its peak in summer, but many insects are evident year-round. Even in the snowy north, you may spot black-pepper flecks bouncing on the snow: tiny springtails active in the depths of winter. More insect signs include:

- Honeybees and other pollinating insects are less active in very hot weather, a negative for fruit trees and for pumpkins, squash, cucumbers, and other vegetables that depend on their visits for fertilization.

- Praying mantises claim territories, and by midsummer they have achieved such size that they are easy to keep track of on your daily strolls around the garden—almost like pets! When rain threatens, they'll vanish from usual perches.

- Spiders aren't insects, they're arachnids (eight legs instead of six), but they link directly to the other bugs in the garden, both as prey and as predators. Admire their beautiful webs on a dewy morning.

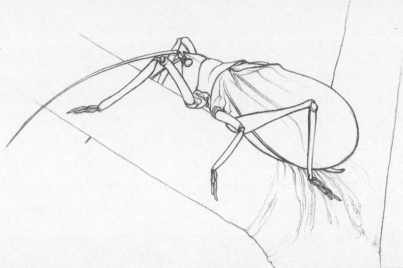

ALTHOUGH BRIGHT GREEN KATYDIDS FEED ON FOLIAGE, THERE ARE RARELY ENOUGH OF THEM AROUND TO CAUSE SIGNIFICANT DAMAGE. LISTEN FOR THEIR SIGNATURE CALLS IN MID- TO LATE SUMMER: ACCORDING TO FOLKLORE, THE FIRST KILLING FROST WILL ARRIVE 3 MONTHS LATER.

- Mosquitoes are extra pesky on humid evenings, and may remain active even during the daytime on overcast, muggy days.

- Listen to the insect symphony that replaces birdsong as heat increases. Grasshoppers in the day, katydids at night, and dozens of other six-legged musicians make life interesting.

- Old-timers believed that 3 months after the first katydid was heard, the first killing frost of the year would fall. It's entirely likely because katydids usually begin rasping their namesake calls in late summer. Just for fun, make a note of the first katydid you hear and count forward to predict the arrival of your area's first killing frost. Check the calendar when hard frost arrives to see how accurate your katydids were.

- Lady beetles have become a seasonal phenomenon in many parts of the country, swarming on houses in fall as they seek entry into crevices around windows or between door frames. In perfect keeping with their orange-and-black coloring, Halloween is the peak of this activity. On warm winter days, the ladybugs may venture out as the sun warms the siding, often appearing inside the house.

Insects and Weather Cycles

Insects are greatly affected by the weather. A mild winter usually spells trouble for gardeners the next year because so many of the bugs survive the season. An extra-cold winter often leads to a relatively pest-free growing season.

An early warm spell can sound the death knell for insects, too. A few days of mild sunny weather are all it takes for cocoons to open, eggs to hatch, and adult six-legged critters to come crawling out. When the weather suddenly swings back to frigid temperatures, those tender bodies usually meet an untimely fate.

> When spider webs are small, the sun will come to call. The more black on a woolly worm, the worse the winter to come. It will be a bad winter if a cricket moves into the house early in fall.
>
> —Folk sayings

If you notice more than the usual complement of bugs around the garden, take measures quickly to curb the population: sticky traps, cardboard collars, hand-picking, and any other deterrents you have in your bag of tricks. Watch for birds and toads to increase in numbers in your yard, too, as they move in to clean up the bounty of extras.

It's reassuring to keep in mind that insect populations rise over a period of years, then suddenly crash to very low levels that are easy for a gardener to live with. When Japanese beetles first move into an area, for example, it may seem they will eat the garden to nothing but lacework. A few years down the line, you'll find that the invasion isn't nearly so bad; the bugs have reached a natural balance.

Count on Crickets

How hot is it? A cricket can tell you. Their chirps are made by rubbing their legs against their abdomen, just as you would run a thumb down a plastic pocket comb. In warmer weather, their legs move faster; in cooler temperatures, their cold-blooded activity slows down.

Interestingly, the insect most of us picture when we hear "cricket" isn't the living thermometer of the clan. The most commonly seen cricket is the fairly large, brown to black field cricket. The one whose voice you seek is the equally widespread but much less often seen snowy tree cricket, which is a delicate-looking insect with long legs and sweeping, hair-fine antennae. It's pale green ("snowy") and, as you might guess, it lives in trees and shrubs. Only males sing, in unison with others of their kind.

This is an easy and fun nighttime project your kids will remember forever. Most modern folks never take time to listen to night noises. Get your family to assist, and you'll all gain an appreciation for the evening summer symphony—I like it better than Bach!

1. First, isolate the rhythmic cheeping of crickets from the diverse symphony of nighttime insect sound. It's a throbbing, fairly high-pitched tone, with a rhythm as regular as breathing.

2. Using a watch with a second hand (or a digital watch that ticks off seconds), count the number of calls in 15 seconds. This works best with a partner: one to watch the watch, one to count the calls.

3. Add 37. That's the temperature in degrees Fahrenheit. Check a thermometer and marvel!

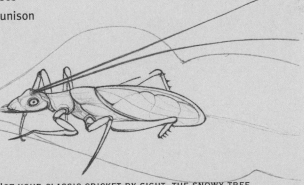

NOT YOUR CLASSIC CRICKET BY SIGHT, THE SNOWY TREE CRICKET IS INSTANTLY FAMILIAR BY SOUND. THE JOINED VOICES OF THESE INSECTS PROVIDE THE STEADY HIGH-PITCHED THROB OF A SUMMER NIGHT. THEY'RE NOT REALLY SINGING—THEY'RE RUBBING THEIR LEGS.

Butterflies

Butterflies are nothing more than dressed-up insects and, like all insects, they're cold-blooded, relying upon the air temperature and the warming rays of the sun to stir their bodies into action. On chilly or cloudy days, butterflies are scarce—if you see them at all they'll likely be sitting still with wings tilted to catch the rays. When the warm summer sun heats their bodies, they are highly active.

- Sunny days increase the nectar in flowers, so butterflies linger longer at individual blossoms. As they dine, butterflies transfer pollen from flower to flower, helping to ensure seed-set for next year's blossoms.

- Butterflies get thirsty, too. On hot, dry days you may see them visiting a muddy spot left in your garden after you water. To encourage their benevolent presence, offer a shallow saucer of wet gravel for a drinking fountain.

TO MAKE BUTTERFLIES TRULY WELCOME IN YOUR GARDEN, PROVIDE FOOD SOURCES FOR THE CATERPILLARS AS WELL AS FLOWERS FOR THE ADULTS. IT'S WELL WORTH LOSING A FEW PARSLEY PLANTS TO PLAY HOST TO THE COLORFUL CATERPILLARS OF THE BLACK SWALLOWTAIL BUTTERFLY.

FALL IS ON THE WAY WHEN MONARCH BUTTERFLIES BEGIN THEIR ANNUAL MIGRATION SOUTH-
WARD. FALL-BLOOMING FLOWERS IN YOUR LANDSCAPE MAY INVITE THEM TO PAUSE BRIEFLY TO
REFUEL BEFORE CONTINUING ON THEIR JOURNEY.

■ Butterflies disappear like magic when rain moves in. The drops can easily batter precious scales from their delicate wings, so they quickly seek shelter beneath a large leaf or other overhang.

■ Those fragile wings can't stand up to strong wind, so butterflies take shelter during such weather. If your garden is a windy one, consider erecting wind-breaks (see page 114) to make it more inviting to butterflies.

■ Like wildflowers, butterfly species have their own seasons. Get to know the cycle in your yard, and you'll know that summer is well on the way when the first swallowtails appear at your zinnias, or that fall is coming fast when monarchs increase in numbers as they migrate southward.

Further Reading

Just as you'd expect, the weather infiltrates reading materials on many subjects because it affects everything on our planet. Once you begin looking for more about this topic, you'll find a deluge of books about the weather, a flood of Web sites on the Internet, and a tsunami of information in every daily newspaper—plus my favorite source of weather news, the Weather Channel on TV.

Books

My favorite book about weather has no words at all, only pictures. It's *Snow Crystals* by W. A. Bentley (Dover Publications), a masterpiece that consists of more than 2,000 beautiful portraits of individual snowflakes, painstakingly collected and photographed by a reclusive and delightfully obsessed Vermont farmer in the early twentieth century. There's nothing better for calming meditation when the winds are howling outside!

Lots of other, more informative weather books crowd the shelves of bookstores and libraries. Many of those listed below are readily available, and all will broaden your weather view, whether you're interested in the sky overhead or the crickets underfoot. For books that are out of print, you can ask your local bookshop to keep an eye out for you, or you can search online booksellers or auction sites. Or try my favorite pursuit on a rainy afternoon: prowling through the shelves of a used-book shop.

Ackerman, Diane. *A Natural History of the Senses*. New York: Vintage Books, 1991.

Asimov, Isaac. *Clock We Live On*. Scranton, PA: Criterion Books Inc., 1965.

Comstock, John H. *Insect Life*. New York: D. Appleton and Company, 1897.

Dennis, Jerry. *It's Raining Frogs and Fishes: Four Seasons of Natural Phenomena and Oddities of the Sky*. New York: HarperTrade, 1993.

Fabre, J. Henri. *The Insect World of J. Henri Fabre*. Boston: Beacon Press, 1991.

Krythe, Maymie. *All about the Months*. New York and London: Harper & Row Publishers, 1966.

Lehr, Paul E., Burnett, R. Will, and Zim, Herbert S. *Weather: A Golden Guide*. New York: St. Martin's Press LLC, 2001.

Levy, David. *The Sky: A User's Guide*. New York: Cambridge University Press, 1991.

Long, Kim. *The Moon Book.* Boulder, CO: Johnson Books, 1998.

Ludlum, David M. *The Audubon Society Field Guide to North American Weather.* New York: Alfred A. Knopf Inc., 1991.

Lum, Peter. *Stars in Our Heaven.* New York: Pantheon Books, 1965.

Meinel, Aden and Marjorie. *Sunsets, Twilights, and Evening Skies.* New York: Cambridge University Press, 1991.

Morse, Edward S. *First Book of Zoology.* New York: D. Appleton and Company, 1876.

Muirden, James. *Astronomy with Binoculars.* Paramus, NJ: Prentice Hall PTR, 1985.

Murphree, Tom, and Miller, Mary K. *Watching Weather.* New York: Henry Holt, 1998.

Palmer, E. Lawrence, revised by H. Seymour Fowler. *Fieldbook of Natural History.* 2nd ed. New York: The McGraw-Hill Companies, 1975.

Rowlands, John J. *Cache Lake Country: Life in the North Woods.* Woodstock, VT: Countryman Press, 1998.

Rubin, Louis D. Sr., and Jim Duncan. *The Weather Wizard's Cloud Book.* Chapel Hill, NC: Algonquin Books, 1989.

Serviss, Garrett P. *Astronomy with an Opera-Glass: A Popular Introduction to the Study of the Starry Heavens with the Simplest of Optical Instruments.* 8th ed. New York and London: D. Appleton and Company, 1927.

Skinner, Charles M. *Myths and Legends of Flowers, Trees, Fruits, and Plants.* Miami: Fredonia Books, 2002.

Spar, Jerome. *The Way of the Weather.* Mankato, MN: The Creative Company, 1967.

Wigginton, Eliot, ed. *The Foxfire Book.* New York: Doubleday, 1972.

Williams, Jack. *USA Today Weather Book.* New York: Vintage Books, 1997.

Wilson, Albert. *How Does Your Garden Grow?* Menlo Park, California: Happy Hours, 1949.

Wilson, P. W. *Romance of the Calendar.* New York: W. W. Norton & Co., 1937.

Young, Andrew. *A Prospect of Flowers: A Book about Wild Flowers.* New York: Viking Penguin, 1985.

Periodicals

Organic Gardening shares garden-tested techniques for stretching the growing season and surviving the elements. Register for the magazine's free online newsletter to receive a monthly almanac of gardening activities for your region.

Organic Gardening
33 East Minor Street
Emmaus, PA 18098
www.organicgardening.com

Weatherwise magazine is informative, entertaining, and written for regular people, not scientists, although the information is top-notch. Photo submissions are welcome for their annual contest; check out the previous winners (displayed on line) for an astounding sampling of the many faces of our powerful, beautiful, always changing weather.

Weatherwise
Heldref Publications
1319 18th Street NW
Washington DC 20036-1802
www.weatherwise.org

Resources

Look for thermometers and rain gauges, from plain to fancy, at garden centers, discount stores, hardware stores, and home supply stores. Those with extensive offerings may also carry barometers, which you can also find by searching on line. Antique and not-so-antique weather instruments often crop up in thrift shops, antiques shops, and in online auctions; check nautical or navigation shops, too, especially for beautiful brass and wooden instruments that are as lovely to look at as they are useful. Sophisticated weather instruments used by professionals and dedicated amateurs are available from scientific supply houses; search for "weather instruments" on line and you'll find a list of many suppliers. Most gardening supply catalogs also carry basic weather instruments, as well as season-stretching equipment, such as cloches, coldframes, and row covers.

Look for antique lightning rods at antiques shops; some are decorative enough to make a centerpiece for your garden. Modern versions are available at some farm supply stores, home supply stores, hardware stores, or online retailers.

Charley's Greenhouse & Garden
17979 State Route 536
Mount Vernon, WA 98273-3269
(800) 322-4707
www.charleysgreenhouse.com

Edmund Scientific
60 Pearce Avenue
Tonawanda, NY 14150-6711
(800) 728-6999
www.scientificsonline.com

Davis Instruments Corp.
3465 Diablo Avenue
Hayward, CA 94545
(800) 678–3669
www.davisnet.com

Gardener's Supply Company
128 Intervale Road
Burlington, VT 05401-2850
(800) 427-3363
www.gardeners.com

Robert E. White Instruments Inc.
34 Commercial Wharf
Boston, MA 02110
(800) 992-3045 (U.S./Canada)
(617) 742-3045 (eastern MA)
www.robertwhite.com

Wind and Weather
1200 North Main Street
Fort Bragg, CA 95437-8473
(800) 922-9463
www.windandweather.com

The Science Company
95 Lincoln Street
Denver, CO 80203-3922
(800) 372-6726 (U.S.)
(303) 777-3777 (outside the U.S. or
  Denver local)
www.sciencecompany.com

Index

Autumn
    droughts during, 132
    garden tasks during, 218
    planting calendar for, 228
Autumnal equinox, 218

B

Barometers, 35, **35**, 40–42, **41**
    aneroid, 41, **41**
    mercury, 41
    positioning, 37
    weatherglass, 41, **41**
Barometric pressure
    altitude and, 42
    changes in, and body clues, 45
    measuring, 35, **35,** 40–42, **41**
Basho, Matsuo, quoted, 90
Bates, Louise, quoted, 168
Bats, 262
Beaufort Wind Scale, 38–39, **38, 39**
Bees, 170, 280
    and temperature, 49
Bentley, W. A., 248
Biennials, for cottage gardens, 154
Big Dipper, the, 96, **96**
Birds, **178**
    behavior of
        spring, 279
        summer, 277
        winter, 279
    and cold air, 241
    feeding, **243,** 252, **252**
    forecasting by, 274–76, 278-280
    as harbingers of spring, **178,**
        178–80
    and leaf mulch, 231
    rescuing baby, 199
    return of as spring planting guide,
        178–80, **178**
    roosting boxes and, 253
    sap and, 174, 175, **175**

    as seasonal forecasters, 278
    songs of and weather, 275–76
    as spring weather clue, 180
    vernal equinox and, 169
    as winter storm predictors, 49, **49**, 244
    winter storm survival of, 252–53, **252**
    winter tracks of, **266**
Black swallowtail butterfly, 284, **284**
"Blue Norther," 13
Brussels sprouts, and fall frosts, 235
Bryant, William Cullen, quoted, 101
Buddleia davidii, **28**
Bulbs, 149, **149**
Burroughs, John, quoted, 23, 29, 44, 259
Butterflies, 284–85, **284, 285**
    and spring sap, 175
    and wind, 29, 107, 285
Butterfly bush, **28**
Butterflyweed, 122

C

Canadian clipper, 244
Cardinals, feather color of, 278
Castings, 171
Catch basins, **146,** 147
Catmint, Faassen's, 117
Cats, as wildlife deterrent, 262
Cercis canadensis, flowers of as planting
        guideline, 176
Chandler, Raymond, quoted, 125
Cherry trees, pruning, 176
Chickweed, **222**
    common, 182, **182**
Chicory, 183, **183**
Chinook, 125
Chipmunks, 262, **262**
    fall behavior of, 267
Chorus frogs, 269
Christmas rose, 254, **255**
Chrysanthemums. *See* Mums
Cichorium intybus, 183

Global warming, 25–26
Goldfinches, feather color of, 278
Gophers, 261
Grafting, by moon phases, 87
Grasshoppers, 281
Gravity, and wind, 8
Grosbeak, red-breasted, **178**
Groundcovers, 148, **148**
Groundhogs
    fall behavior of, 267
    forecasting by, 264, **264**, 265
    as spring predictors, 268–69
Ground ivy, **222**
Ground squirrels, 261, 267

H
Haboob, 125
Hadley, George, 9
Hail, 127
    plants easily damaged by, 196
    protecting plants from, 198
Hardiness zones, USDA, **24**
    meaning of, 238, 240
Harvesting
    by moon phases, 87
    and severe weather, 199–200
Heat Stress Index, 16
Heaving, 241–42
Hedges, as windbreaks, 114–15, **115**
Helianthus × multiflorus and others,
    116
Heliopsis helianthoides, 117
Hellebore, **255**
Henbit, 182, **182**
Hibernation, 267–69
High-pressure air masses, 7, 12–13,
    12
    and wind, 9
Highs, 12–13, **12**
High winds, plants tolerant of, 197

Homemade rain gauge, 43, **43**
Homestead Act, 211
Honeybees, 170, 280
    and temperatures, 49
Horse latitudes, 7, **7**
Hosta, and summer sun, 205
Houseplants
    outdoor vacation for, 193
    and spring sun, 170
Hudson, W. H., quoted, 246
Humidity, 15–16. *See also* Relative
        humidity
    and body comfort, 16, 18, **18**, 65–66
    and dew point, 65–66
    helping plants cope with, 205–7, **207**
    plants preferring low, 196
    protecting plants from, 201–2
    and rain, 17
    and temperatures, 16, 18, **18**, 34
    water vapor and, 61–62
Hummingbirds, 279, **279**

I
Ice storms, 250–51
    and birds, 252
Insects, 280–83
    bats and, 262
    forecasting by, 275
    leaf mulch and, 231
    shrews and, 263
    spring sap and, 174, 175
    weather cycles and, 282
    windy gardens and, 107

J
"Jacob's Ladder" effect, **82**
Jet stream, 10–11, **11**
Johnson, Philander, quoted, 1
Juncos, 253, **253**

effect of sodium-vapor lights on, 29
first aid for frost-heaved, 242
to force for winter color, 256, **256**
fragrant, 99
hardiness of, 66
long-day, 221
night-blooming, 99
protecting from summer weather
    extremes, 197–200
  early harvest, 199–200
  layering, 198
  physical barriers, 198
repairing storm damage to, 200–201
response of to day length, 220–23
short-day, 221
spring ephemerals, 59
for varying moisture levels, 156–57
winter flowering, 254–55
Plant selection
  for drought resistance, 139, 197
  and rainfall patterns, 137
  for summer survival, 195–97
  for windy gardens, 109–12, **112**,
    116–17, 119–20, **119**
Plant supports, 113–14, **113**
  and windy gardens, **107**
Pleiades, 97, **97**
Polar air masses, 243–44
  continental, **4**, 244
  easterlies, 102–3, **102**
  maritime, **4**, 243
Polar easterlies, 102–3, **102**
Polkweed, 183, **183**
Pollinators, 170
  wind and, 107
Possums. *See* Opossums
Prairie plants, and windy gardens, 111,
  119
Praying mantises, 280
Precipitation, 141. *See also* Rain; Snow
  average annual, **136**
  freezing rain, 162, 163

hail, 127
ice, 250–51
measuring, 42–43, **43**
  tools for, 37, 42–43, **43, 249**
and mountains, 70, **70**
sleet, 161, 163
Preserving, by moon phases, 87
Prevailing westerlies, **7**, 9–10, 102–3,
  102
Prevailing winds, 10
Projects
  Homemade Rain Gauge, 43, **43**
  Sound of Cool, the, 215, **215**
  Straw-Bale Windbreak, 118,
    118
Pruning
  and air circulation, 206–7
  and spring sap flow, 176
Punxsutawney Phil, 4, 260

R

Rabbits, 261, **270**
  forecasting by, 263
  and full moons, 86
  winter tracks of, **266**
Raccoons, 261
Rain. *See also* Precipitation
  autumn, 132, 228–29
  average annual, 135–37, **136**
  benefits of gardening in, xi–xii
  benefits to plants, 133
  cloud seeding to encourage, 142
  describing quality of, 143
  freezing, 162, 163
  and humidity, 17
  measuring, 42–43, **43**
  minimum required by plants, 133–34,
    141
  patterns of, 135–38, **136**, 140–41, **141**
    and plant selection, 137
  predicting, 134, 135, 142, 212–13

Stationary front, 125
Stellaria media, 182
Stephens, James, quoted, 273
Stephenson, Robert Louis, quoted, 10
Storms
    air masses and, 125, 126
    birds as predictors of, 274–75, 276,
       277
    lightning and, 128–29
    thunderstorms, 126–29
       protecting plants from, 128,
          197–99
       repairing damage from, 200–201
    to-do list for oncoming summer,
       128
    winter, 243–44
Stratosphere, 5
Straw-bale windbreak, 118, **118**
Summer
    challenges of, 189–90
    garden tasks during, 192–93
    planting in, 150–51
    thunderstorms, 126–29
       protecting plants from, 128,
          197–99
       repairing damage from, 200–201
    "Year without a Summer," 194
Summer solstice, 20, 190–92
Sun
    absorption of by surfaces, **58**
    effect of in spring, 169–70
    effect of on plants, 54
    and humidity, 16
    protecting plants from, 204, **204**, 205
    and seasonal weather patterns,
       19–20
    skin safety in, 190
    strength of, 54–55, 57
    and weather, 6
    weather patterns and, 21–22, **21**
    and wind, 8–9

Sunflower, false, 117
Sunflowers, perennial, 116
Sunrise, 80–82
    mechanics of, 80
    weather forecasting by, 82
Sunset, 80–83, **80, 82**
    colors of, **80**, 83
    mechanics of, 80
    to-do list for, 81
    weather forecasting by, 46–47, **80,**
       82–83
Swallows, 275, **275**
Sweating, humidity and, 18
Symplocarpus foetidus, **254,** 255

T

Taraxacum officinale, 182
Taurus, 97, **97**
Temperate zone, 9
Temperature, 34
    body as gauge of, 50
    in cities, 23, 29, 55, 58
    effect of bodies of water on, 26
    effect of on plants, 54
    and humidity, 16, 18, **18**, 34,
       65–66
    interpreting changing, 34
    mountain elevations and, 68, 70,
       167
    signs of cold, 241
    thermometers, 34, **34,** 40, **40**
       placement of, 37
    and wind, 8
Thermometers, **34,** 40, **40**
    human body as, 50
    positioning, 37
Thinning, and air circulation, 206–7,
    207
Thoreau, Henry David, quoted, 93, 155,
    162

Weather (continued)
    in Midwest, 1–2
    mountains and, 6, 68, 70, **70,** 167
    seasonal patterns of, 19–20
    sun and, 6
    troposphere and, 5
    variety of in North America, 6
    water and, 14–15
    wind and, **7,** 8–10
Weather diary, 50–51, **51**
Weather eye, developing, 44–51
Weather forecasting
    by animal behavior, 263–65
    body clues in, 45
    clear skies and, 54
    clouds in, 46, 71–77, **72, 73, 74–75**
    flower fragrances as clues in, 47, 48
    folklore (*see* Folklore)
    home weather stations for, 36–37,
        40–43, **40, 41, 43**
    intuitive methods, 32
    nature-based lore in, 48–49, **49**
    plants and, 48
    positioning tools for, 37
    predicting rain, 134–35, 142, 212–13
    scientific methods of, 32–35, **34, 35**
    sunrises and sunsets, 46–47, 80–83,
        80, 82
    tools for, 34–37, **34, 35,** 40–43, **40,**
        41, 43
    tools for home stations, 36–37
    wind as clue in, 47
Weather forecasting tools
    anenometers, 37
    barometers, 35, **35,** 37, 40–42, **41**
    rain gauges, 43, **43**
    snow gauges, 37, **249**
    thermometers, 34, **34,** 37, 40, **40**
    wind direction devices, 35, **35,**
        36–37
Weather patterns, seasonal, 19–20
Weather vanes, 35, **35,** 36–37

Weeding, by moon phases, 87
Weeds
    in early spring, 181
    fall-germinating, 222–23, **222**
    growth of as guide to spring planting,
        182–83, **182, 183**
    seed dispersal and wind, 122
    spring germinating, 169
Westerlies, **7,** 9–10, 102–3, **102**
Wildflowers, 59
Wind. *See also* Wind direction; Winds;
        Wind speed
    air pressure masses and, 8–9
    atmosphere and, 8
    bodies of water and, 14–16, **15**
    butterflies and, 107, 285
    clouds and, 77
    cycle of, 102–4, **102**
    global patterns of, **7**
    gravity and, 8
    in Great Plains, 104–5
    jet stream, 10–11, **11**
    mitigating effects of, 108
        conserving water and, 120–21
        by plant selection, 109–12, **112,**
            116–17, 119–20, **119**
        with plant supports, 113–14,
            113
        with windbreaks, 114–15, 118,
            118
    seed dispersal and, 122, **122**
    soil erosion and, 123, **123**
    sun and, 8–9
    temperature and, 8
    as weather forecasting clue, 47
    windbreaks and, 27, 114–15, 118, **118,**
        159
Windbreaks, 27, 114–15, 118, **118**
    and gardens, 27
    planting, 115, **115**
    straw bales, 118, **118**
    Wyoming style, 159